Praise for *Moth*

'A tender and graceful study of parents and children, and a finely judged and measured attempt to capture the flitting, quicksilver shapes of what we keep and what we lose: the touch, the tone, the gaze of the past as it fades. It is a moving and beautifully achieved memoir, and a testament to the writer's skill and generosity of spirit.'

Hilary Mantel

Praise for Nicholas Royle's novels

An English Guide to Birdwatching

'This is a novel operating at the outer edges of the form, deep in the avant-garde...play[ing] brilliantly in the fertile ground between fiction and memoir. *An English Guide to Birdwatching* is Rachel Cusk rewritten by Georges Bataille, full of strange sex, sudden violence and surreal twists. Illuminated throughout with gorgeous illustrations by Natalia Gasson, this is a novel that will charm, unsettle and baffle in equal measure.'

Alex Preston, *Financial Times*

'Great books are still written, they just have to take place in Literature, the continent that never forgets. While reading *An English Guide to Birdwatching*, I travelled in all the time periods, places, countries of literature. It was more than an odyssey...'

Hélène Cixous

'A metafictional fever dream.'

The Guardian

Quilt

'A book of mythological power. *Quilt* is unforgettable, like all those great pieces of fiction that are fed by our immemorial root system, the human dream of metamorphosis.'
Hélène Cixous

'It is quiet, lapidary, and teases out the tangled filaments that link figuration to fact and insight to feeling with the unnerving stealth of a submarine predator.' **Will Self**

'An intense study of grief and mental disintegration, a lexical celebration and a psychological conundrum ... Royle explores loss and alienation perceptively and inventively.'
The Guardian

'Royle's baroque, athletic prose... confers a strong sense of the "strangeness" of English, "which, after all, belongs to no one" and should be continually reinvented ... Moments of delightfully eccentric humour and impressive linguistic experimentalism.' *The Observer*

'A work of remarkable imaginative energy.'
Frank Kermode

'It is in those commonplace moments at the end of a life ... moments which Nicholas Royle describes with such piercing accuracy, when this novel is truly at its strangest.'
Times Literary Supplement

'What deceptively begins as a more or less realistic piece of autobiographical fiction evolves into an astonishing narrative that puts into question the very notion of everyday reality. A highly readable and stunningly original experiment in literary form.' **Leo Bersani**

'Captures the absolute dislocating strangeness of bereavement. While the novel is bursting with inventive wordplay, Royle's use of language is most agile and beautiful in his descriptions of rays... The shifts in point of view have a sort of fairground quality to them, suddenly lurching, demanding your compliance, but it is the way the storyline ultimately develops that takes the breath away.'

New Statesman

'*Quilt* is one of those books I long for but come across rarely... It is strange, surprising, sui generis... with its overturning qualities, its ability to stick in the head while resisting resolution, and its determination not to leave the reader feeling that the end of the text is the end of the reading experience. What my reading life needs – what the literary world needs – is more *Quilts* and fewer comfort blankets.'   **John Self,** *The Asylum*

MOTHER
A Memoir

Nicholas Royle

First published in 2020 by
Myriad Editions
www.myriadeditions.com

Myriad Editions
An imprint of New Internationalist Publications
The Old Music Hall, 106–108 Cowley Rd, Oxford OX4 1JE

First printing
1 3 5 7 9 10 8 6 4 2

A CIP catalogue record for this book
is available from the British Library

ISBN (pbk): 978-1-912408-57-3
ISBN (ebk): 978-1-912408-58-0

Designed and typeset in Perpetua
by WatchWord Editorial Services, London

Printed and bound in Great Britain
by Clays Ltd, Elcograf S.p.A.

For

Sam, Sebastian, Alexi, Elena,
William and Augustus

Pre-word

In my mind's eye she is sitting at the circular white Formica-top table in the corner. Morning sunlight fills the kitchen. She has a cup of milky Nescafé Gold Blend and is smoking a purple Silk Cut. She is dressed for comfort in floral bronze-and-brown blouse and blue jumper with light gray slacks and blue slippers. She is absorbed in a crossword (*The Times*) but not oblivious. She does what always takes me aback. She reads out one of the clues. As if I'd know the answer. Her gift for crosswords is alien to me. I get stuck at the first ambiguity or double-meaning. Whereas she sweeps through all illusions allusions red herrings and anagrams and is done most days by lunchtime. But her fondness for crossword puzzles is inseparable from my interest in words. Where they come from. What they might be doing. Earliest recorded use of 'In my mind's eye': Shakespeare's *Hamlet* (around 1599). Referring to the Ghost.

My mother died years ago. What has induced me to write about her after all this time remains mysterious to me. It is connected to the climate crisis. As the natural historian David Attenborough says: 'the collapse of our civilisations and the extinction of much of the natural world is on the horizon.' In ways I cannot pretend to fathom I have found that writing about my mother is bound up with writing about Mother Nature and Mother Earth. And no doubt it has to do also with my own ageing and the buried life of mourning. The strange timetables of realisation and loss. A memoir is 'a written record of a person's knowledge of events or of a person's own experiences'. 'A record of events written by a person having intimate knowledge of them and based on personal observation.' So the dictionaries tell us. But this memoir of my mother makes no attempt at a comprehensive record. It reveals very little about her early life or adolescence. Friends and lovers. Her education. Travel. Work. It doesn't offer any sort of rounded picture. It seems less a record of events than a grappling with what escapes words. Not just love and loss but fire and air and water and earth. Smell and music. Voice and touch.

I knew from the outset that I couldn't write a model kind of book. For reasons as plentiful as blackberries the classic memoir conforms to certain established principles. The linear and chronological. An orderly unfolding of information and impressions. In a conventional memoir there's no messing about with the strange materiality of writing or exploration of how 'memory' and 'mother' might be inseparable. A memoir has no business with the stuff of crosswords. Anagrams and palindromes. Puns and double-meaning. But in the case of my mother these things are in play from the beginning. MAM. *Mother: A Memoir.*

What is this *mother*? Who says it? To whom? First and foremost the title refers to my mother. But all of us have or had one. Does that distinction between past ('had') and present ('have') hold any real meaning? Isn't a mother not just for keeps but the very figure who keeps watch over keeping? *Mother: A Memoir*: the title might be construed as a sort of crossword clue. 'Memoir' comes from an Old French feminine noun for 'an act of commemoration, especially of the dead': *memoire*. Somewhere down the centuries the word became masculine. I am intrigued by this sense of a buried or repressed feminine. I am drawn to trying to explore the mystery of the mother of memory. Mother *as* memoir. As the act and passion of memory as such. 'Mother' has to do with birth. With the giving and gift of life. But she also has to do with the earth. The sea. The unconscious. Dreams. 'Mother' for me is not only a woman called Kathleen Beatrice McAdam. *Née* as people say. Nay. I love my mother's 'birth names': my father called her Kathleen while her sisters and most others called her Kate. But these names also seem a kind of violence and absurdity. She is prior to names. Pre-name. Pre-word.

Marbles

I have lost plenty of people. Every loss is a lessening. Every loss makes one more aware of how much there is to lose. But the death of my mother was something else. I don't know when she died. She had dementia. For ten years she was among us in the midst of life cut off. An island going down under rising sea-levels. A skyscraper collapsing in a decade-long earthquake. A sunset sleepier than a druid's daydream. It began in her mid-sixties. It was over before her seventy-fifth birthday. It wasn't like an island or a skyscraper or a sunset. These similes are to no purpose. Nothing captures the pace of her descent into where she went.

Like others near and dear I pretended it wasn't happening. I'd ask if she would like a coffee. I'd suggest we go shopping or take a drive down to the sea. I'd say these things as if she was right as rain. I appeared to be unscathed. Not sinking an inch. I would see that she wasn't answering but act as if the pause in the footage was someone else's problem. A technical glitch. It could be ignored. It would come clear in a moment. I could see that she was not listening. She was looking out of the window at the birds around the bird-table. I would repeat the question. She would turn to me with whorls in her eyes. She would look in my direction as if. As if *if*. As if if I could just repeat the question one more time – just once more – it would connect. Repetition the mother of memory. As if if things could just rewind this era might start over. Here we are. Regained. We'd drive down to the coast. Walk arm in arm past the fishermen's huts along the dark Jurassic shore. Drive over the fragile medieval bridge into the little town and sit in one of her favourite pubs. She would have her cup of coffee. I would have my pint of beer.

When does a mother die?

I'm losing my marbles.

So she said one autumn morning in Devon. It was in the kitchen. I had just taken a coffee bean out of the machine and was chewing it slowly.

Losing her marbles. In the past she might have said this of an old friend or elderly family member. My grandfather's cousin or my mother's great-aunt in Scotland whom we would not see for several years at a time. She and I would head north. Like a band on tour. A duo without audience. We would drive through the Great Glen. Listening to the jigging charm and melancholy of Mark Knopfler's *Local Hero* or the road-to-nowhere *Little Creatures* album by Talking Heads. We would stop on Skye or Mull. Or we'd go up east – away past Loch Ness and down again. We would stay in bed-and-breakfasts. Sharing a twin room. At some point on the tour (as arranged in advance by letter) we visited Cousin Nessie in her time-capsule of a cottage on the Square at Drymen. Cups and saucers clinked and teaspoons tinkled. The clock of ages on the mantelpiece stumped up the hour and the half- and the quarter-hours in strange accusation. What is the past? What is a family? It made our hearts knock together. After tea and scones we left and my mother remarked that Nessie was losing her marbles. She said it with all the peremptoriness of a High Court judge. The verdict was sound.

On other occasions the loss of marbles escaped me. I had to reconsider what had taken place. The gestures. The looks. Things said. With a friend of my father's in Somerset it had not been clear. But my mother had picked it up. Visible as an item of litter in an otherwise spotless National Trust garden. She was Acute personified. A bloodhound for lunacy in others. She would note a detail. A failure to retain something just said. An absence of attention. A lower score on the conversation chart. I always imagined her judging what others said – assessing their ability in the arena of wit and recollection and story-telling fast as lightning. And about my father's friend my mother was right. Within months he went from absent-minded to pit-stop care home to pushing up the daisies.

There must have been a point at which we failed to go back to see Cousin Nessie. Solitary in her time-capsule at Hillview Cottage. Her name cropped up only later. She'd passed away. The British way is with 'away'. Americans go without it. She'd *passed*. The *away* may be superfluous but the American idiom has a Christian tint: when people *pass* they pass to the Lord God or to heaven. And 'away' is such a dreamy two-in-one word. Fleet but longing. These details matter. The matter of my *mater*. Matador killing metaphor. My mother's every utterance was a play before the law of written or printed matter. As if her voice threw round each word a gentle mantle of quotation marks. As if she spoke from a love for the provisional that understood that no locution was ever playful enough. A mind mid-clue. On occasion my mother would say that someone had died or passed away. But more often she would fling up some funny everyday idiom. Her father's cousin in the Central Region was *pushing up the daisies* like the man in Somerset. She had *popped her clogs*.

Besides a fine nose for marble-loss my mother had a great taste for irony. 'Irony': I picture the word wrought and looped – gappy and splendid in the manner of the fencing in her beloved Richmond Park. Just another word for the invisible cloaks and lassos thrown. Many people failed to get her. A shopkeeper or dog-owner caught up in conversation could very soon be immobilised by her tongue. Impossible to ascertain the status of what this quick-witted woman had just said. *They should all be strung up.* Did she mean it? *You look so much younger.* Did she mean it? She could pull herself to pieces in a minute twenty times a day but did she ever mean any of it?

Still I don't recall her ever saying in jest: *I'm losing my marbles.* For example at having mislaid the car key. Or forgetting an optician's appointment. Which made the declaration that bright autumn morning with the intensity of the Colombian coffee bean disintegrating in my mouth all the more sickening.

My father and I had understood for months that something terrible was happening. You've been losing them for a good while (one of us might well have retorted). They've been rolling around scattering this way and that – slipping under the skirting-boards disappearing into previously unknown nooks and crannies whizzed off without a murmur every which way in a muted nightmare pinball – for a good while already. Nothing good about it. A terrible while. Hideous wile of a while. For you too must have known. And we had said nothing. Too choked to say. But now for the first time you were saying it yourself.

They were the saddest words ever spoken to me. I wanted it to be a duo's refrain. *I'm losing my marbles.* A playful echo of other times. A riff of her old self making light of fetid fate. I wanted it to be immediately untrue. I wanted the judge to remove her wig and laugh the moment down the plughole. When my brother Simon and I shared a bedroom as boys and at night pleaded with her to come and frighten us by entering the room in different costumes – one minute a sheeted spectre – the next a fortune-teller – the next a shadowy crocodile – how we thrilled to be frightened. Knowing it was our mother in disguise. And now she was making a throwaway colloquialism scarier than a declaration of nuclear war. I was chilled to the marrow. Moribund metaphor. Icing on the cadaver cake. Cold clammy ivy wrapped my innards in an instant. And tears fell from my face incongruous as hot ice. I swallowed the fragments of the coffee bean. I prepared to vomit.

Nothing came. What to say? Rolling down my cheeks. My water marbles.

Ludicrous to pretend: *No of course you're not. Don't be daft darling mother.* Or to effuse: *Yes yes of course. We had noticed. That's why we've been trying to set up an appointment with the doctor. So that we can get you a proper diagnosis and see what medication might be prescribed.*

My father and I were like hooded birds. Seeling our own fates.

Until then I'd never been shot through by dementia. In my late teens I had done some voluntary work at a local mental hospital. I spent afternoons in the company of the raving and sedated. Watched them watching the test card on the television screen from one hour to the next. Listened in fear to their anguished moans and cries. I played chess with madmen. I sang songs on request to old women. And in later years I visited friends who had undergone breakdowns and been sectioned. But I had never felt overtaken – submerged – rooted out by the reality of another's madness. Mad judgment of the judge of madness. Trial of lunacy by lunacy. All the time headlong down a slide with no ground in sight.

If you can't remember

A little boy's prime concern is to be alone in the presence of his mother. Alone. All one. In later years there was the quiet joy of sitting at home or in the pub reading aloud to her. I see that in reading I have never grown up. Whenever I love what I am reading I am in her presence. And then everything is in the voice in which I would read for her. Alone. I sit and read a book with my mother. I read back over these words with her now.

I'm losing my marbles. She never before or again talked of her madness. As if the words had announced her own death-sentence. But when will she have died? This question affects anybody who has lost a loved one to dementia. My mother carried on living. And I was far away dealing with children of my own. It was left to my father to look after her. He was *such a brick.* So my aunt Marion called him. It wore the life out of him. He survived my mother by just a couple of years. She became a phantom-like puppet. The battered shell of a self still harbouring a body. She passed away – passed off – passed through – day after day. She could no longer drive – not after being discovered miles from home with the car slumped in the hedgerow. It seemed a miracle she'd emerged in one piece. The police found her still sitting at the wheel of the 1973 yellow-ochre Opel Kadett. Smoke pouring out of the engine. Flames flickering up from under the bonnet. She seemed not to realise what had happened. She was unhurt. But she would never drive again.

My mother's ability to speak and interact with others withered away. If she had believed in a God and could articulate such a question she might have asked how He could have come up with dementia. Not just invented it as a personal exit strategy for a human being but designed it in such a way that the suffering it produced could linger and deepen and extend – month after month – year after year. Some Gawd that. What is the purpose of an elderly woman mad and sad as locked-up monkeys?

In my mind's eye she is surrounded by fire. A roaring fire. The conflagration of the world. And other images are at work. Like a perpetual flame she is weaving in my words.

Pyromaniac I joked one day. A terrible moment. I realised that she no longer had any idea what the word meant. She continued to smoke cigarettes and my father had a constant fear of her setting the house alight. This was foreshadowed by memories of ten years earlier when an electric blanket caught fire in the night. I was living abroad at the time. I was not informed. But next time I was home it was hard not to notice the new carpets and repainted walls. And that was foreshadowed again by the time in my early adolescence when my mother forked out all of her hard-earned savings on a cream-coloured leather three-piece suite and no sooner turned her back than my father chose to light a fire in the fireplace without first checking on the state of the chimney. When she came home from work that evening her brand-new sofa and chairs were covered in a film of soot that resisted all attempts at making good again. Shadow to shadow. In her latter days the possibility of a cigarette setting fire to herself – or to the house – meant that my father had to shadow her from one room to another. Never a moment's peace.

In my mind's eye she is surrounded by water. I see my mother in the sea in streams and rivers weirs and waterfalls. I see her when I am taking a shower or in the bath. When it rains. When I turn on a tap to fill the kettle. When I fill a hot-water bottle. In the 1960s and early 1970s she and her younger sister Marion used to take me and Simon and Cousin Michael up to North Berwick in Scotland to visit their eldest sister Peggy. Peggy was married to her first cousin Jim. They had no children. On our earlier trips we would stay with them on their farm just outside the town. In later years we shared their bungalow by the sea. For weeks we would inhabit this marine-edged existence unlike any other. We would walk early in the morning or in the long summer evenings along the great pale gold stretches of sand looking out to Bass Rock in the far distance and Craig Leith and Fidra and the Lamb closer to shore. We would wander for miles along the sands searching for the little cowrie shells that washed up every day. Sometimes we might each find as many as fifty. We called them *buddies*. Tiny shells given up by the sea. Looking for buddies was another way of reading with her.

My mother could be ruthless. And despite her claims to lack of education or knowledge of books her reading was voracious. The cottage in Devon had a large garden that needed plentiful attention. Which she gave it when the weather allowed or she wasn't sitting at the kitchen table cruciverbalising or reading a novel or daydreaming or making a shopping list. She must have spent at least six hours every day at that white Formica-top table. She would smoke at least one packet of fags and drink up to nine cups of milky instant coffee a day. Even late in the evening she would drink coffee. And every day she would do the crossword. The *Daily Telegraph* or *The Times*. Neither of these newspapers was appealing to her. My mother's politics were to the left of the left. The paper was just for the crossword. Sometimes I would read to her from the *Telegraph* letters page and we would laugh aloud together. The *Telegraph* letters were funnier than the ones in *The Times* but both could produce a hilarity that stayed with us for hours. The psychoanalyst Jacques Lacan once said that if you want to know how the unconscious works – do crosswords. Often my mother would finish the puzzle by mid-morning. Then the rest of the day could be given over to novel-reading. Interspersed with gardening or a trip out to the local shops or housework or having a natter and a coffee or two with Marion or someone else who had dropped by.

She got through far more books than I did. Considering I was at that time 'reading English' at university I ought to have been embarrassed. But just as I never thought of reading without her so I never thought of her reading without me. When she'd read a book I felt I'd somehow done so too. A mobile library *folie à deux*. She worked her way through Trollope with a sense of purpose I found staggering. Alexander Solzhenitsyn Doris Lessing Thomas Hardy George Eliot Virginia Woolf – nothing seemed to deter her. She would always begin by reading the last page. At the time I found this incomprehensible. A poor final page would not prevent her from turning back to the beginning. She read with a dogged loyalty. But she was never afraid to be outspoken in her judgement. I remember a period when she was reading Iris Murdoch. She'd already swept like one of the ten plagues of Egypt through several of her books. And now she was on *The Sea, The Sea*. One afternoon I asked her what she thought of it. She was very close to finishing it. *Drivel* she said. Just that one word.

It is an irony that Murdoch and my mother succumbed to the same form of insanity. I met her a couple of times. She was married to my PhD supervisor John Bayley. I remember phoning him on occasion at their home in Steeple Aston in Oxfordshire. I never went there but as I write I realise I imagined it as a version of the Devon cottage to which my parents had retreated. Sometimes Iris picked up and sometimes John but it was always a case of staying on the phone for several minutes before one of them answered. I pictured the simple but marvellous lethargy preventing anyone from journeying to the phone. It was the same when I was telephoning home. Even when my father was in his study with the machine ringing right next to him on his desk he would not answer if he thought his wife was in the house. And my mother would never rush – even if she was expecting a call or knew her husband was not at home. The phone was not an object of integrated pseudo-urgency and command as it is today. If the reason for the call were pressing the caller would try again later. My mother liked to recall something her father used to say. *If you can't remember it can't have been important.* This saying was important enough to remember. A way of organising her economy of forgetfulness. Of dedicating her forgetting and not forgetting to the memory of her father.

Surface

I'm losing my marbles.

What resources are called upon when you rise up from the maelstrom of madness to report on it?

Below the thunders of the upper deep;
Far far beneath in the abysmal sea,
His ancient, dreamless, uninvaded sleep
The Kraken sleepeth: faintest sunlights flee
About his shadowy sides; above him swell
Huge sponges of millennial growth and height;
And far away into the sickly light,
From many a wondrous grot and secret cell
Unnumber'd and enormous polypi
Winnow with giant arms the slumbering green.
There hath he lain for ages, and will lie
Battening upon huge sea-worms in his sleep,
Until the latter fire shall heat the deep;
Then once by man and angels to be seen,
In roaring he shall rise and on the surface die.

Tennyson was just out of his teens when he wrote that poem. When I was young I was envious. I was awed by its imaginative power. He had siphoned the spirit of Shakespeare's song 'Full fathom five thy father lies' and changed it into something monstrous and surprising. It wasn't necessary to know anything about the Kraken's origins in the Norwegian word for *twisted* or about its links with the English *crank* and *crook*. Or about the creature's earliest appearance in English in Berthelson's translation of Erik Pontoppidan's *Natural History of Norway* in 1755. 'Amongst the many great things which are in the ocean...is the Kraken. This creature is the largest and most surprizing of all the animal creation...'

All you needed to know was that the *latter fire* referred to the Day of Judgement. At the end of the world everything goes up in flames. As foretold in the Book of Revelation:

> And the sea gave up the dead which were in it; and death and hell delivered up the dead which were in them: and they were judged every man according to their works.

> And death and hell were cast into the lake of fire. This is the second death.

> And whosoever was not found written in the book of life was cast into the lake of fire.

Tennyson had lifted that immortal opening: 'And the sea gave up the dead which were in it.' The sea giveth. Gives out. Gives up.

My King James Bible is among my most precious books. I love the black covers and india-paper thinness. The hundreds and hundreds of pages with gilt edging. The frayed red silk bookmarker. The tiny chunky Gothic black print of the words. Inside I have inscribed my ten-year-old name and the date 'Christmas 1967' in blue biro. At the back of the book is a strand of my mother's hair. A single gray straggle. Stuck in with Sellotape. The strand matters more than the book. She took so much notice of people's hair. She used to say of her sons that they had *such beautiful hair*. As a boy this meant nothing to me. I have hair: what's special about that? If she came back from the hairdresser and we noticed – she was so pleased. She'd got a perm. She'd had her hair done. And her husband or one of her sons had said it looked nice! But more often alas we failed to remark upon it. I remember the way she had of biting her lip. And how upset she could become if no one said anything.

I love the Bible but there are very few mothers in it. The most famous (the Virgin Mary and Isaac's mother Sarah) must puzzle over what made them mothers at all. Otherwise it's all fathers. Begetting this begetting that. But my Bible is also full of my mother. She always has the last word. She is in the last place and never stops speaking.

When I looked up the word 'memoir' I discovered a rare and obsolete meaning: *a memento or something kept in memory of someone*. The dictionary gives just one instance. From an English poet I'd never read. I can hear my mother's playful pronunciation: Thomas *Ken*. She is recalling her Scottish father William McAdam. *D'ye ken?* In a poem dating from 1711 Ken wrote: 'Of Friends whom Death lays fast asleep / They Memoirs keep.' I love the fact that the dictionary can in two lines give an unknown poet a new vocation. Something is missing. The 'they' of the second line are not the 'Friends' of the first. Those who are living are unidentified. The dead friends are identified through memoirs. The preceding couplet runs: 'Terrestrial Lovers Pictures wear / Of those who their Beloved are.' My memoir of my mother is that single gray hair at the end of my 1967 terrestrial Bible.

The Kraken sleeps. He sleeps a sleep that once invaded kills. A sleep betrayed. *Sleep* is the word thrice crowed. The

Surface

Kraken *sleeps* his *ancient dreamless uninvaded sleep.* For millennia he has been feeding on sea-worms in it. Sleep is more cryptic than any *wondrous grot* or *secret cell.* It has no content. It is a world of its own. A law unto itself.

Epistolary

I read 'The Kraken' aloud to my mother one winter evening by the fire in Devon. She must have already come across the poem but she didn't say. She always maintained that she had read nothing. *Your* father *was the educated one.* He had a study full of books. He had read so much. But I have no memory of ever seeing my father read anything besides magazines and newspapers. Like her he never went to university. He must have read a lot when he was young. He knew about all sorts of things. He had an extraordinary vocabulary and always knew how to spell things. He loved the English language and had a compulsive interest in grammatical correctness. My mother was pre-word. My father was word. Or at least that is how I understood them and how they appeared to want to be understood.

My mother also wrote very little. I have many letters from my parents but her contribution tends to be minimal. A 'me too!' and a kiss at the end. Sometimes a couple of sentences or a brief paragraph supplementing what my father had written. There are very few letters composed by her alone. When clearing out what had been the family home in the months after my father died in 2005 I went through the traumatic business of deciding what to keep and what not to keep. Of giving away or taking to the local tip what couldn't be kept even though the parting seemed sorrowful beyond words. Among the smaller items impossible to discard was my father's wallet. I've never used a wallet and wasn't going to start now. I put it in a drawer. I would just look at it from time to time. Register with fondness its continuing presence in the desk beside me. But then a couple of years ago I took it out and examined it. A sort of pickled object I didn't know what to do with. And only then did I notice a small inner pocket sealed with a zip.

Inside I discovered a cache of faded letters. They are little more than scraps. Yet each stirs and moves me every time I read it.

One is a much-folded worn and torn sheet on which my mother has written: '*M, I do love you. K.*' Just that. Without date. Without location. Without reference. The 'do' seems heartbreaking to me.

Another is dated 11.50pm 30 June 1954. It's a Wednesday.

Why are you so far away?

Darling

Third attempt? The first, a page and almost a half and the second only a half. But somehow neither read intelligently and I am afraid that if I ponder any longer you may not hear from me at all before our meeting on Saturday.

Thank you so very much for your letter, thoughts and love. This week is passing so slowly and I am finding it so very difficult to settle down to routine of district again. Each morning I have been awake long before my usual hour, feeling to see if any water might be creeping in and wondering when last I had something to eat.

> *Did we really have two long weeks together? I miss you dreadfully, especially as I write. Have you found my little fern and given it some water? It was left in the pocket on my side of your car. My chestnut tree has several new leaves, but perhaps you saw them last Saturday evening?*
> *Darling.*
>
> > *goodnight and I love you K.*

Would any lover today declare in a text or email: 'I miss you dreadfully, especially as I write'? The core matter of the epistolary – the singular act of committing heart and pen to paper – has gone the way of the passenger pigeon. My mother and father married on 15 November 1956: these are the heady early days. They are just back from a fortnight's holiday. Coinciding with my mother's twenty-seventh birthday (17 June). The 'routine' refers to her job as a district nurse. Early days intimated too in the precarious survivals of the little fern and the chestnut tree.

The third letter is on headed paper from the Chest Clinic at Hammersmith Hospital in Ducane Road W12. She writes:

> *Monday afternoon.*
>
> *Darling M*
>
> *Sitting in the gorgious [sic] sun during lunch break and thinking how lovely it is that I shall be seeing you tonight instead of wondering if I shall have a letter from you in the morning. I hope you have a safe & pleasant journey back to Slaughter and find Kathy & Pete well.*
>
> *It won't be long till we meet again anyway will it?*
>
> *Thank you Dear for such a lovely week-end and making me happy.*

Epistolary

*I do think we ought to get married SOON I'm tired of
going to everyone elses'* [sic] *weddings and just looking on!
Must get back to work.*

I love you.

God Bless.

K.

There is no date on this third document in my father's
wallet zip-pocket. The last may be first and the first may
be last. The second might come after the last. The third
must have been written after Kathy and Pete married. Pete
was my father's brother. A couple of years younger. He had
a petrol station (or rather a single petrol pump) at Lower
Slaughter in the Cotswolds. One day he attached a note
to the gate of the neighbouring field: 'Gone to London to
find a wife.' He returned two weeks later with Kathleen
Elizabeth Green. They married on 2 January 1954 at
Ealing. The tenth anniversary of the death of my mother's
mother. In the following months Pete built their first house
(Fosseway Garage) where they lived till around 1960.

In each of these epistolary scraps my mother expresses
her love with candour: there are no such letters and few
outward signs of such intensity of affection in later years.
But just as poignant is the fact that my father kept them:
they were so dear to him that he carried them everywhere.
So well-concealed about his person that I only chanced
to stumble upon them years after his death. They are so
worn: he must have unfolded and reread them many times.
How much her 'I love you' must have meant to him! Even
though I never heard him say those words to her. He only
once said them to me. That was on the eve of his death. In
response to my telling him amid my own tears that I loved
him. He was not a man to show great emotion. I never in

all my waking days saw him cry. Except – on occasion – with laughter.

A remarkable letter survives from 21 December 1957. It's so speedy and vital. Packed with play. Pricked with the elusion of what is fixed and proper. A proliferation of provisional names or nicknames. A love of the colloquial and euphemistic. The characteristic but gentle un-Christian 'Gawd'. The Humphrey Bogarty 'boid'. And a charming errancy over grammar and punctuation. 'Its' instead of 'it's'. 'Thats' instead of 'that's'. A preference for a dash – rather than full-stop. It's a Saturday. It's just eleven weeks after she's given birth to me (her first child) and she is writing to Marion ('Maryon' or 'old cock' or 'Slobbo' or 'Fanny') on the birth of her own first baby (also a son) earlier that day. In the middle of the letter the newcomer's father (my uncle John) phones:

Sat. p.m.
Dearest Mary-on,

Bravo old cock! I've been throwing Nicholas around in my excitement and keep telling him he has his future play-mate made but so far he hasn't tagged on!

Its rather wonderful to sit back smugly and think how clever you have been, isn't it? I expect you must be feeling shattered but I do so hope you ain't got a sore tail. I'm dying to hear how much he weighed and whether you had to drag out of bed at the early hours to get to the hospital. I'm so pleased it is a boy too. Daddy and Max are very thrilled.

———

John has just this minute phoned to say Michael William weighs 8lbs 12ozs. GAWD! Poor old Slobbo — you must have had a time of it. He says you have no stitches so thats a relief eh? I suppose Nicnax will look really weedy against your son. I hear he has lashings of hair too. Still I'm consoled by the fact that he will probably rub some of it off on his pillow! I hope the nurses & sisters are decent — suppose they will be since it is Christmas.

If we can't get to see you in hospital we shall come & stay once you are home. But, we shall arrange things with John etc when he delivers the boid. I'm so glad it is all over before Christmas — I feel a weight off my shoulders! (8lbs 12ozs in fact!)

Nicnax has big eyes too you know even if his mouth does roam over his face a little! Hope Mickie hasn't got tightlips!

Thought enclosed might come in useful. Let me know if you want anything. Phoned Nettie & she had a little weep too!

I'll be writing again Fanny. Meanwhile we're all thinking of you both.

> *God Bless.*
> *love F.A.B.*

My cousin and future playmate is Michael William Musgrave Morgan. His second name is also mine (Nicholas William Onslow). After our mothers' much-loved father. My mother signs off as 'F.A.B' ('Fatty Arbuckle') in half-serious reference to being (as she would have said) 'flabby'. It's a letter full of love for her little sister. The most touching detail comes in the 'too' as she makes passing reference to their older sister Jeanette (or 'Nettie'): *Phoned Nettie & she had a little weep too!*

Maxwellian

Your *father* was the educated one. Maxwell – or Max (as she always called him) – went to Merchant Taylors' School at Moor Park in Hertfordshire – a public school not far from the family home at Perivale. His younger brothers Pete and Jeff also went there. How their parents afforded this is not clear. Tony Royle and Lola Onslow (née Kathleen Viola Frances Onslow) were both artists. Lola painted and sketched. She also had some success as a children's book illustrator. Her beautiful line drawings and watercolours appear for example in *The Enid Blyton Book of Fairies* (1924) and Ronald Frankau's *'Oh Dear Dear!' Poems and Stories for Real Children* (1929). Tony was well-known as a cartoonist: for a good number of years he did 'Just Jake' and 'Belinda' in the *Daily Mirror*. Could this have brought in the kind of income to support three boys at a public school? In any case my father enjoyed Merchant Taylors' and was pleased to observe that 'old boys' included such literary worthies as Edmund Spenser and John Webster.

Merchant Taylors' gave my father and his brothers a very clear sense of 'proper English'. My father worked for some years as an editor and artist (in heraldic design) at *Burke's Peerage* and later became a director of a small graphic design company based at Sutton (in Surrey) that did illustration work for science books and journals. In his later working years he spent more time copy-editing and proof-reading.

(He was then based at home. Once a week he would drive the three hours or so up from Devon to do a full day's work at the Sutton office and then drive back again.) But he was always a fiend for grammatical precision. I suspect his zeal on this front helped limit production of what my mother called her 'screed'. Likewise if I ever wrote a piece of fiction or an essay and showed it to my father with the clear request that he not comment on spelling or punctuation he always seemed happy to read it and always returned it with the simple remark 'Most interesting' – never expanded upon. Followed by a series of specific observations about where I'd failed to put a comma or misplaced a quotation mark or misspelt or misused a word.

Simon and I coined 'maxwellian' to reference this persnickety quasi-implacable dimension of our father's character. And also to reference any suspicion of its replication or resemblance in ourselves. In truth I have always been guided by my father's love of good grammar and precise locution. But in writing about my mother I have been compelled to respond to what was quirky and singular about her own language. I have experienced a kind of unfettering. And stumbling into a new closeness to her in the very reaching out to shape words and syntax – idioms and ironies – in the wake of her voice and her laughter. In the remembered tricks and turns of her vivacity. I discovered I had to write – for better or worse – without commas. Things linked without notifications or signposts. Continuous but broken. Making more use of dashes. In sentences sometimes lacking main verbs. Or subjects. Discandying flux. Even if at the same time I cannot write a sentence without wanting to pay homage to my father's lifelong maxwellian vigilance as Grammaticality Enforcement Agency.

A single instance of 'maxwellian' *sensu stricto* must here suffice. About five years after my parents had moved from Surrey down to Devon my father became embroiled – in an epistolary way – with a local dignitary called Dr Terry Glanvill. *Honiton News* covered the story of Dr Glanvill's project of raising money for charity through the innovative sport of woodlice-racing. At this point my father intervened. On 18 January 1985 the paper published his letter to the editor: *Sir – I was puzzled to read that Dr Terry Glanvill calls his new sport 'Woodlice racing'. Surely, in accordance with the normal pattern for this kind of activity (e.g. horse racing, car racing, etc), the appellation should be 'Woodlouse racing'?*

Dr Glanvill appeared unable to understand. Or at least unwilling to countenance what my father was saying. In a response published a fortnight later he declared: *Sir – In answer to your correspondent's query, they are called woodlice, not woodlouse...*

Anyone else might have left it there. My father felt it incumbent upon him to write in to the paper once more. As always gentle and courteous:

Sir – Dr Glanvill seems to have missed the point I was trying to make. No one disputes that woodlice are woodlice or, I trust, that a woodlouse is a woodlouse. The matter at issue is the use of the name in the sport of racing, since in all other instances of which I am aware the singular form of the noun is used when conjoined with the word 'racing'.

However, since Dr Glanvill has originated this sport, it is obviously up to him to decide what it is to be called, and he no doubt wishes to emphasise its unusualness by departing from the standard pattern of nomenclature.

I note among my own reference sources that some 24 different species live in the British Isles, of which the

Armadillidium vulgare (the one which rolls up into a ball) 'was formerly employed in popular medicine as a ready-made pill'. This no doubt explains why another name for the woodlouse is 'pill-bug'.

I was delighted to learn that the woodlouse is proving so useful in raising money for charity, and wish Dr Glanvill continuing success in his admirable and ingenious project – particularly as he is so thoughtful as to set the little creatures free after they have played their part.

My father is quite clear about what is appropriate and correct but he is also amenable to innovation: if the fellow wants to call it 'woodlice-racing' he is wrong but not to worry. *All is for the best in this best of all possible worlds*: my father liked to recall this formulation from Voltaire. He loved Latin and would also quote with effusive pleasure from Horace and Julius Caesar. I recall him reading out the response to Dr Glanvill before he posted it and the delight he took in that *Armadillidium vulgare*: he had the pronunciation pat. Whereas my mother and I would be less sure. More inclined to marmalade the armada and dilly-dally on the lid of its delirium. Not to be vulgar about it.

My father loved the sounds of words but delighted in fixed forms. He had a marvellous store of ready-made speeches and recitations. From A.A. Milne's 'Bad Sir Brian Botany' ('Sir Brian had a battle-axe with great big knobs on. / He went among the villagers and blipped them on the head...') to Aesop's 'The Ant and the Grasshopper' (or rather La Fontaine's *'La cigale et la fourmi'*: *'La cigale, ayant chanté / Tout l'été, / Se trouva fort dépourvue / Quand la bise fut venue...'*). He could recite with as much ease from Francis Bacon's essays as from Shakespeare's Henriad. He had a love of books as objects. The laden shelves of his study bore witness. On Saturdays as a teenager I would accompany him to secondhand bookshops in different towns or villages in Surrey or South London – sometimes twenty or thirty miles away. But in these years he seldom bought a book. Any purchase tended to be of some out-of-print reference work relating to his interests in heraldry or genealogy. He read *The Bookseller* and other secondhand and antiquarian book catalogues that came to him in the post. He read his quarterly Buddhist magazine *The Middle Way*. It seemed he had been a very active and diligent reader but then stopped. All the literary and philosophical texts he quoted were from his schooldays. Something must have put an end to his reading. I never asked and no one said.

I suppose it was the war. When he reached call-up age he wanted to go to sea but the navy was full. He was part of the decimation that generated the Bevin boys. He was a coal miner at Worksop in Nottinghamshire. He spent three years underground. By general consensus it was hellish. Many men reported afterwards that they could not wait to get out. But these were the best years of my father's life. He relished the digging. Being underground. The physical camaraderie. The routine. Every day the same. Down the mine first thing. Up at the end of the day. A meal served to him in his digs. A few beers at the pub. *Thirsty work down t'mine* (as he liked to reminisce). Then sleep and start again. Digs to digs.

Who's turned the lights out?

In the early stages I was committed to the idea of a memoir that would contain no photographs or other illustrations. I could not *not* think of Alice's incredulous question in Wonderland: 'What is the use of a book without pictures or conversations?' But I wanted more than anything else to evoke my mother's voice. Her sayings and tricks of phrase. The veering polytonal quality of her speech. I was driven by the desire of what Philip Sidney and William Wordsworth call *prosopopoeia*. Giving a voice to the absent or dead. From the beginning I was also mindful of Roland Barthes' little book about photography. On the surface *Camera Lucida* (1980) is not about his mother with whom he lived most of his life and who died in 1977. If there is a surface. That is the question. Does a photo have a surface any more than a page of print? In any case Barthes' book is haunted by a photograph of his mother as a girl aged five in a winter garden in 1898. The picture is not reproduced. He found the thought of its inclusion unbearable. And so the most powerful image in the book is not present.

I was drawn to the thought of a memoir that would call on the reader to imagine: to see but also and perhaps first of all to hear. Might there be a way of experiencing a memoir with pictures but still in sound? Of letting the silence of photographs speak? Or if not speak at least in some ghostlike way enter into the conversation? Isn't Alice in the end suggesting something of that with her 'or'? An *or* of gold like the roar of which George Eliot speaks: *If we had a keen vision and feeling of all ordinary human life, it would be like hearing the grass grow and the squirrel's heart beat, and we should die of that roar which lies on the other side of silence.* My mother loved Blake and would sometimes quote him. Often out of the blue: *To see a world in a grain of sand / And heaven in a wild flower...* But she also loved Eliot and her call to hear the grass grow and the heart of the squirrel. I imagine a sort of mystic photo pad in which the words that surround and respond to each picture have the effect of making the photograph disappear. Translated into the roar on the other side.

Here is a photograph of the McAdam family at Drymen in around 1905. There are six people in the picture. Four men and two women. A mother and father and four offspring. From left to right standing up are Helen or Nellie (b. 1879) and Walter or Watty (b. 1887) and William (b. 1891).

Who's turned the lights out?

Seated are John (b. 1882) and parents Helen (b. 1851 *née* Helen Millar King) and John (b. 1847). The picture is the work of A and G Taylor Artistic Photographers of 127 Sauchiehall Street Glasgow. An albumen print in cabinet card format. It is formality personified. Everyone is dressed in their Victorian or early Edwardian best. Everyone is watching the photographer or the birdie. But photographer and birdie are no more present than you are. The people in the photograph are not smiling but the mouths of Nellie and her little brother William suggest some disposition to amusement. All the mouths are uncanny. Tight-lipped. Akin.

Roland Barthes asks: what *pains* in a photograph? He coins the term 'punctum' to designate some detail that has an unexpected and inordinate capacity to wound. There is something painful that moves over this Drymen family photograph. A punctum is first of all the opening of a tear duct. The photograph trembles in the eye of the beholder. At one moment it is the awful sense of composition as decomposition. The mouths all arranged. And then the hands. Then the jarring distance between the bodies. Then the creeping force of the ivy and other vegetation that surrounds and envelops them in our certainty that all of these people are dead. The boy on the right is my mother's father. Or rather he will be. In the bizarre instant of the picture William is just a young lad of fourteen standing in placid concentration alongside a father whose facial hair looks like the overdone product of a low-budget Victorian TV melodrama. But spectral excess is the very oxygen of the picture. Like Philip Larkin's 'MCMXIV' it is engulfed by the future. They will all die in time. Never on time. The McAdam offspring will live on till the 1950s and 60s. But my mother's grandfather John will die at Drymen in

1926. And her grandmother Helen will die in 1938. In a room in broad daylight in the time-capsule overlooking the Square these will be her dying words: 'Who's turned the lights out?' Isn't that also what pains in a photograph? The way it can say not 'Look at us in the brightness of now!' but 'Who's turned the lights out?'

Out of the picture

The village of Drymen held a kind of enchantment for my mother. It had to do with poetry and song but also mourning and silence. So many McAdams lived in and around and are buried there. At various times they ran the Square Inn (now the Winnock Hotel) and the Clachan Inn. The Clachan is the oldest licensed pub in Scotland (1734). Its first landlady was Rob Roy MacGregor's sister: Mistress Gow. The McAdams belonged with the MacGregors. My mother's contempt for the pettiness and inanity of nationalism came out of a deep swirling attachment to her father's Scotland as much as to her mother's England.

There was a well-established link between inn and kirkyard at Drymen: coffins would stop en route for mourners to drink. My mother's aunt Nellie died four years before I was born. But her uncle Watty was still living when we visited on at least a couple of occasions. He spent most of his life as a farmer but was landlord of the Square Inn from 1924 to 1928. He was a lifelong bachelor. He once made the eighteen-mile journey south to visit the city of Glasgow. Not at all to his liking. He never went again. I remember him sitting in the time-capsule cottage on the Square without a word. Like a character in a late Beckett play. So much dwelling in silence. And then there was Cousin Nessie. I suppose they were sharing the cottage then. I only recall her as gap-toothed and ruddy-cheeked and gray-haired. For many years she ran the tearooms on the Square as well as the Clachan Inn. She had a tendency to say 'Och – that's *terrible!*' Simon and Cousin Mike and I internalised this declamation and parroted it for years. It was key to our love of a Scottish accent. A 'ter-r-r-rible' stretched out to implausible length. As teenagers visiting with our mothers (our fathers more or less never came with us to Scotland) we would strive to tell Nessie things that might elicit the response: 'Och – that's *terrible!*'

In the latter part of her life she became quite deaf. Only now does it occur to me (like a tacit gong of memory) that my great-uncle Watty's silence might have been his *modus vivendi* for dealing with Cousin Nessie's deafness. My mother in her final decade became quite deaf too. My hearing is on the decline. In my twenties and thirties I had no time for obscure cousins or great-aunts and -uncles. Let alone for their physical foibles and frailties. But the past catches and joins up. It trembles. It courses back and loops in. It calls out. It cries. It howls. It sings. It doesn't happen when it happens. In the mind's ear. It sears.

My mother's father was not the first William McAdam. I remember walking with her among the graves at Drymen and finding more than one headstone bearing that name. But *he* is not there. His ashes are at Mortlake Cemetery in southwest London. He was born on 12 May 1891 on a sheep farm at Slachristock in the Kilsyth Hills a few miles from Drymen. (Submerged in 1939 as part of the Carron Valley Water Scheme – its watery ruins another kind of time-capsule. Dissolving in silence at the bottom of one of the largest water-supply reservoirs in the UK.) My mother's grandfather John – he of the cascading sideburns – managed the farm until 1903 when he inherited from a second cousin the lease of the Square Inn and moved there with the family. The inn itself belonged to the Duke of Montrose.

How many William McAdams does it take to make a Kathleen Beatrice? Her great-great-grandfather William McAdam married a Mary Logan of Drymen and they had a son called William McAdam and he had a son called William McAdam as well as a son called John. And John had a son called William McAdam (my mother's father) and all of this may sound dry as dust or as the dry men of Drymen – a mere dree tale of a string of men with the same name – but there's liquid refreshment and even music at the end of the day. For the William McAdam who was my mother's great-grandfather was a fine singer and a celebrated figure at the Square Inn long before his son John and later his grandson Watty became innkeeper there. This William McAdam was for many years gamekeeper to the Duke of Montrose – and later to a Glasgow stockbroker called Holmes-Kerr. He would sing at the Inn for Holmes-Kerr and the collective company at the end of a day's shooting. His best-loved rendition was of 'The Lea-Rig':

> When o'er the hill the eastern star
> Tells bughtin time is near, my jo,
> And owsen frae the furrow'd field
> Return sae dowf and weary O;
> Down by the burn, where birken buds
> Wi' dew are hangin clear, my jo,
> I'll meet thee on the lea-rig,
> My ain kind Dearie O.
>
> At midnight hour, in mirkest glen,
> I'd rove, and ne'er be eerie, O,

If thro' that glen I gaed to thee,
My ain kind Dearie O;
Altho' the night were ne'er sae wild,
And I were ne'er sae weary O,
I'll meet thee on the lea-rig,
My ain kind Dearie O.

The hunter lo'es the morning sun;
To rouse the mountain deer, my jo;
At noon the fisher seeks the glen
Adown the burn to steer, my jo:
Gie me the hour o' gloamin' gray,
It maks my heart sae cheery O,
To meet thee on the lea-rig,
My ain kind Dearie O.

I encountered this story about my mother's great-grandfather many years ago in notes about the family's history but never troubled to reflect on the singing of 'The Lea-Rig'. The song exists in various forms. There's a version in David Herd's *Scots Songs* (1776) and another by Robert Fergusson and William Reid. But I now realise that William McAdam the gamekeeper must have sung the Robert Burns version (dating from 1792) with its concluding verse about the hunter.

I check out some details of the vocabulary. A *lea-rig* is the grassy ridge left at the edge of a ploughed field. *Bughtin time* is the hour when you bring the sheep in to be milked. *Dowf* is listless, lacking in spirit or energy, sad, melancholy, wanting force. *Eerie* here means fearful or timid. *Jo* (a sweetheart or darling) I already know: it's a nifty little J-word my mother taught me when we used to while away long Devon evenings playing Scrabble. Then on the internet I click up a wonderful YouTube recording of the song. As if out of the gloaming gray of decades I am invaded by this foreign body of old Scottish music. Engulfed by the realisation that my mother also sang it:

Gie me the hour o' gloamin' gray,
It maks my heart sae cheery O,
To meet thee on the lea-rig,
My ain kind Dearie O.

Gugga

My mother's father William McAdam served in the Great War as a veterinary surgeon (or 'horse doctor'). He met Emily Gibbs – his future wife – when his Scottish regiment was billeted at Chelmsford in 1916. Prior to going off to the continent. After the war they spent time in Canada and Scotland before setting up home in London.

William and Emily had four daughters – the youngest (Marion and my mother) both born in the house they rented on Hotham Road in Putney. [*Left to right: Peggy, Marion, Nettie and my mother, February 1930.*] His eldest brother John inherited and sold property in Scotland and bought two houses on Ongar Road in Fulham. He gave one of these (no. 24) to his little brother William and lived next door. John McAdam was an air mechanic with the RAF during the war. In later decades he established himself as a draper and William joined the trade. They later sold carpet and linoleum. One of my earliest memories is of my right big toe getting broken by a roll of lino in the basement at Ongar Road.

My mother and father lived with her father for several years. This was my first home. And here too my own brother Simon was born on 10 February 1960. I remember nothing about my great-uncle John who died in May 1965 at the age of 83. I only know that – while my grandfather was always partial to whisky – John was teetotal. Even when they were adults living in Fulham little brother

William had to be surreptitious. He used to conceal his whisky bottle in the old Drymen family grandfather clock.

The day my mother's father died still clangs and clamours. We called him Gugga. I loved him very much. Many of my earliest memories had to do with him. The two of us together at the house in Fulham. My parents out at work. He would be in his Parker Knoll chair beside the bubbling coal-fire. I would be on the rug. We would play with coloured wooden building bricks together. He would prepare an apple with his penknife in a single snaking curl of peel then slice it up for me. He had what seemed an endless supply of bars of Fry's Chocolate Cream. He would break off a single piece. My relished quota for the day. Then he lived with us in a three-bedroom semi-detached house in Cheam. He was the first person I ever saw dead. He was seventy-four. I was seven. 6 September 1965. The previous evening he had taken his customary fifteen-minute walk down to The Harrow for a couple of pints of Guinness. Everyone else must already have been in bed when he came home. He had fallen asleep in his Parker Knoll in the sitting room. I was the first up in the morning. He was asleep. I was going to school. I tried to wake him. I touched his right hand as he sat there. I went to school. Only later did I remember how cold his hand had been. How still his face.

My mother put on an incredible show. She picked us up from school in his 1964 purple and black Ford Anglia and drove us to a toy shop. *You can choose anything you want.* She had never said such a thing before. I suppose I could have opted for some large and expensive item. An Action Man. A space-station. But I was troubled by the unprecedented offer. *Anything you want.* I chose a miniature plastic Dalek that moved about on a ball-bearing.

Gugga

The silver-painted body had a stripe of blue around it. My brother chose the Dalek with the red stripe. My Dalek soon enough split in two and the pieces were thrown away. But I still have the ball-bearing. A marble of sorts.

My aunt Marion was back at the house with my uncle John and my cousin Michael. Now my mother was at the kitchen sink washing up and crying. She began to make noise I'd never heard before. She wouldn't stop. My uncle took me and my brother and cousin out. He led us with his walking stick up a familiar alley to Seears Park. I don't remember us ever reaching the park itself that afternoon. Just the alley. (And only now – more than fifty years later – I reflect on the resonance of this strange French-English word *alley* as 'going'.) He told us that our grandfather had died. He made it sound simple and natural. Our grandfather was old and in due course this happens to old people. I was struck by the contrast. My uncle gentle and matter-of-fact walking along but at the same time probing and studious as if in consultation with his walking stick. My mother transformed into an inconsolable unrecognisable howling creature too scary to be in the house with.

About a dozen years later we were living in a somewhat larger house in the same Surrey village. I was in the garden when my mother came out of the house to Auntie Marion and burst into tears as she told her their eldest sister Peggy had breast cancer and would be having a mastectomy. These were horrified uncontrollable tears shared by the two sisters as they clung together in the middle of the lawn in the hot summer afternoon sunshine. But nothing like the engorged wailing of my mother at the death of her father. With my cousin Mike and other school friends I collected and swopped cards about the American Civil War. They came with bubble gum. Pink and sugary all too soon gray and tasteless. Our excitement was for the cards not the gum. They showed soldiers maimed and killed in a wide range of poses and situations. They were gory and macabre. Oozing with death. But their effect bore no comparison to my mother's crying at the kitchen sink.

Simon

That kind of howling returned only once. It came when my brother Simon died downstairs in the cottage in Devon. My mother couldn't have been expected to be aware that he was dead because – unlike me – she wasn't in the room. It was around 10.45 in the evening. Sunday 28 September 1986. She didn't have to be present. She couldn't but didn't need to be. She knew. She locked herself in the bathroom upstairs and howled and howled and howled. For hours she refused to come out or let anyone in. From that death none of us recovered. But my mother it did for. She it by degrees sent mad. My father and I understood this without ever speaking of it. Grief at her son gone in his mid-twenties drove her into any and every bush and ambush in mental and physical flames drowning buried for miles in every direction.

Permissive

In memory of my brother every word would be in grief. Without relief. To the end. After his death my mother never spoke of it. Every word in tears. Torn to pieces. Everything broken down the middle: before his death – after his death. Take the word 'permissive'. It's about permitting or sending through. Letting loose. Letting go. Before Simon's death it was easy to connect my mother with such a word. She *permitted* us everything. But after? How could a mother let her son – who was gone – go?

What incredible freedom she gave us. Of course she must have found us challenging and even plain impossible. Simon and I were not good boys. But why were we so bad? My mother and father and Gugga seemed kindness and indulgence personified. I got expelled from my first primary school. I used to be convinced this was because I refused to pray in assembly (which is true). But I also still remember the filthy white taste of the sudsy soap a teacher made me put in my mouth. Which suggests bad language rather than no language at all. When we were about six and eight – and my seniority must have led the way in this – Simon and I were for some reason alone in the house. Our father was at work and our mother had had to go out for some brief period. I suppose it must have been in the months after Gugga's death. In our mother's absence we investigated the bathroom. In particular the mirror-fronted cabinet above the washbasin where she kept her cosmetics. There were various shades of lipsticks. At first we had fun pouting and putting it on our lips. But then we started drawing or painting or writing on the mirror. And after that we began to graffiti the walls of the bathroom. Our mother was livid. How could she not be? What did we think we were doing?

I became less insubordinate during my school years. Or insubordinate in different ways. By the end of his life my brother was as gentle as a saint. But in earlier years he was quite wild. He got expelled from his secondary school for a plethora of reasons – some more plausible than others. My parents had an interview with the head teacher who presented them with an inventory. A list of fifteen or more cases of unacceptable behaviour. I only remember two: 'throwing smaller boys over fences' and 'thinking that he is an eagle'. The first of these indeed sounded and still sounds bad. In fact I suspect it was only one boy on one occasion and more an easing over than a catapulting. But still. Not commendable. But 'thinking that he is an eagle' seemed bizarre. Would you seek to expel someone from school for thinking they were a llama? At least llamas can't fly. (In later years I came to feel that there were preternatural affinities between my brother and J.A. Baker. He read T.H. White's *The Goshawk* but – so far as I know – never encountered Baker's *Peregrine*.) My parents fought against the school's decision and lost. As it happened I was at a different school and my own relative anonymity as a pupil helped persuade my headmaster to take my brother in as well.

My mother had no limits. If my brother wanted to train a kestrel (like the boy in the Ken Loach film *Kes*) he could. If he wanted a gyrfalcon she would help him acquire one. If he was interested in collecting owl pellets. If he wanted to collect skulls (a vole or a crow or even a hippopotamus). If this involved cooking the head of a small mammal found dead in the Cornfields. When he was fifteen the local paper ran a story about his naturalist passions. It features a photograph of Simon with a barn owl on his gauntleted fist and another in which he appears to be conversing with a jackdaw. The jackdaw is perched on a sheep's skull in my brother's hand. Even the journalist baulked at some of the things on which he was reporting. 'Dead cat? No problem' ran the strapline for the article. But my mother didn't mind.

She seemed to understand 'permissive' society in ways no one else did. It is true that she had no apparent problem in later years with her sons sleeping with young women. But she herself had a sort of horror of sex. My mother would often refer to something 'rearing its ugly head': by far the worst and most recurrent offender was sex. But 'permissive' for her was not about sexual antics. Rather it had to do with a more general and more radical conception of freedom and possibility.

Not long after the newspaper article was published disaster struck. In those days a paper didn't scruple at providing the more or less precise address of someone featured. In any case the story must have got around because some nefarious person or persons came into our back garden at night and made off with the gyrfalcon and the barn owl. My brother was devastated. As was my mother. The aviaries were in the back garden but the crime seemed as intimate and violating as a domestic burglary.

A key to the wildlife world of our years in Cheam was to be found in the Cotswolds. This is where my father's brother Pete lived with Kathy and our four cousins: Heather David Vincent and Caroline. Having served some years as a one-man petrol station Pete turned to selling advertising for a newspaper in Evesham. Then he and Kathy started up an estate agency in Winchcombe. In the early years the family lived in a rambling eighteenth-century house in the heart of the town. Here we would go for weekends or longer stays several times a year. My mother got on well with Kathy and liked Pete too. I remember the house as a wonderful space of laughter and music and song. But I know my mother also found the chaos of their domestic scene extraordinary. She couldn't believe *the state of the place*. She had a low tolerance for untidiness in her own home. She would often voice her disdain for how *in need of a good spring clean* a place was by exclaiming (in the voice of Bette Davis from *Beyond the Forest*): *What* a *dump!* 'Permissive' in my mother's sense did not apply to domestic hygiene. Our cousins' house was a spectacular dump by my mother's standards. There was a playroom that you had to take a step down to enter. But it was so full of discarded toys that it was more or less impossible to access. It resembled (as I now think of it) a microcosm of the South Pacific Garbage Patch. Somewhere off an upstairs corridor there was a mysterious high-ceilinged room creaking with old furniture and other objects: a combination of pickings from my uncle's estate agency work and stuff from Perivale. The curtains were always drawn. Which doubtless gave further force to the leopard. There was a real leopard – its skin and glassy-eyed stuffed head – waiting on the floor in the dark. When we were back in Cheam my mother used to refer to the state of the house in Winchcombe from time to time. Always with a visible shudder.

But outstripping everything was the sheer range of animals living in the house. The kitchen at Winchcombe

as an idea must have driven my mother potty. For this was the room in her own house in which order and cleanliness were paramount. The Cotswold kitchen was more like a zoo without keeper. Amid all the other clutter of unwashed dishes and laundry there were budgerigars and chameleons and terrapins and cats and dogs and stick insects and lots of white mice as well as a bushbaby that was released from its cage every night after supper and leapt about for an extended period. So the pets and other creatures my brother and I kept (and often left to our mother to look and clean up after) followed in this Cotswold tradition.

Around 1968 Pete and Kathy moved out of the town into a beautiful house on a nearby hill: St Kenelm's. It was a former eleventh-century chapel surrounded by fields and woods. There's a charming photo of my mother and Kathy (whom my mother always thought very glamorous) posing either side of the back-garden gate. Another shows all the members of this Cotswold idyll. (Excepting the photographer: my Uncle Pete.) [*Left to right: my father,*

David, Vincent, me, Caroline, my mother, Heather, my aunt Kathy, Simon.] My brother and David would wander in the fields and woods for hours birdwatching or looking for owl-pellets and dead animals. Simon and I loved visiting our Cotswold cousins. We were like the bees in Keats' 'Ode to Autumn'. As if warm days would never cease. Our parents left us all to our own devices – in the days before there were devices – while my father and his brother Pete smoked and reveried by the fireside in the drawing room and my mother and my aunt would sit in the kitchen by an Aga that never seemed to go out. Like having a double: two Kathleen Royles. (Both married to men whose mother had also had this name.) Yakking. That was my mother's word. Sharing girlish laughter and regaling one another with stories. Yakking and laughing away into the night.

Nurse

My mother was a nurse. Her being so calls for a new vocabulary of nursehood. *Nursehood*: a sort of cryptic condensing of my mother and a Robin Hood. Robin Hood or Rob Roy: in my unconscious – and in hers – this couple were always mixed up. She who'd be a fantastical *hood*. The nurse who'd be always the she you wanted her to be. Nurse *who'd*. And at the same time I think of my mother also as the creator of a new kind of nursery. Not something in modern steel and glass with government vouchers but ancient in the mood and blood of what it is to care to support to nurture to look after.

A tiny newspaper clipping survives with the headline CHELSEA NURSE LEAVES FOR FULHAM:

> Chelsea's loss is Fulham's gain. That is what her patients are saying now that Chelsea District Nurse K.B. McAdam has been transferred to Fulham.
>
> Nurse McAdam is a very popular nurse with her many patients.
>
> One, Mr Malcolm Mackenzie, is particularly interested in her hobbies –painting and pottery.
>
> 'She has great talent as a water-colourist, with a wonderful sense of colour and form,' he observed this week.

End of story. So minimalist yet mysterious. The desirable footballer image. A jokey idea even then: getting a transfer from Stamford Bridge to Craven Cottage. The solitary alleged testimony of a patient called Malcolm Mackenzie. The evocation of my mother as interested in pottery? A talented water-colourist? Where was this cutting from? *Sporting Life*? A local newspaper? A nursing gazette?

That my mother was a nurse is the fact of the matter. A fact that in another clime Gertrude Stein might opine one must sublime and resublime again and again. I think of my mother's patience. *Her many patients.* I think of the play of 'patience' and 'patients'. Remembering for example days in early boyhood starting with the rattle of the milk float. The milkman in his uniform in the dark leaving bottles with silver or gold tops on the doorstep for a blue-tit to peck open if it could. Days before central heating when our house was warmed by an open fire and a gruff sooty-faced coalman lugged enormous sacks and opened and dumped them in the coalbunker. Days when breakfast was dippy egg with toast-strip soldiers or Gugga's salty porridge with milk and butter or golden syrup. Days when a horse-drawn rag-and-bone cart came down the street to the jangling of a bell. (Whenever I told people we lived in Cheam they connected it with Tony Hancock. The rag-and-bone man in *Steptoe and Son* and prior to that the not-very-successful comedian from East Cheam in *Hancock's Half Hour*. In reality there was a North and a West and a South but never an East Cheam.) My mother's patience with me as I'd sketch and then sketch again a pencil drawing of the Beatles as seen on TV in December 1963. Her patience every day when I wanted to sit on the lavatory for what seemed like hours resting on my knees a cork mat with a jumper on top to provide a hillscape in which I manoeuvred one by one large groups of Air-Fix soldiers or cowboys and Indians. Meanwhile she would be downstairs tidying or in a neighbouring upstairs room making beds. Singing in full-throated ease 'The Skye Boat Song' or Judy Garland's 'Over the Rainbow'. She had such patience for everyone. And everyone her patient. With never a hint of fluster or condescension.

Thirty years later no different. I was writing a short story called 'Light Lunch' and talked about it with her at the white Formica-top table in the kitchen and read it aloud to her in a quiet corner of the Tucker Arms at Dalwood. It began: 'Rosemary and Kenneth lived in a house that was rather too large for them.' Then I drove us home and we established ourselves in the kitchen. She made a coffee and filled a hot-water bottle. I poured myself a Glenmorangie. And we returned to the subject of the final paragraph. Vexing to me but to her it seemed nothing but pleasure. The story is about a wealthy childless couple in their late forties who develop an all-consuming desire for food. Their consumption becomes an enormity in every sense. The final paragraph presented the crucial dilemma. I was divided. Should it be a story that concluded with cannibalism and if so how? Or should it be a story that in a more literal way consumed itself? A story in the vein of Maurice Blanchot's 'The Madness of the Day'. About how the light goes mad. Or about how you might go mad for the light. The male protagonist would not only devour his wife but eat the streets the Houses of Parliament the entirety of London and at last swallow up the light. I don't know how long my mother spent listening to my prevarications and contemplating variant possibilities with me. An hour? Two hours? Two coffees? Three drams of whisky (plus a splash in her instant)? She favoured the simpler ending.

Nothing hifalutin'. But also not too explicit. We ended up with Kenneth telling his wife he has a surprise for her. After asking what it is: 'Rosemary noticed that he was still strangely absorbed by the table-top, or perhaps by her plump arms resting on it. Then she caught the light in his eyes.' In the story the table is dark mahogany but in reality it was the white Formica-top kitchen table. I can still remember the thrilled light in my mother's eyes as we settled on that final sentence.

She had extraordinary presence of mind. The sort of attentiveness and calm required to hold a kestrel on your fist as my brother does in a photo taken outside St Kenelm's in the early 1970s. It is a classic amateur shot. The main

subject almost edged out of the picture. But the field in which Simon is standing as it slopes down behind him into Dingle Wood was the scene of a dramatic event close to the time of this photograph. My uncle Pete was a collector of all kinds of objects – from eighteenth-century oil paintings to vintage cars. There was an old pale green Vauxhall Victor Estate among the various automobiles on the large forecourt (or area of mud) above the house. Did the car work? Could it be made to run? My cousin Heather (just a year older than me) recalls sitting with my mother under the chestnut trees below the garden. (The area away to the right of where – in the photo – my brother is standing with his kestrel.) Talking as they looked out across the field. My mother inviting her teenage niece to 'give voice to her thoughts and feelings'. My mother 'made everyone feel that what they were saying was worth listening to'. Then they became aware of 'some commotion and frantic shouting' up the hill to their left. Followed by the 'surreal vision' of Simon tearing alongside the green Vauxhall. Hanging on as if for dear life to the door handle as the vehicle freewheeled downhill out of control. Breaking off from the tranquil conversation she was having with her niece my mother yelled at her son: *Let go! Let go!* At which Simon disengaged himself and stood stockstill in shock. The car crashed in Dingle Wood. A complete write-off. Heather recalls how my mother 'as usual took calm control of the situation'.

Calm and control came to the fore on another life-threatening occasion. Also in the early 1970s. She took me and my brother on holiday to Welcombe Bay in Devon with the mother and son and daughter of a family called the Breens. A holiday without fathers. The Breen father was an alcoholic who beat and abused his wife. My brother and her son Tom were friends. My mother felt compassion for all of them but to Sally she was a special strength. It was a great relief for Sally Breen to have some time away from the husband. (He died a year or so later. Discovered on the stairs at night. Asphyxiated by his own vomit.) One day we were down on the beach. Simon and Tom were playing on the sand. My mother and Sally were relaxing in the sunshine. I was swimming in the sea. As was Sally's daughter Amelia. (She was a year or two younger than me.) I didn't feel as if I had swum out too far but then in an uncanny shock I felt below me the sudden and immense shifting of a powerful cold body of water and I was swimming to the shore – I knew straight away – for my life. I'd never felt anything like it. A monstrous undercurrent out of nowhere. I managed to get back to the beach but I was gasping for breath. Only then did I realise that the real event was taking place behind me. Millie was being dragged out to sea. Sally was beside herself. My mother took control in her own way. She shouted and shouted at the men on the beach to do something get help phone the coastguard. And to demonstrate the seriousness of the situation she walked firm and steady with all her clothes on into the sea. It was the spectacle of this seeming madness that aroused effective notice. Someone or other must have run or driven to find a phone and dial 999. A helicopter was scrambled. Millie had been washed away. Dashed on some distant rocks. She had bad cuts and bruises but was winched to safety.

Something Oscar Wilde grasped and writing this book has enabled me to appreciate anew: the perverse and marvellous importance of being cousins. Vanessa was the only child of my father's youngest brother Jeff and his Anglo-Irish wife Joan. She was a beautiful young woman who in a sense never stopped being young because she

developed multiple sclerosis in her early twenties and
spent the rest of her life in a wheelchair – in what was at
once gruesome prison and Snow White suspension. She
died in 2018 at the age of 51. She outlived her parents by
just a year or two. Vanessa and I were close in ways that
required no speech. Even when her face was half-paralysed
we could read one another without a word. I was ten when
she was born. I had no idea what was going on. But one day
my mother had a baby. A sister? How did that happen? The
term 'postnatal depression' was never used but I suppose
Joan suffered it. She was unable to cope. Another mother
must be found. Vanessa lived with us for six weeks or so.
My mother loved her as if she were her own baby. No
one had any sense as to how long the newcomer might be
staying. It was wonderful. I was allowed to bottle-feed her.
Did her mother's condition or my cousin's sojourn away
from home have some connection with the much later
development of MS? That question has haunted me. And I
never knew if Vanessa knew that she had spent those weeks

with us in her early infancy. If my mother was anything other to her than the unknown nurse.

Some of the most moving photographs of my mother are related to her life and work as a nurse. There is the picture of the State Registered Nurse award ceremony. At first glance stationary – but in truth an action-shot. My mother second from the left in the front row. The one with the book (*Textbook of Medicine*) and diploma secure in her lap. The one in the instant of clapping. With her white gloves and the fullest most embracing smile. And visible in the dimness of the right side of the picture in the second row are her father with her sisters Nettie and Marion. My mother didn't *support* the National Health Service – she didn't *believe in* it: she *was* it. To me and many others she was its simple extraordinary embodiment. As a district nurse who worked at Hampstead General Hospital and later at Hammersmith General (where she gave birth to me) she treated private as well as NHS patients. All received alike her devoted attention and what people today call empathy.

SHE WON
TWO PRIZES

Winner of the silver medal presented annually at Hampstead General Hospital, 25-years-old Nurse Kathleen McAdam, of Fulham, was also awarded the surgical prize.

But her primary passion was for the spirit of free universal healthcare. There is a newspaper clipping that shows her proud and glad at twenty-five years old when she was employed at Hampstead General and North West London Hospital: 'she won two prizes'. The photo says this. The caption seems to mimic it. In another photograph she has paused on her bicycle. I imagine she has just arrived for work and come in through the main entrance at Hammersmith. There is pleasure in her face. Pride along with wry self-effacement. A disposition to amusement akin to her father's in the 1905 Drymen picture. But above all something solitary and single. Quiet but indomitable. The nurse alone.

Even in the photograph where she is standing in the sunshine of the back garden at 19 Carlisle Road in Cheam in around 1967 she holds our lovely cat Tatty Too with the care and poise of a nurse. My mother nursed everything and everyone. She adored children. She might be down in

Honiton on market day and fall into talking with a child who'd tripped and fallen on the pavement until the parent or carer was drawn in and the conversation would become the most lively and significant event that morning on the high street. She'd remember the child and they'd speak again on future occasions. Her attentiveness to children was part of her pre-word world. It was an aspect of the unspoken invention of a new kind of nursery.

She loved to listen – but how she also loved to talk! She nursed conversations. She nursed thinking and feeling. She nursed my brother's pictures. She nursed my poems and stories. She nursed her flowerbeds. Her cup of coffee. Her crossword. She nursed whatever she looked on.

Chote

My uncle John called her Nurse Chote. I don't know where this name came from. It sounds demeaning or at best ambivalent. It acknowledges her importance as a nurse while also reducing her to that function. And the 'Chote' conveyed no sense to my ear besides rhyming with *goat* and *stoat*. I suspect it said more about my uncle's jealousy of Marion's attachment to my mother than about my mother. In this family portrait he is in full regalia as RAF wing

commander alongside his much shorter and younger wife. Holding both of Marion's hands is my cousin Michael. And in the foreground on the right is their poodle Boodles. My abiding memory of Boodles: standing on his hind legs in the Morgans' Mini sticking his head out of the open window to enjoy the streaming breeze.

I was very fond of John. I called him Nuncle. At the time of this photograph he was commanding officer of the Joint Services School for Linguists based at RAF Tangmere. Service personnel were taught Mandarin and Polish and Czech in addition to Russian. In our early years I most associated him with a solitary short phrase: 'Defend yourself!' He would exclaim *Defend yourself!* then start tickling you. My cousin had to endure this on a daily basis. I came to feel there was something troubling and cryptic about it. The irony of crying 'Defend yourself!' while attacking. The vigour of the tickling (for it was never altogether gentle: you often came away with aching ribs). It was only years later that I discovered that John had been married once before and had older children in California. And it is only in recent years that a fuller sense of him has emerged as a spy. After a 'good war' in the RAF he was commissioned to study Russian at Cambridge. Thereafter he had a close involvement with Donald Maclean. John never forgave his perfidy. While based on the Czech border in Germany my uncle gathered thirteen months' information from behind the Iron Curtain into a single folder. He was flown by armed escort in an RAF plane to the Ministry of Defence. He knocked on Maclean's door and passed over the folder. *Thank you John.* After Maclean's defection he came to discover that all his various contacts had disappeared without trace. But my uncle himself was some years dead before we learned that he'd once smuggled himself into the USSR and dressed and talked as a local peasant as part of an elaborate but successful operation to help a defecting Russian scientist escape from Moscow.

When we were growing up Nuncle was often travelling. He had a job with Marconi. In his spare time he read books of history and biography with a studiousness that impressed and inspired me. I was also captivated by his habit of inserting memorabilia in the pages of a book: a newspaper cutting or letter or concert ticket or photo or dried flower. It was like the private elaboration of a mysterious other story – the memoir of another life – within the book. And then there was his more or less diurnal habit of going off on long solitary walks and cycle rides. He was also on a regular basis 'gone fishing'. Sometimes for several days at a time. Mounted on the wall of the Morgans' dining room was a glass case containing the preserved rainbow trout he had caught in 1959 at Chew Valley Lake in Somerset. About the same age as me and Simon and Michael: our embalmed unspeaking contemporary.

In 1973 my mother wrote him a poem. She inscribed it in a card on his fifty-seventh birthday (21 March):

The winds of March are fiendish strong
On certain Downs they swirl along
Be warned! For they are on the search
'Twixt bracken, scrub and Common Birch
To bare the one that's doing his Thing
(While skylarks soar and sweetly sing)
Come ding-a-ling-ding. Ding-a-ling.
Rheumatic pains in limb and joint
Brings Chote to make her vital point

And her advice free – not unwise
(Though draped in this poetic guise)
'Oh! Keep it from the cold wind's spite!
Warmly clad and out of sight
Till warmer days in later Spring!'
Come Ding-a-ling-Ding. Ding-a-ling.

The poem is signed 'Anon' and accompanied by a cartoon pencil drawing of a fish by my father. It seems at once tender and barbed. Suggesting a knowledge or understanding of her brother-in-law with a 'ding-a-ling' all of its own. I suspect 'Nurse Chote' was my uncle's equivalent of 'Defend yourself!' He showed affection but he kept himself at a distance. He shared with my father a quiet deference to the power that was the bond between

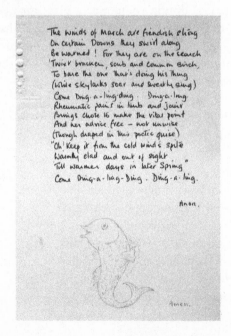

Marion and 'saucy Kate' (as another birthday inscription has it). The sisters were in together deeper than secret intelligence.

Over my cousin Mike my mother has had a lifelong influence. He remembers her as the reason he decided to study medicine and become a GP. She passed on to him a love of the NHS. And the spirit of that passion lives on: two of his own children are also now doctors.

Demonic

'Then she caught the light in his eyes.' My mother loved her middle name (Beatrice) and associated it as much with Dante as with her aunt Beattie. The name means 'she who makes happy or brings joy' and insofar as any word becomes her 'Beatrice' does well. But my mother was no softie. The light in her eyes could also suggest something of the demonic. It's there in the 'She Wins Two Prizes' photograph. As my cousin Mike recalls: 'She would literally roll up her sleeves.' She set about things with a vigour and intensity that could be alarming. As if something had taken over.

She also took cryptic pleasure in murder mysteries and horror films. She used to remark from time to time: 'All's fair in love and war.' This was a saying of hers that I never felt I understood. On one occasion I remonstrated: *But that can't be so. You don't murder your husband. There has to be a concept of war crimes...* But like everything else she said she had thrown a strange mantle over it in advance. There was always the matter of context. She never said 'All's fair...' in response to news of a particular disastrous military event. And there was always an ironic or hyperbolic lilt to the aphorism. Along with a sort of detached projection that suggested she understood all too well why for example a woman might do away with her spouse.

She was fascinated by Bette Davis and all the characters she played. I don't know when I first saw *What Ever Happened to Baby Jane?* I imagine it wasn't until I was in my teens. But I remember I watched it knowing that my mother was already an admirer. When *The Nanny* came out in 1965 she and Marion went to see it in Sutton. At the flicks. I was still awake when my mother came home. I wanted to know how it was. What happened? *It was scary.* But what happened? *It was for grown-ups.* But what happened? I insisted on knowing. And my mother told me something about a child drowning in the bath. It was about that and about a nanny. Whatever it was my mother said it was enough to silence me. And I remember the light in her eyes. Mischievous without malice. Murderous but vicarious. With a glint of demonic pleasure. In my memory I associate it with the twinkle of admiration she had for Alec Guinness in *Kind Hearts and Coronets* – a delight in black comedy that messed about with the supposed distinctions between social classes. For that in the end is what the demonic in my mother seemed to be about. A possessed dedication to something like the common. Something belonging to everyone. The common touch. The common good. And therefore a devotion to the destruction of class differences and sexual and material and educational and all other forms of inequality. In laughter and in spirit. In her furious dream of a common world.

Polar bear

Drivel said she of *The Sea, The Sea*. My mother's withering verdict on numerous books. Recalling the irony of Murdoch's madness about which Bayley wrote in the final decade of his life I also see as if never till now the resemblance between him and my father. Both almost comical in their mildness and benignity. The idea of John and Iris as versions of my parents – thanks at first to the figure of the umbilical cord of the telephone back in the day when I would wait and wait for a response – seems at first absurd. The eerie effects of identifications we pretend to tame by calling unconscious or unforeseen. They show up as if by chance in dreams or writing.

But in truth Unconscious and Unforeseen have no telephone number. They are ex-directory. Unavailable. No knowing if they are even living together.

The death of my father on 30 July 2005 broke the World Bank. All symbols of authority were dissolved. Language died in deference. But his death had strange positives. It seemed quick. He was in hospital for a single night and died in it. And then it was a way for him to enter into a sort of ethereal second adulthood. He had reached the point of wanting to be dead and in a surreal mysterious abrupt manner he was granted his desire. On the eve of his going he spoke to me of the attractions of euthanasia.

Being dead his influence on my life never stopped. In many ways he became more present. It fell to me to listen to him in different and more reflective ways. The mildness and benignity became more powerful. It has led me to wonder how far the point of a father is to be dead. In the last years of his life it was on Sunday evenings we most often spoke. I can still catch myself on a Sunday night on the way to thinking I must phone him.

But what of my mother? *I'm losing my marbles.* The words rose up like a Kraken. The effort behind them! She manifested in her life a madness that no one should receive. In time it was diagnosed as Alzheimer's. But that word was never spoken. Either to her or between my father and me. It was taboo. I don't know if my father used it in conversation with others. For instance with Marion who would come to think him such a brick. Or with his own brothers to whom he spoke on the phone every three or four weeks. But he and I never used the word. I refused to contemplate my mother as the member of a kind of sub-society designated by the word 'Alzheimer's'. In part because it seemed to deny the life of my brother. My brother was not called Alzheimer. In those days rapid search facilities on a hand-held device did not exist. Still I could have gone to the local library and tracked down Aloysius Alzheimer. But I had no desire to do so. I dismissed the idea that the life of my mother could be encapsulated by a proper noun that had nothing to do with her. She carried on. She carried the death of her son. She bore on where only she could go. Into the valley of a moon half the size of the sky. The desperate minutes hours and days every one of them without remedy in those sinking years of maternal oblivion.

Some sufferers from so-called Alzheimer's can lead lives with a degree of happiness. They can find things funny. They can be moved in moving ways. A friend's mother for instance loved the music of Neil Diamond. The daughters fixed up for her to go to a concert. They accompanied her to the event. There were many thousands of people in the audience and the words 'NEIL DIAMOND' blazed in bright lights high above the enormous stage. Their mother loved it. So many songs she had loved since her youth. And at one point she leaned over to one of her daughters and shouted in order to be heard. She shouted with joy: *I don't know who this guy is but he sure can sing!*

My mother was not like this. She veered between black and blank. There were no diamonds for her. All the time every day. She was like the great white polar bear we'd once seen at Edinburgh zoo. Compulsive circumnavigation. To this corner of the enclosure. Along this stretch of the glass frontage. Under the water and back up to this corner of the enclosure. Along this stretch of the glass frontage. Under the water and back up. For all to gawp at. My mother would walk from one end of the house to the other in fretful unknowing. Agitation without respite. She would walk to the kitchen to fetch herself a cigarette and light up without remembering she already had one smouldering in the ashtray in the room she had just vacated. In a kitchen cupboard she kept a substantial stock of chocolate bars and assorted nuts. She ate these with the energy of a famished squirrel. She became overweight as she had never been in her lucid days.

Snap

For all the speed and sharpness of modern teletechnology we remain in a state of arrested development when it comes to photographs. They give us phantasmagoria on a plate. Here is my mother at the age of four and a half (in January 1931). Around the same age as Barthes' mother Henriette Berger in the unreproducible image in his *Camera Lucida*. I call this person my mother but the appellation is crazy. She inhabits an impossible world that

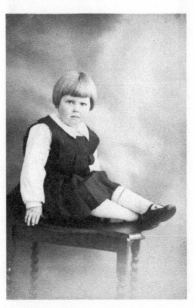

is nonetheless real. I could never have known my mother at the age in which she appears in this picture. Kathleen Beatrice looks thoughtful but also a little in disbelief. As if to implore the viewer to indulge some incredulity in turn. *Why have you given me this pudding-basin haircut and dressed me in this gruesome stiff pinny and tight socks and shoes and placed me on this idiotic little table and requested I keep as still as a stone?* As in other pictures of my mother as a young girl she looks plump. Like the baby that Sylvia Plath talks about in her poem 'Morning Song': she resembles 'a fat gold watch'. And in her face and form I recognise myself and my own beloved daughter.

Photographs can be sites of strange defamiliarisation and disidentification. I gaze at the picture of my mother [*see*

Frontispiece] taken (I suppose) in the early 1950s. It's a posed 'art studio' photograph: she looks like a film star. With a bit of that demonic allure in her eyes. Was my mother ever like *this*? Or was she ever *not* – at least a bit – like this? There is another picture [*left*] in which she appears to be on holiday. There is a date (1949) pencilled on the back. And then in the frame directly below her is a young man in jacket and tie. Smiling but macabre. Who is he? A snapshot of my nemesis. Exposure of a father I could never have had. Radical phantasmagoric dissociation. Another photo features my mother in what looks like a caravan. Leaning out of a narrow window with a bespectacled smiling toothy stranger so close you cannot

be quite sure at first whose arm is whose. Inked on the back: 'Devon 1956'. A year before I was born. Or – who knows? – just nine months.

And then there are pictures in which I do recognise as my father the man accompanying her. The picture of them together as engaged or just married. A formal but beautiful photograph. He is sporting his Old Merchant Taylors' School tie. They are looking into one another's faces with love. My father with one arm around her and the other holding an umbrella. Or the picture of them together in the sea. Awash in foam. Somewhere in Devon. My father with a moustache very similar to his own father's and a dark hairy chest as if poised to rise out of the water. Only the head of my mother visible in the foam. Laughing. And her

laughing in this wildness of foam and the crests of white waves beyond her recalls a holiday in Sidmouth (the town where my mother once told me I was conceived) when my brother and I were around ten and twelve and we couldn't get out of the sea. The waves were breaking and throwing us up on to the beach and dragging us back in again and my brother and I were laughing like sea drains. We had never found anything so funny in our lives. We were incapacitated by the churning white horses of the waves horsing about trying to get out only to be pulled back in. But my mother became frightened. *Get them out Max! Get them out!* But my father would do nothing besides try to pacify her. He could see that we were not in distress. This was something that I know my mother prized in my father. Even if his slowness could be maddening – still she found in him an unflappable calm.

Like the photograph of him from around the same time. Standing rugged and at ease in a Norwegian-looking heavy

cream-coloured jumper. One hand in his pocket. The other holding a cigarette. The white foam of the sea washing up close behind him on the Devon shore.

Never in my life did I see my father snap. Whereas my mother could. She had a spontaneity and impulsiveness quite contrary to my father's nature. She didn't dilly-dally over anything. She was always *in* what she was doing. And then it was time to be in something else. So that this capacity to snap never seemed at odds with my sense of her patience and control. I suppose this is just a way of saying I never imagined my mother could lose her mind.

In the Christmas holidays at the end of 1966 she took me and my brother to the cinema in Sutton to see *One*

Snap

Million Years B.C. For my birthday a couple of months earlier my father had bought me (for the then gob-smacking sum of thirty shillings) a huge hardback volume called *Prehistoric Animals* by Josef Augusta with full-page colour plates by Zdenek Burian. My interest in dinosaurs at that time went along with a passion for drawing or painting volcanic explosions. This film with Raquel Welch and John Richardson appeared to offer the perfect cocktail. The cinema was crowded and stuffy. I recall the embarrassment of squeezing our way to three empty seats. But far more acute was the embarrassment of leaving. We watched the film for about five minutes. It wasn't the crashing loudness of the explosions of volcanoes and earthquakes and screams of prehistoric people being propelled into ravines or the bellowing and intimidating ferocity of the dinosaurs filling the screen. It was the almost naked Raquel Welch and the attention she was receiving not just from the cavemen on the screen but from those in the audience. This was not (my mother decided) a film for her nine- and six-year-old sons. She pulled us to our feet and we were dragooned down a row of goggle-eyed viewers who resented having to stand to let us pass. Out we went. Blinking in the afternoon light we'd left just a few minutes before. Something wrong had happened but my brother and I had only a vague stirring of what.

My mother's snaps: lifelong unfurlings.

Emily's analyses

I always wanted to be a poet. Publishing one slender volume after another until one day there would be a single chunky tome called *The Collected Poems*. Poetry is about immersing oneself in what Wallace Stevens calls 'maternal sounds'. Every poem is a work of love launched by the mother's face. I wrote none while she was losing her marbles or after she'd lost them. But I used to write and read poems aloud to her. And although I stopped writing in lines with rhythms and rhymes I have never stopped trying to write in her spirit.

Isn't there a risk of diminishing her by speaking of 'spirit'? Of setting her aside from the physical and real? Allotting her some significance that corresponds to the religious? There is more to be ventured about ghosts – *anon* (as she liked to say). But the spirit of my mother is spit and polish. It is trip and spright. Irony and dream. Spirit unlike any other. With a mercurial cape of laughter thrown over it.

What of the mother of the mother? Emily Esther Gibbs (born 25 July 1889 [*shown here, with my mother as a child*]) is a ghost figure in the story. This goes back to the *née* and nay-saying. The subordinated and precarious 'maternal name' and 'maternal lineage'. Together with the fact that she died when my mother was only sixteen years old. She

is a phantom grandmother to me. (I never knew any other kind.) But in dying so early she deprived my mother of so much — life unlived and memories unshareable. A memoir is about what survives. But it is also about what is enigmatic and irretrievable. Cryptic and unknown. Starting in this case with the mother in the mother: a pre-word lineage. Even 'lineage' is inept. It is more flux or emanation. There is no document of civilisation that is not also a doing-down of the mother. A memoir of the mother would be a study in maternity — from ma to eternity. Would be. Should be. Dreams of being.

Emily was one of six sisters. There was also a brother called George. Here they are in around 1926. [*Clockwise*

from top left: Ettie, Beattie, Minnie, Emily, Mabel, Lilith, and George (centre)] They grew up in Little Dunmow in Essex. The closest town was Braintree. The nearest 'big' place Chelmsford. Today Little Dunmow is almost part of Stansted Airport. Little is known of Emily. Still less of *her* mother. Her father was a butcher in Maldon. With his field behind the shop. Several of Emily's sisters were primary school teachers. Emily worked as a seamstress. Ettie became Mrs Hazelwood. Beattie became Mrs Green. Mabel became Mrs Gozzett. Minnie became Mrs Brown. All the names swallowed up.

Emily's analyses

At some point in the early 1980s I explored the idea of writing *as* my mother. A maternal ventriloquy. I imagined her mother speaking through my mother speaking through me and wrote a story called 'Emily's Analysis'. It was a sort of explosive political Molly Blooming of a woman in a therapy session taking psychoanalysis and every other psycho-social structure to pieces. It was an attempt to write in the land of pre-word. A torrid failure. No writing in that land. One can only write about or towards or in its wake.

About ten years later – not long after she told me she was losing her marbles – I returned to this thought of maternal ventriloquy. My mother had always had terrible dreams about school exams. Even in her old age – for as long as she continued to be able to tell me her dreams – she had nightmares of being back at Putney High School for Girls sitting her School Certs. As a schoolboy and university student I experienced a good deal of anxiety around exams as well. But I had also had an early taste of their comic and absurd dimensions. Throughout her life my mother was wont to declare British secondary education – with its division into public and state schools – nauseating. Vile. Egregious. The inequity and the iniquity. My parents could not afford to send me to a private school. But like any mindful socialist of the day she wanted her children to have the best education possible. She and my father arranged for me to sit a scholarship entrance exam for a place at a local public school.

I can close my eyes and be there now. The solemnity of the cavernous exam hall. The stomach-churning hush. Surrounded by desks at which dozens of unrecognisable strange boys were sitting as stiff and nervous as myself. We were ordered to turn over our exam paper. There were ten essay topics. We were supposed to choose a topic and write about it in the allotted time of one hour. I was so keen to please my parents and win the scholarship to the posh private school that I attempted to write answers to all ten questions. Recalling my crazy zeal and catastrophic performance that day was a recurrent source of shared laughter with her.

In any case – following the dismal failure of my first 'Emily's Analysis' – I decided to try to write another. About taking an exam. A short text in the voice of my mother. My mother's voice in me. The narrator is studying at university in Scotland. I based it on Glasgow. (I happened to be teaching at Stirling at the time.) I wanted to articulate my mother's anxiety about exams while querying the assumptions of knowledge and authority that underlay it. To transform her anxiety into the playfulness and satirical incisiveness with which I most identified her. To mess about with the idea of memorising quotations and the mechanics of learning by rote but at the same time to drive on with the sort of speed that she and I loved in another Emily (the author of *Wuthering Heights*). The narrator has certain attributes identifiable with my mother. A fondness for listening to classical music on BBC Radio 3. For coffee and the occasional banana. And for using a hairbrush every day. But at the same time I wanted to leave the sexual identity of this 'I' up in the air. Like the car they are in.

It's called 'Exam':

The exam starts at nine and I'm on the motorway. It's one of those muggy early June mornings you don't know if it's going to be asphyxiating or a gift. I get up extra early to be sure I'm on the road in plenty of time. I decide against breakfast, or my stomach does. I pack a banana in my bag for the car, just in case. But I don't want to think about the banana. The idea makes me queasy. I drink a cup of coffee to wake up, and then another in the hope it will have me wishing to pay a visit before I set out. But instead I find myself standing in the bathroom picking as clean as possible a hairbrush I haven't so much as looked at in twelve months. I ought to be checking I've memorised all my quotations properly, but there I am standing over the waste-paper basket plucking dead hair and bits of gray fluff from my hairbrush, like some demented harp-player. It's funny isn't it, the way you choose to do the most practical of things at the most impractical of times and then the way the most practical of things turns out to be a nightmare and a half. For nightmare and a half read: interminable. I stupidly imagine it's going to take sixty seconds at most, but the operation sends me into a trance. Ten minutes later I'm still at it. It reminds me of the fairytale about the boy and girl who must set an impossible task for a giant, otherwise he's going to eat them, and in the end, in desperation, they ask him to straighten out a single curly hair, not a pubic hair needless to say, but a single strand of that kind of curly hair that children have in fairytales. A nightmare and a half, as I say. Somehow I manage to drag myself out of it. I put the brush back on the shelf and get going. I've lost valuable time but haven't we all?

The car starts like a dream, and I'm off. It's 7.50. As it's rush-hour I'm allowing myself forty minutes to get into the city and find a space in one of the student car parks, then another five minutes to get across to the main building. *Déjà-vu* for a moment, just thinking about that. But I'm on the motorway. I'm on the motorway and it's a beautiful, bright but hazy June morning. The road seems unusually clear, I'm sailing along at such a rate I can feel myself making up time. There's hardly another car in sight. Keep this up, I tell myself, and I'll be there with minutes to spare. Perhaps even long enough to grab another cup of coffee. But the thought of that has my innards churning and I realise a third cup would be out of the question. One moment I'm as calm as one of those S.O.S. orange call-boxes that punctuate the hard-shoulder, the next I'm overtaken by nerves. I'm one of those people who take exams really seriously. I can't help it. I find myself taking exams really seriously, I mean taking the idea of taking exams, really seriously, even when I'm trying my best not to take them seriously at all. Anyway this is the last one, my final finals, and a lot's at stake. My life, if you really have to know. Or that's how it feels. I'm sailing along but then I'm overtaken by nerves. I switch on the radio and it's a classical music station playing something peaceful and sad, but then the voice of the guy in between freaks me out. I don't even take in what he's saying but the way he announces the composer's name and title, it's as if he were announcing a nuclear accident. Panic stations. I lurch forward and kill it, suddenly feeling quite ready to be sick. I run my hand quickly through my hair. Calm down, I tell myself. But running a hand through my hair reminds me of my neurotic behaviour with the hairbrush and the disgusting tufts of gray. I try to focus my attention on something else. I'm in the middle lane, travelling at the maximum legal speed, but still there are cars regularly overtaking me. For a while I concentrate on timing it so that I turn my head to look at the driver in the outside lane at precisely the moment of overtaking. But it seems that, no matter how many times I do this, the other driver simply ignores me. It's as if I didn't exist. I fumble in my bag and eventually extricate my all-important cassette. I stick it in the machine, press play and wait, as I drive, eyes on the road straight ahead.

Shut up, Heathcliff! (That's me, talking to the dog.) The exam starts at nine and I'm on the motorway. (Did I say that? Don't quote me on it. I listen to the tape, which is a recording of my own voice, recounting all the significant facts and reading out all the key quotations.) And there I am, speeding along at top notch, when suddenly it happens. I come over the brow of a gentle upward incline and spread out before me, dazzling and glittering in the June morning sun, is a great sea of frozen traffic. It's like being unexpectedly face to face with a shimmering corpse. The way the sound of screeching brakes and smell of burning rubber fill the air is appalling. It's impossible to tell who's going to hit who, or up ahead, who's already hit and already dead. This is the moment, I know, in which the whole of your life supposedly passes in front of you. The whole story, in one fell swoop, a single polaroid snapshot. It's the split second in which you see the light streaming at the end of the tunnel. It's the time, it's said, that a person is most susceptible to having an out-of-body experience. All that happens with me is that I hear a voice. I hear myself saying: What's an exam if it's not an out-of-body experience?

Write an essay about this story, giving particular attention to tone, imagery and narrative perspective. Time allowed: forty-five minutes.

I wrote 'Exam' with a view to reading it aloud to her. I also imagined her reading it to herself. I hoped she might find it very funny. She alone might share with me the hilarity of the final exam question rubric (*Write an essay about this story...*). Who says it's a *story*? Who would have *the gall* – that would be her phrase – to assume that 'tone' or 'imagery' or 'narrative perspective' might be appropriate terms or authoritative criteria for responding to it? What on earth would one write in such an exam?

Reading this piece again now I am struck by details I haven't thought of before. Being face to face with a shimmering corpse is of necessity about my grandfather. My first witnessing of a human cadaver is an ineffaceable memory. Seeing my mother's father dead without knowing and much later imagining her encountering his body still propped up in his Parker Knoll in Carlisle Road. The fairytale with the single strand of hair is something she once read to me. There is a Scottish hint (via Macduff's 'one fell swoop') of the loss of children. And then it occurs to me that the length of this drive would locate the speaker's starting-point as Drymen. (Not that there's a motorway between Glasgow and Drymen.) I see the development of a phantasmagoric photograph. A single Polaroid snapshot: 'Who's turned the lights out?' Concealed associations and buried memories. Come forth in a disinterring writing.

Next time I was down visiting from Scotland I read 'Exam' to my mother over morning coffee at the white Formica-top table. First I read it aloud. Then she read or appeared to read over it herself.

What's it all about then? she asked with a gentleness of yore. Like a mimicking of Jack Warner in *Dixon of Dock Green.*

It's an exam Ma... I started to explain. *It's whatever you make of it.*

It was beyond her. She hadn't laughed. Not even chuckled. She was losing her marbles. And I was losing her.

Way-on-High

My mother wrote so few letters. They almost never bear a date. Sometimes the letter got sent without my father's perusing it. More often it shows signs of having been 'corrected' here or there. A missing word inserted with a maxwellian caret. An apostrophe or other item of punctuation added. By courtesy of the Grammaticality Enforcement Agency. There is a letter that must have been written in the autumn of 1987 – soon after I'd begun a one-year lectureship at the University of Tampere in Finland.

I'd been trying to get a university-teaching job but Thatcher's cuts made it nigh impossible. Over the course of about five years I'd applied for upward of sixty-five positions – temporary lectureships and fellowships – and been shortlisted (without success) just twice. So when out of the blue someone at a university in Finland phoned me early one Monday morning and offered me a one-year post and gave me twenty-four hours to think about it – I knew I had to say yes. It was approaching the first anniversary of my brother's death. I'd moved back from Devon to Oxford. I was about to begin another year in that super-fortified vampire town without any sense of what I was doing or why. I'd been trying to make ends meet with a smattering of English literature A-level students and a bit of undergraduate teaching. This phone call in September 1987 was from a complete stranger in a strange country with which I had no links. Offering me a job I had not even applied for.

The man said he was called Gurney. I had never met anyone with that name. At the time I was trying to make headway writing a book about telepathy and literature. *Gurney*? It's a stretcher a support a life-saving form of transport. But Gurney was also the name of one of the founding members of the Society for Psychical Research. A key figure in early writings and experiments on thought-transference. Author of an intriguing book about speech and music called *The Power of Sound* (1880). Fascinated by hypnosis and 'deathbed wraiths' and telepathy (a word invented by his friend F.W.H. Myers). A character mysterious also in the manner of his death in 1888 (aged forty-one): an overdose of chloroform in a room of the Old Ship Hotel in Brighton. I associated him most of all with the phrase *'phantasms of the living'* (the title of an enormous book he co-authored). The strangeness of first hearing someone's name over a telephone: *Did you say 'Gurney'*?

Having already decided I was going to accept I phoned my parents to talk to them about it. As usual my mother picked up the phone.

I've been offered a job.

Where?

Finland.

Oh Christ!

In a mixture of surprise and unease I laughed. I hadn't expected that tone from her. It sounded like despair. I knew I couldn't turn the job down. I stressed that it was just a one-year post and Finland wasn't as far away as some places and I'd come back to Devon in the vacations. But the tone of that 'Oh Christ!' still scrapes like something down a blackboard in my mind. I would love to believe that my going to Finland had no impact on my mother's mental deterioration – but I cannot.

The letter from my mother in November 1987 starts: '*Darlin' Nic...*' She liked to syncopate her darlings and spell my name that way. There are just a couple of signs of my father's proofreading. On one occasion my mother has written '*Friday*' and he has added in his precise spidery hand just above: '*(Saturday?)*'. And then a little later he crosses out the place-name '*Ross-on-Haye*' and writes above it: '*Haye-on-Wye*'. The fact that my father has in turn misspelled (a very unusual thing for him to do) is a cause for momentary delight: I hear 'Haye-on-Wye' as 'Way-on-High' and my mother in ecstasy oblivious as to whether she is alone or not in the house singing at the top of her lungs 'Over the Rainbow' *way up high*. Way up high Haye up Gee up Giddy up Heigh on Why...

In any case this letter is characteristic of everything she wrote to me: it snaps and slips from one topic to another and is written at various times over a couple of days or more. (At one point she comments on the fact that I'd sent a card to my eighteen-month-old nephew Sam and his mother Cris – my brother's widow – wished to thank me: 'This, she asked me to add when she noticed that I'd started this drivel.') The letter has all the features I love in my mother's writing. At once staccato and flux (threaded along with plentiful dashes). A sharp eye for what others do and ear for what they say. Most of all: no sign of marble loss.

She is just back from a 'grand tour' with her dead sister Peggy's husband Jim: it 'came very suddenly and passed as quickly and now it seems I never left home!' He came down from East Lothian to Devon and they drove up north again (Jim at the wheel) in his bottle-green Jaguar to North Berwick and then back down via Blackpool and Ludlow and other towns. I must have told her I was in a flat on the seventh floor of an apartment block in Tampere for she expresses her hope that I'll be comfortable and trusts there is a lift. She wants to know how I manage with washing my clothes and whether the university provides any meals. She devotes several sentences to recounting her efforts to get my father to sell some of his many books or – if only as an interim measure – build some shelves upstairs along the hall (or 'passage'):

Your bit about your meagre collection of books made me smile [doubtless I lamented about this in an earlier letter: I had only what I could take with me on the plane to Finland – I must have cut a ponderous figure as I struggled down the aisle with my carry-on bag bulging with books and my Barbour coat heavy with a *Chambers Dictionary* in one inside-pocket and a French dictionary in the other] – *I've at last persuaded Dad to transfer the shelves from the bedroom to the passage and he seems to be making rather a long job of it – c/o broken drills and lack of nails & screws – now lack of time with too much proof-reading & an excessive number of 'competition's to fill in & send off. I'd half hoped to see all the books in situ on my return* [from Scotland] *but in fact it was as I'd last seen it. The ever reluctance to 'do' anything about books in this household must be unique! Fairly recently there was a mumble about contacting a dealer (with a Wilmington* [i.e. local] *Tel. No.) to see about selling a few – to help pay for a new oil tank, but the mumble only lasted a day & a half while the urgency of a tank has dwindled since we are finding your fire in the kitchen so useful.*

It is so strange – melancholy but also uplifting – to be able to cite her words and linger on the singularity of her handwriting. Her quirky use of 'c/o' (for 'care of') in 'c/o broken drills and lack of nails & screws'! And then her use of 'quotes' (such as 'competition's' and 'do') – as odd as anything in Henry James. I've transcribed her 'and' as '&' but no keyboard symbol does it justice: it is more a tiny 'looped' plus-sign that recalls for me her lifelong love of knitting and the fact that her own mother had been a seamstress. Along with her little knotted *and*s go her dashes – everything knitted up & cut off at once.

I imagine she intermitted the composition of this letter with knitting. She spent so much time in autumn evenings at work on jumpers for family and friends. That autumn I asked if she would knit me a balaclava. When I came home at Christmas she presented me with a beautiful heavy wool sooty black and grey headpiece – complete with modest slit for mouth and eyes. Perfect gear for any terrorist comedian operating in a cold climate.

The letter then veers off into a touching account of Cris failing her driving test (and remembering that her own sister Marion failed hers *four* times) before returning to the subject with which the letter had begun:

From here to N. Berwick took us exactly 12 hrs 7 mins last Thursday. Jim suggested taking our time – and we did – stopped at practically every service station for coffee – cream doughnuts & a cigarette. My collection of brown sugar packets is VAST. N.B. [i.e. North Berwick] unchanged – very quiet – most shops closed or up for sale. On the Friday I was taken to visit his friends – they were all very pleasant & generous with booze and on the Friday

[∧ Saturday?] James was busy all day while I 'did' the beaches & searched for buddies — naturally — when I wasn't birdwatching. There were masses of starlings flying around the Bass and other rocks — which was surprising. I did the museum to find nothing new There — There never has been anything added to it since I first went there 40 odd years ago. On the Sunday we went to visit Nessie in Drymen — had our only real meal of the holiday in the local hotel where Nessie gazed nostalgically on the inglenook fire place seeing Grand Father & grandmother sitting either side of it — Then to Hill-View and listened to Nessie playing a lot of very old Scottish songs on the piano with considerable talent — much to my amazement. She moaned at one time about the cold weather & when I told her you were in Finland she looked astonished — then said 'Oh dear! that's BAD — he will have to be <u>very</u> warmly clad there I'm sure.' Then 5 mins later — 'I'd nae like to be HIM.' From Drymen we headed S.W. & ended up in Blackpool just missing the lights festival by one day. My first time in Blackpool — never even imagined seeing it as it always sounded such a ghastly place but, I actually found it quite impressive. From here we went down to Northbridge-Leominster and Ludlow (where we stayed the night — beautiful little town with loads of Elizabethan houses) on to Bradford-on-Avon — [Hay-on-Wye] — Ross-on-Wye & Monmouth (where we stayed another night) then to Bath where we spent the day doing the baths & museums — arriving home the following day. All in all — I quite enjoyed it! But the weather was v. poor — the sun came out once for ½ hr. otherwise gray mist & rain.

She evokes the Scotland we loved together: the buddies and the birdwatching and the little museum at North

Berwick that never changed (the stuffed albatross so majestic and incongruous — suffocated and lugubrious — in its glass case never moving a millimetre year after year). She captures the melancholy of this little seaside Scottish town in out-of-season but also the sense in 1987 of more general economic hardship ('most shops closed or up for sale'). And in a few sentences she brings Nessie to life as I never encountered her. Dreamy in Drymen. Funny about Finland. Musical in Hillview. So much has altered in the forty-odd years since my mother wrote this letter. Including the art of letter writing. In its vitality and charm — as well as in its shifts and solecisms — her writing seems closer to the letters of Keats than to today's texting and instagramming.

Of course not a word about my brother anywhere in her 'drivel'. That would never be talked of. Mum ever after.

Painter

My father encouraged his sons in their drawing and painting. This 'ran in the family'. On the walls at home were numerous framed paintings and drawings by Lola Onslow and Tony Royle. My father also painted with some skill. And in our boyhood he would delight us with black-line sketches of cartoon characters he'd invented – such as Woby Dan and Sebastian Greep. He'd enthuse in unusual fashion as he showed us books with illustrations by Arthur Rackham and Edmund Dulac and Gustave Doré – as well as by his godfather John Hassall. My mother always claimed that she couldn't draw or paint at all. But then what was that remark by Malcolm Mackenzie about? My brother and I were always led to believe that the passion for drawing and painting came through our father and our father's family. Yet it was our mother who seemed to oversee and nurture this. At painting and drawing I was never much good. At any rate I didn't keep at it. At some moment when I was around thirteen – and my brother just eleven – we made an explicit agreement: he would be the painter and I would be the writer. An unwritten contract – followed all our lives.

It was easier for me to see after my brother's death – and then easier again after my mother's – how much she had watched over his painting. How she inspired and nourished his artwork just as much as she did my poems and stories. Clearing out the family home following my father's death I found numerous letters from my brother to 'Mummy' (as he called her all his life) in which he writes about the photographs he has been taking and the pictures he is painting. And about all the materials – oils canvas different kinds of cartridge paper brushes drawing pens and so on – which he needs and which she then helps him obtain. My mother also did everything she could to get him a place at art school in London. In a letter to my cousin Mike (written around July 1978) she writes: *I took Simon up to St Martin's Art School in Charing X Rd to give in his 'portfolio' and await results but we were both rather horrified by the sordidness of the place. At the Slade Sch of Art – part of University College we looked around & had a chat with an elderly professor who emphasised the importance of doing A levels so I'm hoping Simon took it all in & will change his attitude.* In the barn owl and jackdaw newspaper story about him at the age of fifteen my brother is quoted as saying: *I don't really like school. I can't stand living around built-up areas. I don't care what I do for a living as long as I live in the country. Maybe I could work as a freelance artist.*

Wallace Stevens entitles the second part of one of his poems 'The Westwardness of Everything'. It has to do with Ireland. But for me this phrase is about my family's relation to the West Country. At the age of fifteen my brother seemed to know just what he wanted to do. The Cotswolds were not quite the West Country but they were westward enough to be going on with. His yearning to live in the country was bound up with our Cotswold cousins – just as it was aligned with my parents' increasing determination to move out of Greater London and head west. He never did A-levels but on the basis of his portfolio got a place at Taunton Art College. He moved down to the West Country a couple of years after our cousin Mike had

moved to Bristol to study medicine and a year before our
parents – and Marion and John – left Surrey and moved
to Devon. But Simon was not to be institutionalised. He
got kicked out of Taunton (for possession of cannabis) and
started another course back at Kingston in Surrey. And
then the illness began. At which point he dropped out of
Kingston and moved west again.

What might have become of my brother's art? His life was
so short and he left behind little. But he was very gifted.
All the drawings and paintings that survive have such life
and humour. Such accuracy and strangeness. My parents'
bedroom in Devon always seemed more my mother's
domain than my father's. It had windows on three sides
– as well as an en-suite bathroom looking out over the
valley. This was where my mother took her baths. (My
father would always shower in the downstairs bathroom.)
This was also the room in which she locked herself when
my brother died. This bathroom was her domain. Here she

would stand smoking a Silk Cut at the open window early
morning or evening and watch the house martins weave
and shoot about the air. (Or after dark the bats.) She always
kept both bathroom and bedroom very well ventilated.
Windows wide open for extended periods of the day.

Walking into the bedroom always gave me the sense
of stepping aboard a boat of light. At the furthest window
was a small white Formica dressing-table on which she
kept various trinkets and jewellery. Behind them on the
window-ledge stood a couple of my brother's paintings.
One was a painting of an alligator. He had painted an inner

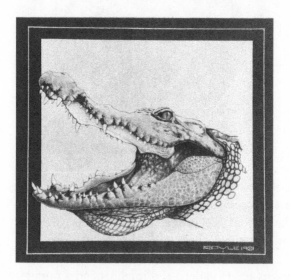

frame for this sinister-looking beast: its head seemed to
be coming out of the picture. The other was a night-scene
of a badger minding its own business pattering down a
moonsplashed lane. Then on the wall of the bedroom there
were a couple of watercolours. One of a nuthatch. Another
of a lamb playing in a field of green — with rather childlike

and implausible ruins in the background. Although we never spoke of my brother after his death I know she cherished these little paintings. Sometimes as I came upstairs or along the passageway from my own bedroom I saw my mother in the company of her lost son's pictures.

Once she was sitting at the dressing table with her back to me. I advanced towards her. She didn't turn around. She was looking at the badger in the moonlight. Tears were flowing down her cheeks. Neither of us spoke.

You go to an art gallery and might spend a minute or two looking at a painting. My brother's last painting was in another category of existence. We all knew it was his final painting. (In fact he began another but this was the last completed.) He was working at it for months. Sometimes he had no time. At no instant was there enough. Sometimes he was too debilitated smashed up washed out by medication and the cancer's advances. Other times he could work with care and patience for several hours. We all lived with this painting. Throughout the final months when my mother and Cris were nursing him my brother worked on at this picture about which nonetheless none of us ever said anything. Nothing besides some vapid remark such as *Looks wonderful...* or *Amazing colour...*

No one asked *So what is it?* because it was obvious what it was. It was his last painting. It is a painting of his last painting. A painting of his life. It is within a ruined building in broad daylight. Timber-framed. Gray stone. Dilapidated and open to the sky. In the centre is a porthole window without glass. Like an eye. The suggestion of some kind of torture chamber is clear. A thick rope descends from a beam in the background. A black metal chain from another. Beyond the doorway are grasses and sand reminiscent of the beach at Farr Bay in northern Scotland where we had stayed the previous summer. (Farr was the limit. As far as we could go. Farr Bay was the unspeakable 'terminal point': the furthest point of our Scottish adventure. From the moment we left the inn there with its desolate quicksandy beach we were on the road home. The terrible fifteen-month final straight.) In the foreground of the painting like a misshapen mouth below the porthole window are stone steps leading underground. Sitting at the top with one foot on the second step and the other dandering on air is a sylph-like spectre-thin young man with ears like an emaciated Captain Spock. He is looking off. Awry. Away from the viewer but also away from the bulking principal presence in the picture – a man with gray hair and moustache. Dressed in a blood-red cassock fit to die for his faith. Light sandals make his feet match with those of the forlorn being on the steps. He has a benign expression but wears dark glasses and holds one arm behind his back. The sinister. Under his right arm is a gigantic dreamlike snail. For all the apparent emphasis on the male I see it as a painting about the mother. Not only the mother who had in March 1986 brought my brother a son but the mother who had brought my brother himself into the world. As if wrapped in the swaddling clothes of a snail. This was the painting that accompanied my mother and the rest of us through the worst months of our lives.

Speechless

My father never talked much. Except on the phone to his brothers. The occasional old school friend or work colleague. He could be very loquacious on paper. But he spoke little to me or my brother. Just as he didn't dream at night so he refrained from speech by day. His not being able to remember any of his dreams seemed a get-out clause for the very idea of having an unconscious. His self-proclaimed status as non-dreamer infuriated me. How could he not dream? Or at least how could he not accept that he dreamt but could not remember what he dreamt? How repressed must he be!

Likewise I could be riled by his silence. I would become incredulous that he had nothing to say. Or that so often his one line in conversation was about the weather. This never altered. Even after my mother died and we were the sole survivors. Even then when he might have opened up he didn't. Every morning he would be downstairs before me and as I entered the kitchen he would greet me (sometimes in a West Country accent: *Mornin'!*) then summarise his meteorological gleanings regarding the day. Drawn from the latest forecast on Radio 4. Compared with the previous day's radio and TV and newspaper predictions. Just the weather. Then silence. Every day. As if there were nothing else to be said. But as the years passed I became less exasperated. More tolerant. Even heart-warmed by his ritualistic formulae and expressions.

It was a great boon having a brother. We could share and verify the reality of our feelings. Our father's taciturnity annoyed us both. He was a strange figure. Strange to all. Even to his own brothers. And of course to my mother. Freud coined the term 'oedipal' to refer to the welter of feelings – negative as well as positive – irradiating any so-called nuclear family. His contention that we should deploy this word to designate the fundamental tenor of a mother-son or father-son relationship always struck me as questionable. Why Sophocles rather than Shakespeare? Wasn't the kind of psychic dynamic Freud claimed to have discovered more evident in *Hamlet* than in *Oedipus the King*? Was there not in any case something strange about basing life on literature in this way? And then again: why give it a general name at all? But Freud also understood the profound links between the name and magic: how a word can spirit up and spirit away. How a name can be a source of dispossession as well as power. How a name can affect the person saying it as much as the person named. And how these links can carry on beyond death.

In many respects our family was conventional. The unfab four. As in the photograph on the beach at Soar Mill Cove in Devon in 1965: a just-like-any-other-family snapshot. There's no doubt that my brother and I felt aggressive towards our father for being himself. My brother and I fought one another and fought our father for our mother's love and attention. If I was alone with my mother and my father came into the room the current of hostility that passed through me did not alter over the decades. As Walter Pater says: *Each one of us keeps prisoner his own dream of a world.*

I always thought it funny that there was a writer called Father. A writer moreover who seemed in many ways

more a mater than a pater. Dreams are mother. From the mother and in the mother. They mother us. And in one's own dream of a world there are also magical words like 'maxwellian'. We do not dream in Sophoclean Greek. The charm of 'maxwellian' lay in its capacity to encapsulate the behaviour of a man in silent mode. To introduce laughter into the scene. And to make some gesture towards recognising the singular stamp of our father. Towards registering his own – strange because reputed dreamless – dream of a world.

Death releases among other things the banal but terrifying reality of writing. Private communications. Personal documents. Of course I did not read the letters my brother wrote to my parents. But after his death and after my parents' deaths these letters came to me and forced me out of the absurd narrowness of supposing that my mother was my mother rather than my brother's. Of making me at least a little more aware of how far my mother was my brother's mother as much as mine.

Following my father's death I had to contend with a certain faded light brown folder bearing the title *Widworthiana*. I had been aware of its existence. He'd told us that he was writing the thing and even gave occasional intimation of topics he was covering. But it was only after his death that I studied it in any detail. It is divided into some seventeen instalments dated between June 1985 and August 1990. My father's graphic design company did a lot of business with a publisher in New Jersey. Over the years he'd become friends with a couple of the women who worked there. They exchanged Christmas cards and letters and had the occasional chatty phone call. He only once flew over – for a week in 1969 – to meet with them. At some point during that week my mother took me and my brother to a toy shop and said: *You can choose anything you want*. To my ears a horrifying repetition of what she'd said the day following her father's death. I supposed my own had died. Falling from the Empire State Building. At any rate his time with the ladies in New Jersey must have cemented the relationship. For many years his company was reliant on this publisher for a steady flow of illustrative work. *Widworthiana* emerged out of my father's interest in the local and particular and his American colleagues' expressed interest in English rural life. This singular opus was not addressed to his New Jersey colleagues as such. But the obvious pleasure taken in describing aspects of English everyday life was not for home-grown consumption.

Widworthiana was – in a curious fashion – for an American market.

While my father never spoke of his love for my mother and his children and grandchildren there was no doubt that it was deep and constant. Which is what makes his *Widworthiana* so unbearable to read. He writes it in periods when there's little or no proofreading to do or when he has a few days' holiday. On one occasion he makes reference to the fact that Kathleen (as he always calls her in the text) is away on holiday (doubtless visiting Scotland with Marion). There is no sense that this is a furtive document. On the contrary it is pitched towards a general reader. Like a whimsical cross-current to Alistair Cooke's *Letter from America*: *Widworthiana* is a 'letter to America' in the form of notes from rural life. My father writes about the weather and the state of the stream that runs down (or has stopped running down) the garden. About his various pond-digging and related spring-seeking exploits. About his lawn-cutting and hedge-trimming and endeavours to make certain useful implements and other contraptions. Other humans make fleeting appearances but the main *dramatis personae* are three geese (Charles and Brownie and Griselda) and a fox. A black rabbit that turns up in the garden then disappears (feared taken by fox or crows due to its poor camouflage) but comes back (as if from a magician's hat). Some white doves up the lane at Kitty West's house for which my father constructs a dovecot. (He also details what transpire to be fruitless plans for establishing a dovecot of his own.) And the house martins that fly about the eaves through spring and summer and whose arrival and departure each year my father records with maxwellian precision. Interspersed through the seventeen instalments are a series of exquisite diagrams and line-drawings of the garden and the position of the cottage relative to nearby woods and fields and other houses.

Here is a paragraph from the first instalment (dated 4 June 1985):

> *Perhaps the most significant Widworthy item at present is the geese: we have two geese and one most ferocious gander. I have at last (I think!) come to an understanding with the latter, and can go freely in whatever part of the garden I choose, but unfortunately I am the only one who can do this — even Kathleen, my wife, will not by herself step over the fence into the half acre or so of garden that is goose territory, and any visitors who want to be shown round the garden can only do so if closely chaperoned by me. Sometimes I have to grab Charles (the gander) by the neck, and usher him away on such occasions.*

It was always unclear to me how or why we came to acquire these birds in the first place. I imagine it was my brother's idea and my parents were happy to facilitate. But my father's description gives a nice sense of what Beckett might call *how it is*: the geese just are. Their arrival and the rationale for their presence in the garden are beyond anyone's control or understanding. The 'even Kathleen' is a fine phrase. As if in tribute to her otherwise intrepid spirit.

It can feel uncanny to read something written by a loved one who is dead. It's not so much (as in the case of the letters tucked away in my father's wallet) the sense that one is reading something one shouldn't be reading. It's more how writing opens up and changes the past. One sees and is seized by unexpected thoughts. Unfamiliar perspectives and new insights. There is eeriness but also strange solace. There is the return or fresh emergence of a beloved voice.

Speechless

Speaking in a manner at once recognisable and unfamiliar. In Instalment XV (9–14 May 1990) my father writes:

> *Due perhaps to the alleged 'greenhouse' effect on our climate, the growth patterns in these parts seem to be changing somewhat. I had, for example, to mow all the lawns near the house on 22nd February this year, which is at least a month earlier than I've ever had to cut them before. Conversely, I have not yet been able to cut a large area of the grass beyond the stream at all, due to the fact that it has so many groups of daffodils, narcissi, primroses and bluebells growing in it. The daffodils and narcissi have now all finished blooming, but many of the bluebells are still in full flower and will probably continue thus for another week or so, with the result that when I do finally get around to cutting these areas, most of the grass will be at least a foot tall. I hope my old tractor will be working efficiently when the time comes!*
>
> *The house martins returned three or four days ago from wherever they'd been spending the winter, and we frequently see them swooping around with their usual grace and speed in the air at the back of the house, and then going up to the nests in the eaves that they had abandoned at the end of last summer. I think I'll have to go out to the Small Pond soon, to make sure that plenty of the silt/ mud that has built up in it lately is readily available for the house martins to use in refurbishing their nests; there isn't much other mud available in this area at present, due to an exceptionally low rainfall over the last month or two, which has left everything very dry.*

I love my father's capitalisation of 'small pond'. Elsewhere in *Widworthiana* he speaks of the Black Pond and the Green Pond as well. But most of all I love his discreet 'we': 'we frequently see them swooping around with their usual grace and speed'. Alongside the evocation of climate change what most strikes me in these paragraphs is how they reveal my father to be more like my mother than I'd come to assume. That Royle 'we' is at once poignant and disorientating. Like the tracery of the house martins.

In earlier instalments my father recounts the sad fate of Charles and Brownie: they are taken off by the fox. He does not demur at describing the specific nature of their decapitations and gruesome remains left in the Spinney (his name for the steep slope of pine trees at the farthest edge of the garden) and in the hedgerow forty yards down the lane. For the surviving Griselda my parents in due course found a local farm happy to take her. As my father reports in Instalment IX (June 1989):

> *Griselda is now fully settled into her new home and appears to have taken over leadership of the small flock of other geese there. She has laid quite a few eggs, so we have great hopes that she will achieve motherhood at last. Kathleen calls at her new abode at least once a week — partly to buy things from the farm shop and partly to give Griselda a few crusts of bread that she has saved for her — so we'll always be able to keep up-to-date on her progress.*

That tender 'we' once again!

But the only human death in *Widworthiana* is recorded in Instalment XVI (2/3 July 1990):

> *I regret to have to tell you that Kitty West died last week, but as she was aged 86 I suppose it is a thing that one has to accept. Certainly this will eliminate the likelihood of*

our acquiring any more white doves — though curiously enough a couple of weeks ago (the first sighting of such things for many months) I heard a great fluttering of wings one morning and on looking out of the kitchen window I saw that three white doves had landed on the roof of the garage...

For me this is the breaking point in my father's entire document. It has to do with what is concealed behind the formality of his 'I regret to have to tell you' — as if his readers in the United States or elsewhere might be expected to have some personal attachment to Kitty based on the knowledge of her that has accrued in the pages of *Widworthiana* — and the stoicism around Kitty's death as 'a thing that one has to accept' (though even this is hedged as a supposition rather than a conviction).

My father began writing his *Widworthiana* soon after we learned that my brother had only a matter of months to live. The family was falling to pieces. I'd applied to attend a six-week summer course at the School of Criticism and Theory in New Hampshire. In the spring of 1985 I heard I'd won a fellowship. All travel and accommodation expenses paid. In jubilation I called my mother. She said without a moment's hesitation: *You can't go.* I felt acute disappointment but I knew she was right. Instead I moved back home from Oxford to spend as much time as I could with my brother and Cris. Among other things that summer our mother gave us money to hire the Peugeot Estate which he and I (with Cris and my girlfriend at that time) drove up and all around the very north of Scotland. As far as Farr. The final holiday. And meanwhile in wordless grief my father repaired to his book-lined study and began to write.

In all the pages of *Widworthiana* no reference is ever made to the fact that his son is dying or has died. My father talks in detail about his first grandson Samuel (born six months before my brother's death and a month after Simon and Cristina married) and the games they play together and the toy cars acquired or constructed for these games. He talks also about Cris. But of Sam's father there is not a word.

Instalment XII (dated with an antiquary's precision '11th Oct. et seq. 1989') includes a reference to the black rabbit:

> *When I was returning from Sutton on 3rd October I saw the black rabbit again, this time in the lane near our entrance drive. It ran back down the drive ahead of me and as I advanced very slowly and carefully it had disappeared into some other part of the garden by the time I eventually parked the car outside the front door, but at least we now know that it's still around somewhere.*

I imagine my father after an exhausting day at the office in Surrey. Driving the long dark autumnal journey back. My mother alone in the house. Waiting for the headlights of his car to hit the hedge at the top of the driveway. After coming in and kissing her on the cheek (as she always let him do but without ever returning the kiss) he might have remarked: *I just spotted the black rabbit again.* But if he did so it would have been without any further elaboration. Only in his writing – and even here it goes unremarked – he gives the date. My father was a lifelong scrutineer of dates and times. 3 October 1989 was the third anniversary of my brother's funeral. My father was not religious in any conventional sense: he had great loyalty to his own eccentric kind of Buddhism (without any Buddha). He was very interested in numerology and superstitious thinking. But he had no special apprehension about what happens after death. Or at any rate none that he ever talked about to me. But the sighting of the black rabbit ('Blackie' as he calls it elsewhere in *Widworthiana*) seemed to pulse with possible meaning: 'at least we now know that it's still around somewhere'.

My father was an enigma to the last. I visited him about a fortnight before he died and we found ourselves going upstairs to bed at the same time. At the foot of the stairs on the window-ledge (a deep ledge characteristic of old Devon cottages) stood a rather old and battered-looking brown and black painted clay owl that my brother had made when he was a teenager. I never paid much attention to this object but that night it became clear to me that my father held it in particular regard. Every night before going up to bed (he now revealed to me) he patted the owl on the head as if it were his son and murmured: *Good night, mate!*

Speechful

If *maxwellian* was synonymous with 'reserved' or 'un-speaking' – in a world of one's own – no word seemed apt to capture the speechful aura around my mother. To enter into a conversation with her was never a decision. It was already happening. You were bobbing on a tide or washed by a wave whose crest had preceded you. Talk was a flood. Awash. But there was never a sense of anything gratuitous or pointless. Wonder and danger were never remote. In part this was because of the unconscious power of her speech. As my cousin Mike recalls: 'She'd say something that would silence a room but never rebound on her.' This unrebounding seemed innocent. Any politician would give their eye teeth for such a gift. It was the genius of a speech belonging to no one and everyone. But you would never think to respond to her with the claim: *You don't know what you're saying.* Her words were charged with might. Meaningful but wild. Without pettiness or spite. Still any interlocutor had to proceed with care. An old friend from my schooldays remembers her as 'a strong-minded lady'. He recalls: 'I needed to tread carefully, I felt, or I would merit her scorn (albeit never articulated), so very different from the mothers of every other friend I ever had.' And then there was wonder and danger also in what Shakespeare might have called the frame of her discourse. You never knew what she was going to say next. You never knew where a conversation might be heading. You couldn't tell what kind of conversation it even *was* or could be. You could never feel quite sure about how she'd got from one topic to the next. It went so fast. It all went with such ease – even amidst the pauses – that you were often left puzzling over not just how it had ended but also how it began.

Family conversation had always revolved around my mother. But with her disintegration it became untenable. More hopeless than with a lover with whom one has just broken up. No one wishes to remember sentences that end – bobbing about.

Unfinished.

Tumbleweed connections.

To witness my mother in talk's abyss. In the black hole of a full stop you could never see

The life of her speech knocked out. And this crushed banana childlike space of speech was the smashing of the frame of mourning. When were we to acknowledge that she was no longer with us? What words what order of words could make sense?

Conversation conservation life supportive paradise lost.

Before she was ill my mother loved to talk to anyone. And she was an inveterate listener. She loved to hear what someone had to say. She had a dislike for social privilege and snobbery of any sort. And for the kinds of behaviour that accompanied it. Like her husband she was sickened by fox-hunting. Living in the suburbs of London this didn't much matter. But it was different in the depths of Devon. The hunt came up and down the lane. (This was in the early 1980s – years before the arrival and departure of our geese.) On several occasions the fox had scarpered across the garden with the hounds and a horse or two in pursuit.

At last even my father felt prevailed upon to speak. He attempted to reason one morning with the woman who lived down the lane and who helped organise the hunt. He had no success but conveyed the family's sentiments well enough. Thereafter he acquired a little rubber stamp and used it to darken every envelope he posted. *For fox sake ban the hunt.* This was more or less the most outspoken thing my father ever said. Or wrote. Or at least rubber-stamped. He never swore. The most extreme expletive to which he ever resorted was a very occasional 'Blast!'

But my brother – a short while afterwards – got into an intense altercation with the fox-hunting lady down the lane. He spoke his passionate animal-loving mind to her. She returned fire. He was upset by the encounter. I wasn't there and nor was my mother. But a couple of days later she and I were driving up the lane and saw the slick dark form of the neighbour on horseback beside her stable. My mother asked me to stop the car – and then she rolled down her window. *You silly cunt!* she cried. So foreign to her idiom and thus all the more shocking.

The hunt never crossed on to our property again.

My mother otherwise liked to talk with any and everyone. That is what it was to be Nurse Conversation. A nurse of and in and for conversation. Nurse Hood. After we moved from Fulham to Cheam in the early sixties she became staff nurse at a local BP factory. And after moving to the West Country she worked part-time in a nearby nursing home. She nursed all the sanity of her days. Wherever she went she listened and she talked with a sympathy that seems only more remarkable as time passes. She once said to me: *Never lose the common touch.* Like much from her lips impossible to judge. Did she say it because she thought I was already losing it? And with *common touch*

I knew at the time what she meant. But like other phrases that I recall with piercing accuracy I am left looking at them as I might graffiti. *Never lose the common touch.* It remains a yardstick. It watches over me every moment. Do I have it? Could I ever know if I had it?

She had it in any case. And her conversation was as prolific as a jungle. To rich or poor junior or senior known or unknown she'd talk and listen as if there was no tomorrow. When I was a teenager my friends would come over after school and she would engage them in conversation in the kitchen on arrival. I would chip in but after a while found myself saying I was going up to my room. Come and join me whenever. And sometimes my friends got past conversing with my mother and sometimes they didn't. For the most part I felt unbothered by this. But I felt rather miffed when one or two of them developed such a rapport with her that they'd turn up and not mind in the least if I wasn't at home. Conversation with her had a therapeutic power. Troubled teenagers felt better. The lives of their parents and others were enlivened. She raised the tone and spirit. A physician to all men and women young or old. I could never talk like that but what a mother to have in one's kitchen!

In later years when I brought a girlfriend home it was the same. I didn't feel as if my mother was vetting – though of course she formed judgments sharp as breaking glass. My overwhelming interest was in having sex with the young woman who had just arrived. Mother and girlfriend must have shared this unspoken. Was the lovemaking more intense as a result? I never thought about it in that way at the time. Reading a book or listening to music in my bedroom waiting for my mother to stop talking or listening to my girlfriend was like being a mimic octopus with an unseen tentacle wrapped around downstairs.

With best wishes

My earliest sexual experiences I talked about with her. There are phrases that still make me wince to think I said aloud. Like Monica Lewinsky in reverse. I did have sex with that woman. Mother I did. My mother and I had read *Sons and Lovers*. We had also read *Lady Chatterley's Lover*. We were advanced Lawrentians. When I was seventeen I gave my father the small Penguin volume containing *Psychoanalysis and the Unconscious* and *Fantasia of the Unconscious*. What is now most bizarre to me about this is that I inscribed the book to him: 'Christmas 1975 – With best wishes'. Was I incapable of writing *With love*? What son writes to their father *with best wishes* for fox sake? The lifelong enigma of names and anonymity. A child is expected to move from *Daddy* to *Dad*. *Daddy* comes to sound infantile – or demonic. But I never felt comfortable with *Dad*. It always seemed a kind of brutality. I wanted him to have a name unlike anyone else. In the end I proposed *Alias* and he seemed pleased with this. I still think of him by that name. And as a child moves from *Mummy* to *Mum* the glibness feels still more indecent. I tended in later years to call her *Ma* or *Mother* but neither seemed right. I tried using her forename – Kate or even Kathleen – but that was no help either. But could I ever have inscribed a book to my mother *With best wishes*?

And this present to my father in 1975 seemed an intriguing choice as well. By then I had already encountered

Heidegger. A book about him had circulated in our A-level history class. Like a porn magazine under the desk from one boy to the next. I spent a while with it. It seemed simple as pie. The thrownness of being. The crossing out of tired words. As easy as Neil Young's 'Tired Eyes'. Heidegger's dream of a new language for describing the world and human life. No problem with that. But I was also aware of the existence of Freud and this elicited a different response. I was determined not to read him. Not because I suspected he was baloney but because I was intensely interested in the question of how to write about the mind in a way that wouldn't get sidetracked by his vocabulary. I had not read *Psychoanalysis and the Unconscious* or the *Fantasia* essay by Lawrence. I'd skimmed and skipped. I'd read enough to see that Lawrence was trying to huff and puff and rebuff without at the same time quoting a single sentence from Freud. I was impressed but sceptical. Giving this book to my father was another case of finding a way to not read a book myself.

With best wishes? Was I out of my head?

It was many years before I read anything of any great length at all. But I had grasped the correlation between a piece of writing and a bomb. Poetry did this. To read a novel by Jane Austen was as impossible for me as eating meat was to become. But a poem by Wordsworth or Keats or Eliot was like jumping into a clear lake on a burning hot day in the Alps. As I did with my brother in the Austrian Tyrol in the summer of 1969. Our ever-watchful gentle anxious mother standing by.

In the same year that I gave my father his Christmas reading I discovered Wallace Stevens and Walt Whitman and Frank O'Hara. I would read to my mother late into the evening at the kitchen table. And I was writing poems by the dozen. I had no idea what I wanted to do in life except be a poet. To read or write a poem was to work with explosives like Guy Fawkes. An encounter with even the flimsiest lyric in *Palgrave's Golden Treasury* had a potential for clear and present danger. But in the world of novels I had at least read *Sons and Lovers*. In part it was a terrible book of prophecy. I cannot recall it without subsuming it in the death of the brother. But the book was also a shocking scene of recognition. The ebullient intensity of a mother's love and the love of a mother. Not that she and I spoke of it like that. But reading *Sons and Lovers* she knew I knew she knew we knew. Waiting for my girlfriend to finish talking with my mother was an integral part of my love life. Why would anyone want to terminate a conversation with my mother in order to have sex with me? Why would one wish to deny that conversation itself can be a way of having sex?

Air

With such a portfolio how dire the decline. The endless days of unfinishable sentences. Thoughts begun but. Only disconnect. The obscene unseen undoing of short-term memory.

And then the sickening smiling terror of the day I went to the care home. She'd been there a month. Her husband no longer able to cope. He and I visited together. She looked at me and didn't recognise who I was.

At first I thought I'd mistaken myself. As if I'd entered in error and needed to go back out of the woeful building and come back. As if if re-entering this time my mother would see me sure as eggs are eggs. I was catapulted away on an elastic band of myself. Even when I tried to recover my senses and accept that I hadn't moved an inch I felt several yards along the corridor. Negotiating with a nurse and some other sorrow of a scarecrow of a former person. I was floored. As if getting to my feet after a fainting episode like the one I had with my mother in the supermarket in Cheam one too bright morning twenty-five years earlier. (It was an epileptic seizure. I felt driven to track a light moving across my field of vision till I smacked my head against a freezer and passed out. I'd bitten my tongue and for some minutes slept as if in Eden. I returned to consciousness to find my mother kneeling beside me on the floor and an ambulance waiting to take me away.)

Afterwards I asked my father was it the same with him? No. He believed his wife still recognised him. Nothing of this nature had ever happened to me before. She looked and didn't see her own son. It was worse than her telling me she was losing her marbles. Her mind was my loss alone. All one. Still the horror of the encounter had to be kept. To hold my mother's gaze across the air in the supposition that some change would occur in the whorls of her soft blue eyes and a spark of remembrance restore her to me. But she shuffled her feet and turned away.

In my mind's ear she is air. In the air. Of the air. Every poem goes back to her. All tune and melody. All music and all atmosphere. In front of my mother Simon and Mike and I danced dizzy with delight non-stop round the dining table in the winter of 1962 singing along to the forty-five revolutions per minute of The Beatles' 'Love Me Do'. To her I introduced my passion for songs by Dylan and Bowie. With her I'd listen to Lennon and then hear her love of his voice in it. Already dreaming of the past. Only much later catching that I couldn't have loved it without her ear for it in the first place. The heights of Joni Mitchell were in imitation of my mother's song. To come into the house unnoticed and hear her singing upstairs alone 'Love is a Many-Splendoured Thing' or 'My Way'. Or to find her sitting at the white Formica-top table in the corner of the kitchen singing along to some Haydn or Elgar or Dvorak or Vaughan Williams on the radio. Humming was next to impossible for her. Her joy in life broke through. To Bach's 'Air on the G String' or Barber's 'Adagio' she sang. Even with Brahms she sang. She never went or expressed any desire to go to a concert hall or to the opera. She was content to have it on the radio as and when it played. Stunned by Maria Callas my mother's listening penetrated me more sharply than the voice. The day cancer killed my brother the music died. No music from that day on. End of all airs and graces.

Ghosts

My mother loved Walter de la Mare's 'The Listeners':

> 'Is there anybody there?' said the Traveller,
>   Knocking on the moonlit door;
> And his horse in the silence champed the grasses
>   Of the forest's ferny floor.

My sense of listening comes out of that poem. Listen with Mother. *Are you sitting comfortably? Then we'll begin.*

My father liked to tell ghost stories. How he squared that with his Buddhism is not clear to me. For he loved squares and symmetry and 'noble reason'. I suppose it was linked to his predilection for fixed forms. Stories that were neat and firm. All boxed up. His fondness for ghost stories seemed bound up with his attachment to particular houses. His attachment to our cottage in Devon was matched only by his love for the Elizabethan manor house in which he grew up. Perivale Grange was a fire-victim. Even its 'demolition' ghostly. Filmed burning down in around 1961 as part of a Hammer horror. But never caught on camera was the secret panelling in the dining-room. That ancient trickery of woodwork is one of my earliest memories. I must have been just three at the time. It slid back to give on to an encrypted oak-panelled sitting room. My father liked to recount the occasion when his own father Tony sat there one evening by the fire with a friend and both became aware that someone was standing – equidistant between them – looking into the flames. An Elizabethan gentleman complete with ruff and pike.

My father also liked to reminisce about the secret passageway that led from somewhere under the house to Perivale village church some hundreds of yards away. This priest hole and getaway retained special spookiness as it never got beyond hearsay. And this despite my father being granted permission by his parents to dig various experimental holes along the border of the garden and then (the following summer) to excavate below the floor of the pantry – till it filled up with water and mosquitoes.

For someone of such taciturn bent he also relished to a surprising degree regaling us with tales of the occult powers of our great-grandmother. Kathleen May Blood had received the gift from an ancient man in India when her father was working on the railways there in the early 1880s. She befriended him and brought him gruel for breakfast at the end of the garden each morning. He was so old his limbs had turned to jelly and could be tied in knots. Which to solicit charity is what his friends did with him every day in the local marketplace. My father liked to recall visiting her in her old age – a white witch as he described her – living alone in the heart of a wood in Middlesex. Under the pen-name Irma Blood she was author of a curious Lombrosian spiritualist book called *Faces and How to Read Them*. As witch she had asked my father one summer holidays was there anyone he hated and he named a teacher at his school. The man's death was announced in assembly on the first day of autumn term. My father also enjoyed recounting the occasion of visiting his grandmother just before she died. (All of this must have been very painful.

She died in December 1952. She had already outlived by some ten months her own daughter Lola. My father was embroiled in a double mother mourning.) And how with a squeeze of her hand she transmitted the gift to him.

My mother never told such tales. Life itself was the ghost story. And de la Mare's poem epitomised it. The anonymous traveller and the knock at the door. *The lone house* and the commitment to keeping one's word. *The quiet* moonlight. The *starred and leafy sky*. The *strangeness* of the other's heart and one's own. The *plunging hoofs* of the horse. The silence that *surged softly backward*. And the *host of phantom listeners*.

I have no recording of her voice. Some phrases from her lips have the quality of psychic fossils. Auditory coelacanths. *That's not like you* she said one day with reference to a can of shaving foam I was taking to the bathroom. She thought I had bought a chlorofluorocarbon canister. Whereas I had been careful to choose an *environmentally friendly* product. Containing no CFCs. This was back in the days when saving or destroying the planet was a personal consumer choice.

The pain of false accusation. Still the line can ring like iron on stone. *That's not like you*. The words might jump out at me at any moment anywhere. Listen with Mother.

And then watch. In my mind's eye the pitiful etiolated fragility of the post-war world of imminent atomic catastrophe (what Jonathan Schell years later would call *The Fate of the Earth*) is best caught in children's television. *Bill and Ben the Flower Pot Men. The Woodentops. Tales of the Riverbank. Watch with Mother.* As if this wasn't her one chance to do something else.

But like reading poems the memory of watching television is inseparable from her. My other own heart. *The*

Ghosts

Magic Roundabout. *Blue Peter*. *Captain Pugwash*. *Popeye*. *Tom and Jerry*. *The Flintstones*. *Bewitched*. *Flipper*. *Animal Magic*. The test card. If we weren't watching with mother we weren't aware of it. The vast *trompe-l'œil* of the history of the goggle-box. Our being together before the irradiating screen. My father liked wrestling and boxing and football. *The Invaders*. Diana Rigg in *The Avengers*. My mother liked *Upstairs, Downstairs*. *The Forsyte Saga*. Anthony Hopkins in *War and Peace*. I was young but watched Kenneth Clark's *Civilisation* and Jacob Bronowski's *The Ascent of Man* with them. TV as edifying. And what eddies it made. Gary Glitter on *Top of the Pops*. Jimmy Savile everywhere – from the savvy evil tours of children's hospital wards to the lock-you-in mock-safety advert: *Clunk click every trip*. The eerie retrospect of having watched paedophiles and other gruesome abusers entertain us.

For years after this we had no television in the house at all. Like processed sugar its absence soon went unnoticed. But in the final years my parents came to depend on *Coronation Street* and *EastEnders* like heroin. Every evening the volume bumped up and the sound crashing out. As if they were making up for all the rock concerts they never went to. A screen covering life *in absentia*. As the soap operas boomed out back to back from the other end of the cottage I crouched in my mother's former crossword seat in the corner of the kitchen.

Wit

My mother's love life. An aerial photo of forest fires. Without acridity. Still too far away to see anything in detail. *This* ancient cedar. *That* stretch of dusty meadow. She told me of suitors who preceded my father. She was not a virgin when she met him. But my brother and I were content to suppose that our parents only twice had intercourse. My mother once quipped that my father would come to bed at night with a condom in the breast-pocket of his pyjamas. The same condom. Was she joking? Even during their marriage a question mark hung over her relationship with a local solicitor. His wife was close to my father. Their sons were close to me and my brother. I caught my father and the solicitor's wife in a clinch one evening in his study. But I never saw anything between my mother and the other man.

Still she always attracted men. She was Nursehood. The embodiment of comforter. She was warm and funny and compassionate. She talked and listened with wit. As if Wit were the lover. When we lived in Surrey she would recount some aspect of her day working as BP factory nurse. A man with a minor injury with whom she spent a full couple of hours chatting. Any inference of the man's sexual interest in her left dangling. He was not alone. Numerous factory workers came to see her with no specific injury or ailment. She gave them a chance to talk. Like a brilliant new kind of psychotherapist: without appropriate qualifications or known aim or recognised vocabulary.

She had an admirer in a diminutive cook called Bill. He worked for Shell and had known her and her sisters when she was growing up in Putney. He went on living there all his life. In a tiny coal-fire-smoky flat with his tiny decrepit parents on Lacy Road. (Until his old folks passed away and he was moved on to a brand new council flat not far away.) He drove a Triumph Herald and would take me and my brother and cousin to football matches at Craven Cottage. He would buy us hamburgers and hotdogs at half-time. At Easter he would make each of us a beautiful individualised chocolate egg filled with more chocolates and encased in a floral green decorated cardboard box almost big enough for a pair of shoes. He would take us to play lawn tennis at the Shell employees' club at Teddington. The Lensbury. My mother and Marion and me and Simon and Mike. My mother was very good at tennis. We would have drinks in the palatial bar at the end of the afternoon. Bill loved my mother. She was his one flame. He was older. Very short. Balding with wisps of reddish hair. Blubbery mouth and oversized nose. Long-suffering watery blue eyes. Not a body to jump into bed with. But a sweet and generous man besotted with her all his adult life. My mother flirted. That was her relationship with Wit. With Wit she dallied. She dillied. She danced. She delivered.

But did she know what she delivered?

When she died it was Marion who wrote to Bill with the news. I suppose he and my mother had not been in touch for some time. He replied in a shaky hand from his council flat in Upper Richmond Road. The letter is dated 5 April 2003:

It was with every sadness that I received the news of Kate this morning. I'm so sorry. Life doesn't seem fair. I'm so much older than Kate I can't believe it.

I've had some experience with Alziemher [sic]. *Both my parents had it, but they were older than Kate. We had some happy moments together for which I'm profoundly grateful. She will be in my thoughts for as long as I live.*

I'm enclosing a cheque for £80.00. Perhaps you can donate it to whatever charity she was interested in.

So [the next word is illegible], *I will write again in a more cheerful way so for now*

> *My Deepest Sympathies,*
> *Yours ever...*

A week or so later Marion received a letter from Bill's brother's wife – a woman she had never known or met. It began: *'"Marion" – I found a letter from you whilst going through Bill's belongings and I thought you would like to know that he passed away on Saturday, April 5th 2003. He had not been ill but had a slight stroke so he didn't suffer...'* Why the writer felt compelled to specify '2003' who knows? She wouldn't have read Bill's letter to Marion: she was quite unaware of the heart-stopping coincidence of the date.

Earth

In my mind's eye she is earth. Even in the abysmal depths of the sea there is the ground out of which enormous ancient sponges swell. A place to lie down or be lain. To dive into. Surrounded by mysterious grots and hidden cells. She is in the earth in the village churchyard alongside her husband. Less than half a mile along the lane from where they lived. Her younger son had to be earthed alone in the churchyard at the top of the nearby town of Honiton because she could not bear to walk or drive past his final resting-place every day. She did not even attend his funeral.

She was not a religious woman. She believed in the principles of a socialism that might in due course lead to world government. She wasn't an idealist but still – like John Lennon – she liked to imagine. She embodied compassion and an extraordinary force for justice. There was nothing ostentatious about her. As boys we sang in the school choir. Once after a carol service she complained to me about another mother wearing make-up. *Disgusting. You could see where the tears had streaked!* Church was a place for thoughtful solitude or the sublime song of choirboys. Not for Jesus Christ the Lord or women showing off their emotions.

Still she had to go somewhere and the ground seemed the place. She loved the little village church. No bigger than George Herbert's Bemerton. I must have acquired my love of graveyards from her. We would drive to churches all over the place. She is in the earth. On her gravestone beside her name and *beloved wife and mother* is the date of her death (25 March 2003) but no mention of when she was born. An oversight I cannot explain. The funeral director never raised any query. A monumental omission. And so there she lies to this day. As if she had not yet been born.

A dream

My mother is in everything. And she is not here. The straggle of hair at the end of the Bible. What am I to do with it?

The night after writing 'she is not here' I had a dream. I was on a long blank residential street in a town in the north. Small terraced houses as far as the eye could see. No cars. No pedestrians. A hot afternoon. My mother was at the house. Somewhere down the street. I was also aware that Peter Townend was due. He was expected to announce his arrival by sending an unmanned perambulator along the street. It looked more like a carrycot but large enough for an adult squeezed knees-up into it. It was motorised and had been programmed to stop when it saw me. I was to drive it back to the house for Townend's arrival. I was nearing the house when I first heard the perambulator. Trundling mechanical like a horror film prop. An oversized old Singer sewing machine on wheels. Faded rose-coloured bedding and cushion. It was coming down the uneven cobbled pavement towards me. A feeling at once comical and terrible. It didn't stop but slowed down. As if uncertain. Then it rattled to a halt and I retrieved it. But when I got to the house it was another house altogether.

On awakening I was convinced that it was a dream about my mother. She was not there. She is not here. But as permissive poet and voice of free association she is everywhere. My Singer. No dreaming without her. It is in dreams that I feel most in touch with her. Even when she doesn't appear.

In conscious daily life I can go for weeks without ever thinking of Peter Townend (1921–2001). But here he was – coming from the other end of town. Before petering out. Peter Townend was social editor of the *Tatler* back in the days when it featured non-salacious accounts and pictures of aristocratic young ladies. When 'coming out' meant something quite different from being gay. Debutantes ceased being presented at court in 1958. The *Daily Telegraph* obituary describes Townend as having more or less off his own bat kept the 'deb season' going for a further forty years. He was a strange celebrity in his own right. He knew every upper-class family in the land. He was the closest thing England had to a national organiser of arranged marriages. My parents had nothing to do with 'high society' and yet he was their own matchmaker. He introduced them to one another at a party in London not long after the death of Lola Onslow. He and my father were colleagues at *Burke's Peerage*. [*Burke's Peerage editorial office,*

A dream

Fetter Lane: my father, pipe in mouth, seated towards the back on the left; Peter Townend seated furthest away, in the middle, with L.G. Pine to his left.] But I have no idea how he knew my mother.

My father in mourning for his mother was the man with whom my mother fell in love. My mother who had been mourning the death of her own since she was a teenager. In one of the lucid moments of her final decade she remarked how much she'd come to see that love is pity. As with other memorable remarks this took on the character of cryptic graffiti. At the time I supposed she was referring to her own marriage. But might she not have been referring to her love for me or her imagining of mine for her? If love is real – as Lennon sings – it is also pity.

My mother must once have held Townend in affectionate regard. If only out of gratitude for having introduced her to the father of her adored sons.

When we lived in Cheam he would come for Sunday lunch a couple of times a year. For all his gregarious matchmaking Peter's private life was a matter of well-guarded silence. My mother said he had a young man in Chelsea but we never met him. Certain things about Peter Townend's Sunday visits came to infuriate her. If there were no gravy or no pudding he would cavil. 'The cook' wasn't doing her duty. And she wearied also of the extent to which he and my father presumed that they could talk together throughout the afternoon without accommodating anyone else. Peter was a brilliant mimic. He recounted anecdotes about the Royal family and other hifalutin' folk. My father would puff on his pipe with pleasure but say very little. I was fascinated by the relish Peter took in storytelling. There was a stagey delight not a thousand miles from my mother's. Tina Brown described him as having a face like a dolphin. He had extraordinary skin. The pale creamy softness of hands suggestive of someone who has never-done-a-day's-work-in-his-life. A larger than life head but small eyes. Lank sweep of gray-black hair. Breaking the surface of the sea.

I can count on one hand the number of occasions in my life I've been in London and seen by chance an old friend or acquaintance or family member. I last saw Peter Townend that way. Each of us was looking for someone else among the restaurant chairs sprawled out in the late summer afternoon sunshine beside the Thames at the Southbank Centre. He didn't see me and I chose not to see him.

To catch a mouse

There were so many non-human animals around the house as we were growing up. That is to say besides mice woodlice spiders flies daddy-long-legs silverfish butterflies moths bees wasps. The brief recollection of a mouse must stand in for all these other gentle intruders or cohabitants. We had a multivolume Children's Encyclopaedia with gilt tooling and bright red bindings. But the ordering was strange. In addition to running from one to twenty-four there was a baffling alphabetic alternation. Volume 4A or 10B and so on. I'd look something up and get lost in the other volume of the same number. That must somewhat explain why the set remained so little delved into. But there was also awe for its thick-paged newness. Its solidity and voluminousness and heavy smell. There were Things to Do as well as information about nature, 'great lives' and famous books. There were fairytales alongside scientific inventions. There were diagrams and line drawings and black and white plates and even a few in colour. Of the Things to Do I remember only two. One was instructions on how to cut glass underwater. If you took a small pane of glass and filled a bucket of water and immersed the pane you could cut it with an ordinary pair of scissors. It didn't sound plausible. I tried and it worked. It felt like a miracle. The magic of Ali Baba.

The other was instructions on how to catch a mouse without hurting it. My mother was against any kind of cruelty to animals. As was my father. Even at the end of his life he would go to great lengths not to kill a wasp or a fly that was being a nuisance in the house. How did I come to put into effect the directions for catching a mouse? What kind of collusion with my mother made it happen? For me aged ten or eleven the very existence of mice in the kitchen seemed fabulous. I had seen no such creature but my parents must have been aware of 'activity' (in the nice euphemism of rodent pest-control). They must have talked about what to do. I suppose a mousetrap was on the agenda. I happened upon the alternative measures in an odd or even volume of the Children's Encyclopaedia. My role was as proprietorial and pleased as a child could be. Like cutting glass with scissors it was not rocket science. One had to prop up a wastepaper basket with a matchstick and place a tiny cube of cheese on the floor next to the match-head. I can still picture the light metal bin with its swirling brown and red floral decorations on the outside and its white interior. Next morning it was as if the tooth fairy had been captured alive. We hadn't looked yet she was in the bucket. I recall the glimpse of that otherworld quivering quick creature before releasing her at the bottom of the garden. I imagine she found her way back to the kitchen by nightfall. She or he.

Giftie

I doubt that was the first time my mother recited to us from Robert Burns: *Wee, sleekit, cow'rin, tim'rous beastie.* More than any other poet he was hers and in the air. Because I heard Burns long before seeing it on the page there were no boundaries between one poem and another. As far as I was concerned the cowering timorous little mouse came from the same poem as *O wad some Power the giftie gie us / To see oursels as ithers see us!* These latter lines might sound at any time. With them my mother could paralyse in a flash.

There was an Irishman called Pat O'Grady who did occasional painting and decorating for us. He liked a glass of whisky. At least this is what my mother provided and he always seemed happy to drink it. He would linger at the end of the afternoon talking to her twinkling his eye at me and my brother and saying he must be off but never turning up his nose at another Bell's 'afore ye go'. I have little sense of the dynamic between Pat and my mother. Her father had been partial to a Bell's at the end of the evening. Pat was no father-figure but it is possible she enjoyed remembering Gugga through him. Pat liked to talk and tell stories himself but he was as vulnerable as anyone to the sharp and unpredictable turns of my mother's tongue. One time he'd been regaling the company for quite a while about something or other that had happened and my mother cut in to observe: *O wad some Power the giftie gie us / To see oursels as ithers see us!* I don't think she realised what she'd done. Blind to her own strange power of speech. Pat went pale as a waxwork. I could see him thinking: What did the woman say? Was she talking about me? What did I say now? *O wad some Power the giftie gie us... !*

These words of Burns seemed always in the wings. Sometimes she would invoke them and the target would be clear. At other times her interlocutor might be quite at a loss to understand. This rhyming couplet punctuated life. It was a dart from a blow-pipe distilling all of Freud and more. Delicious delirious poison of the maternal unknown. We can never do it. Narcissus is blind. Self-observation impossible. And yet it was my mother who said this and who therefore to me was the seer. She could see me myself as I never could and she said so. She stood in for all the *ithers*. The ither of the mither. My mother in the mire of the beholder.

O, what a panic's in thy breastie! How much of the agitation of my mother I shared without knowing. And where could the transfer of such unknowledge end? There is no point at which to conclude a reflection on memories of my mother. That is her uncanny gift. With every instant another depth. Another angle. Another resonance. How for example could the bad dreams she had – even when she was in her sixties – about being back at school taking her exams be separable from the trauma of living in wartime London and the death of her own mother? And how could her agitation be unrelated to my own – not just as regards my own experience of 'taking exams' but as regards an anguish of writing in general? For each sentence is deadly in so far as it threatens to fix or arrest the otherness of my mother flowing through – over and under – the world of my thoughts and feelings at every instant.

Little creatures

For so many tiny creatures there are webs and burrows and burials of memory over which my mother watches. *I'm truly sorry man's dominion / Has broken Nature's social union.* Her conception of social union didn't stop at the human. She marvelled at the silverfish flashing behind the kitchen sink as much as the Red Admiral to be rescued from a cobweb in the shed. When we were wanton boys in full sadistic flower with magnifying glasses setting fire to ants and flies in the summer sunshine of the garden we knew without exchanging a word that she was looking on from the kitchen window aghast. But there were so many other animals in the forests of our youth. Forests doubtless nurtured and encouraged by the menagerie-minded madness of our beloved Cotswold cousins. In earlier years we had hamsters and rabbits and gerbils and guinea pigs and goldfish and tortoises and Mexican jumping beans. Then as a teenager – alongside his aviaries for the kestrels and barn owl and gyrfalcon – my brother had aquariums with angelfish and neon tetras and catfish and Siamese fighters and piranhas and vivariums with terrapins and a chameleon and a North American garter snake which – within twenty-four hours of joining our household – gave birth to thirteen tiny squirming snakelings. The lid of the vivarium had not been designed to contain such an event. So the influx became outflux and that Sunday evening by torchlight in the upstairs rooms in wardrobes and under beds we were all obliged to play Find the Snakes. And then accompanying us through so many years was the beautiful half-Persian white and tortoiseshell Tatty Too (who lived to be almost eighteen) and a sweet-natured miniature long-haired dachshund we named Glimpy.

We understood that a dog was for life not just Christmas. But it was my mother who dealt with the many end-of-life scenarios and what must down the years have amounted to a veritable hillock of poop and vomit. Of smaller mammals the guinea pigs were the last and worst. My brother's was white and ginger and mine tortoiseshell. They lived in a raised hutch in the garage. We were supposed to clean out their run but of course it was our mother who did this. They developed some kind of scurvy. They had sores in their fur. Pet you wouldn't. Pet no more. They became unpleasant to look at or think about. So we didn't. My mother continued to nurse and clean and look after these creatures we were quite old enough to realise and disavow. That she would also have dealt with the end of their lives – along with those of all the other domestic creatures who shared our roof from one month or year to the next – we never considered.

When my father was no longer able to look after her and she was in a nursing home and I had young children of my own and was unable to visit as often as I should she was the white and ginger and the tortoiseshell guinea pig. I didn't do right. I didn't do my duty. I wasn't there. And when I went that time just before she died and she didn't recognise me I became the guinea pig in turn.

Bombs away

Here is an extraordinary photograph. It reminds me of the surprise of seeing Parmigianino's *Self-Portrait in a Convex Mirror* in Vienna: it is so small that its very miniaturism brings moisture to the eye. There is an eerie sense also of mannerism and surreality. It has something of a convexing swirl. In the receding darkness of the garden-fencing. In the roundness of the mound on which the figures are sitting. My mother is on the right. Marion is second from the left. The girl beside Marion is called June. The boys are Ray (in the middle) and Don (next to my mother). They are in the back garden of the house in which my mother was born: 19 Hotham Road in Putney. The earthwork is the

family air-raid shelter. It is summer 1940. War fills the air and ground. Such strange incongruity. The formality of the boys' shirts and ties. The posing of youth on a tumulus-like barrow. What does this smiling picture say? What do these happy-looking children see in us?

My mother and Marion were due to be evacuated to Bristol on 25 November 1940. The day before this the Bristol Blitz began. Gugga and Emily changed plans and sent them to Edinburgh instead to live with their eldest sister Peggy. They returned south the following year and continued their schooling at Queen Anne's Caversham near Reading. What a bonding experience all of that must have been for my mother and her little sister. What a war. What life exams. They both recalled being enthralled by the flashing lights and shadows from falling bombs on gravestones in Brompton Cemetery in the blackout. My mother also gave a vivid account of listening to doodlebugs overhead. The sound of an engine. Loud and very fast. Then gone.

There is next to nothing documented from this period. Just three or four short letters written by Emily Gibbs to Marion or to Marion and my mother. (The sisters were at Queen Anne's at this time.) One indicates that they were all going to travel up to Drymen for a holiday in July 1943. Another urges her daughters to remember to go to see the dentist. And a third (headed *24 Ongar Rd., S.W.6, Sunday*) starts: *Dear Marion, I was pleased dear that you sent that P.card. I heard it afterwards from nurse & then Mrs Jones that bombs had been dropped in Reading – now if you had not sent that card I would have been so worried about you both...* Nurse? Emily has a nurse? Then just a few months later the bare fact: on 2 January 1944 the death – of heart failure – in her sleep – at the age of 54 – of my mother's mother. *O, what a panic's in thy breastie?*

Woman reader

For a long time I didn't read Virginia Woolf. She said that to become a woman writer you have to kill the angel in the house. My mother was the angel but she also changed with the years. She never became a 'woman writer'. She never killed the angel. But she became a unique kind of 'woman reader'. Her older sisters Peggy and Nettie read Georgette Heyer and Jean Plaidy. My mother had no time for such stuff. I remember when it was Doris Lessing. Various novels lay one at a time by the radio and Silk Cut and lighter and ashtray in the kitchen. In my mind they all merged. Was it just one summer or did it last longer? My mother sat in the corner of the kitchen in Devon reading *The Grass Is Singing The Golden Notebook Briefing for a Descent Into Hell The Summer Before the Dark Memoirs of a Survivor*. I suspect they did something to her. One day she pushed *The Golden Notebook* across the table and said I'd be interested. My mother never pushed books. I took it away and tried but couldn't get on with it. I was busy with other things. I was teaching a lot and supposed to be writing a PhD about Wallace Stevens. I vaguely apprehended something underway but we didn't speak of it.

'Consciousness-raising' was no more relevant to my mother than 'Alzheimer's'. Like 'stream of consciousness' the phrase seems miles off-target. She was unconscious embodiment. A dreaming range of liquid volcanoes and airy interruptors. If *wit* evokes her better than any other word it is with a will-o'-the-wispishness. Endless veers and vanishings of humour and knowledge. Awash in the un- or under-said. One evening I presented her with a photocopy of Woolf's 'The Mark on the Wall'. In contrast to her slapdash dilatory son she read it straight away. 'Contrived' was the acid verdict. My mother's critical judgments were like no one else's. They were off the wall. Off Woolf's wall and everyone else's. But while she seemed to resist all the grids and classifications of culture and history certain shifts occurred. Submarine seismic passivities. Seething fires in the dark.

Meat

In earlier years she had indeed lived up to Woolf's angel. If there was a draught she sat in it. If there was chicken she would have the leg. But against draughts more and more she wrapped herself up. The purple-padded chrome-legged chair she sat on at the white Formica-top table was tucked in beside a radiator. The snuggest corner of the house. And then that chicken leg. Or the whole chicken. Along with the Sunday 'family roast' of lamb and potatoes with Brussels sprouts and swede and Yorkshire pudding and gravy and mint sauce. Along with the obligation to get up at the crack of dawn every Christmas Day long before anyone else to prepare the turkey for the oven. Our family was 'animal-loving' yet year after year seemed to have no qualms about meat-eating. The lambs massacred for the day of rest across the British Isles had no apparent connection with the sheep in the fields or with our cat and dog or with the bunny rabbits Snowy and Samantha in their hutch in the garden.

How does disavowal subsist so long? And then how does it come to such an abrupt end?

When the cancer first hit my brother it was with a lump in his upper arm. He was twenty years old. The size of an Adam's apple it bit into him and planted itself hurtful as the best-aimed punch. He would recover and endure almost to the magical point of all-molecule-changing seven years.

And then a ten-ton applecart would be dumped on his head lungs back brain overall all over in a monstrous refused fused forever fifteen months. But when the bump first arose tender as a button mushroom in his right arm he became vegetarian overnight. My mother and I did likewise. Meat-eating was no longer possible. The encounter with the cancer in the house was translated into a hundred languages most of which were in silence or tears but another was a new five-word commandment: *Thou shalt not eat meat.*

The abstention from meat-eating was not just in solidarity with my brother but went to the heart of the cruelty of human life. My mother had never enjoyed consuming the flesh of other animals. Nor had I. My father did not feel this way. He ate what was put in front of him. He never cooked. A part of him considered that food itself was a superfluity. He claimed never to feel hungry. This did not preclude him from having a sweet tooth: he took obvious pleasure in consuming apple-pie and Devon double cream or toffees or cake or choc-ices. Anything in fact enriched with milk or cream. When my brother and I were not yet teenagers our parents took us on holiday to a bed and breakfast farmhouse in Dorset. More or less on arrival we had tea and scones with strawberry jam and clotted cream in the rather formal dining room. Other families sat somewhat awkward and subdued at adjacent tables. We remonstrated with my father when he – having waited his turn like the gentleman he was – shovelled a huge quantity of clotted cream on to his plate. He explained without demur: *Seemliness does not apply to cream.* After my brother fell ill my father gave up meat more by default than by design. But for my mother and myself the renunciation came with an overwhelming sense that we should have done so years before.

Meat

Mourning has to do with taking the lost loved one inside oneself. He or she is no longer to be found in the outside world. The loved one must now survive within others. In memory. Psychoanalysis talks of the danger of a kind of magical cannibalistic incorporation in which the dead loved one is buried alive. Gobbled up like a shot but concealed within. The mourner deals with the impossibility of accepting the loss by an act of swallowing whole. Even by denying that the beloved once existed in the external world. But however mourning happens there is the trauma of taking the beloved within. To be faithful is to keep him or her alive in memory. Living on in oneself. Other to oneself.

One thinks *if*. *As if*. As if if that time were today we would have gone about everything in a different way. I knew that my father would never be able to speak. But my mother and I could have talked about what was befalling our family. In fact we just descended into an unspoken abyss. Nothing to be said. Either at the outset or at any point in its some-times hopeful long-drawn-out death-carving aftermath. We never articulated our feelings before or after Simon's death. Not a word. Nor did he himself speak about it. If he talked with my mother I'll never know but I doubt he did. The family way of dealing with the enormity was to say nothing. Except regarding matter-of-fact issues. How he had slept. How he was eating. What discomfort he was in. What other painkillers might be tried. The date of the next doctor's appointment. The next chemo or radiotherapy. What was there to be said?

A couple of years before his death Simon and Cris moved into a tiny terraced cottage in the centre of Honiton. It bore the simple name 'Mousehole'. One evening about a year later he and I were alone together in his former bed-

147

room at our parents' home. Out of nowhere he said: *You are everything to me.* He always had a piercing stare but now he was on the last straight the stony force of his look was insupportable. He knew he was going to die whereas I refused to accept it. Even on the night it happened. I could have told him that he was everything to me and also to our mother and father. I could have said we were all vegetarian cannibals. I could have eaten him up like honey. But I don't believe I said anything. I was too moved by his words. He came back to the family home for the last few weeks of his life. As he lay dying in the ebb and emaciation of consciousness and morphine on the final day I sat beside him reading Chaucer's *Wyf of Bath's Tale.* I was supposed to be teaching it in Oxford the following week. You have a little book and along with the sweetness in your mouth there is bitterness the rest of your life.

Someone phoned the undertakers. I suppose I did. I who denied he could have died till he did. Everyone else in the house withdrawn by then howling or silent into locked or other blank places. Was the GP still present as well? I don't remember. He skulked away. It was the middle of the night. Two undertakers. Furtive as thieves. Doing their best to be polite and show dignity but after they'd huffed and struggled with carrying my brother out the younger couldn't refrain from remarking to me it must be a blessed relief the state that body was in.

Perspectives

In Shakespeare's *Richard II* the Queen expresses her fear that 'Some unborn sorrow, ripe in fortune's womb, / Is coming towards me.' The King's counsellor Bushy replies:

> Each substance of a grief hath twenty shadows
> Which shows like grief itself but is not so;
> For sorrow's eye, glazed with blinding tears,
> Divides one thing entire to many objects,
> Like perspectives, which rightly gazed upon
> Show nothing but confusion – eyed awry,
> Distinguish form.

Shakespeare is referring to figures or pictures that look fragmented or confused except when viewed from a certain angle. In this reflection tears themselves become optical instruments. Like the 'quaint mirrors and perspectives' in Chaucer's *The Squire's Tale*. Bushy's words project a strange perspective of their own. They turn things back to front. 'Rightly' gazing meets only with confusion whereas eyeing 'awry' brings lucidity and coherence.

None of us has the gift to see ourselves as others see us. Yet do we even have the gift to see others as they are? I can distinguish the form of my mother as sharp as ever in my mind. Her words. Her voice. Her body and ways of moving. Her face and hands. The play of different smiles and lights in her eyes. But how memories of my mother come to form in words are also thanks to her. She traces and colours every word and feeling. And as I find myself recalling some detail about her I am shaken by the memory into some new perspective. Reminiscing collides with unexpected things and words that collide with other memories. I used to think that 'colliding' was the source of 'kaleidoscope'. In the late 1980s I discovered the novels of Elizabeth Bowen. I fell in love with them. Bowen's intelligence and humour and 'powers of observation' were a revelation to me. I encouraged my mother to read *The House in Paris* where the feeling of being shaken like a kaleidoscope is a key to the lives of the characters but also to how the novel is written.

I don't know which came first but around this time a cheap and cheerful kaleidoscope took up long-term residence in the kitchen by the radio and my mother's cigarettes and lighter and ashtray. ('Cheap and cheerful' was another gentle but fraught item in my mother's lexicon. It might be a phrase of withering contempt or quiet delight. Another of her life-crossing undecidables.) She had acquired it for her beloved young grandson Sam. But like the best toys it seemed of more enduring interest to the adult than to the child. Resting up there on the white Formica counter-top it was not within sight or grasp of my young nephew. My mother used to enjoy *Desert Island Discs*. Was she one of the listeners six months before my birth when Bowen told Roy Plomley she'd like to take to the island as her 'one luxury item' a kaleidoscope?

The future is as much an abyss as the past. Obstetrics has moved on since Shakespeare's day. Ultrasound can make life in the womb seem as ordinary as watching TV. Certain physical defects can be detected before birth. Sex can be determined. The fears of monstrosity attendant on childbirth have diminished. Still we can be haunted by the Queen's image of 'unborn sorrow'. It's the pressure of the time. The ripeness that is all. The sense of imminence and what is coming but cannot be seen: 'Some unborn sorrow, ripe in fortune's womb, / Is coming towards me.'

My nephew Sam was such a wonder for my mother. A beautiful little creature who gave new purpose to her and to my father's existence. They looked after him as often as they could. He lit up their days. The beatific impossible replacement.

Beyond recognition

Early 2003. There is the care-home mixture of electric and winter daylight in the corridor. Fusty carpet. Chintzy decor. My father a few steps away in conversation with a senior staff member. The bodies of strangers flickering fussing faltering at different distances around me. Then the isolation of my mother. As if the camera crew could relax now homing in on the most transporting face in the world and she is not a guinea pig or polar bear or cowering mouse it is my living magical mother. We've been told she had a fall. She took a knock a few days earlier and has a cut on the back of her head. That is why the film crew has come. You are on location the failed film director at last coming to the home homing in on the face that launched your lives.

Back down the frazzled tunnel twistings of the years I can only picture it with the help of this flip-flop phantom film crew. My brother of course among them.

Not to be recognised by your mother. Since that day it's centuries. But the moment has stayed. Long-stay eye park. Hers settles. A whorl fixing on my face. There is contact between our looks but nothing identified. Words like 'spark' or 'glimmer' all out. Tennyson recalls in the long elegy for his friend Hallam how *All the wheels of being slow* and catches the reader up in the time of seeing that that 'slow' is not an adjective it is the end. I am looking into this blue swirl – my mother's eyes – but she fails to register that it is I. In trying to register her failure to register all the words slow. Slow down. Right down. The first poem I ever wrote down (I was eleven) began: 'Down, down, down, / Down to the depths of the sea.' Ah! My mother's delight at reading it. And now? Two 'I's parked in dateless dark. It's a lot. Each a slot. I see you. You see no son. The day is done. I am in translation. Into the nothing you see. We park apart. Under the hill. All the dancers. It's too much of a lot and no lot at all. Richard III carried a car park on his back. Five hundred and forty years later his lot acquires *scheduled monument status*. What is my mother's lot? *How is it to be borne?* All lots are lost. The odds is gone.

In Richmond Park as a child the trees were taller than my eyes could track. [*My mother with her parents and sister Marion, Richmond Park, 1940.*] At the base of the massive bole moss and acorn cups and rivulets. Kneeling in suspense. Watched by mother. The morning sun a glitter in the cobweb of this tiny velvet soft diorama. Life of the little folk between roots. All asunder. No haven under the hill.

Water

Public wells were once ubiquitous. The only other connection we had to the village containing my mother's 'specialist memory care home' was water that gushed from a wall in the street. Constant free drinking water from an ancient Devon spring for all comers. Just bring your canisters and fill up.

In and around my parents' cottage water was always a topic. A key attraction when buying the place was the stream running down the garden visible from the kitchen window. And the house itself was fed by a spring in the field just above. After heavy rain the lane at the top of the drive was a wild intoxicating gush and gurgling. Snowdrops primroses daffodils flourished in the banks. 'Enfolding sunny spots of greenery...' There was a watery affinity in the thought of the author of 'Kubla Khan' having his own 'sweet birthplace' just four miles away on the banks of the River Otter. And it was easy to think too of how autobiography might arise in response to flowing water. Hadn't Wordsworth begun *The Prelude* questioning the River Derwent about the meaning of his life: 'Was it for this...?' When I was living in Finland letters from my father would detail the state of the stream as well as the supply of spring water for the house. By chance I had a colleague called Ralf Norrman who was writing a book about Swedish hydronyms. Ralf was passionate about the relationship between water and place-names. He died of a brain tumour at fifty-three. I loved him because he wasn't my father but resembled him: somewhat mad but very gentle. They never met but shared a serene eccentricity. I picture the placidity and pleasure in which they might have passed an afternoon together. Speaking of water and names.

When my parents first moved to Devon my father compiled meticulous records of the activities of stream and spring. *Stream almost dried up. Steady flow in the stream. Stream overflowing and water running down the hill all over the garden. Spring most satisfactory. Spring rather low. Spring a trickle. No water at all coming through to the house from the spring.* My father's love of digging met up with his love of streams. If the boyhood search for the priest hole and subterranean passageway to the church had led to water filling up the pantry at Perivale the search in Devon focused on the garden. He made divining rods from coat-hangers. Then he made some from copper. Then he splashed out (forgive me) on brass-tipped hazel rods by mail order. The nagging absurdity of all these maxwellian implements lay in the sense that there was *water water everywhere*. But the rationale for digging knew no bounds. Over a number of years he excavated deep holes all over the property. Such was the origin of the Green Pond [*overleaf*]. And the Black. And the Small. The largest was at the bottom of the garden. Lined with plastic. Home for the geese. From the kitchen window we could watch them gliding about like beautiful gray and white sails. But they soon punctured the lining with their webbed feet. The pond turned marsh. The green hydronym. Or was it the Green Pond because that was the colour of the lining?

My father carried on digging. He shifted as far away as he could. Into the hidden area of pine trees he called the

Spinney. His younger son was being as all the wheels slow rutted by cancer. My father withdrew into the Spinney and dug. He dowsed and made numerous trial excavations. To visitors braving that steep and shady section of the garden the resemblance to hasty ineffective graves dug by a serial killer was inescapable. In the end he succeeded in constructing a large and for the casual walker dangerous pit in the heart of the Spinney with an elevated length of black plastic guttering from which in triumph flowed a tiny but constant trickle of spring water. If you stood at the lower end of the Spinney and gazed up at this earthwork amid the pines it was hard not to see it as some arcane shrine.

But there was a period when the flow of water from the spring above the house became so feeble that a couple of times a week we would drive the five miles with empty five-litre bottles and other containers to this village with its well-in-the-wall. Collecting water with my mother was simple and lovely. With my father there was always a modicum of pressure. ('Modicum' was a word of which he was fond.) As if the operation were military and precision paramount. The need to fill each canister as far as possible to the brim. With my mother there was ease. Here is beautiful spring water gushing out of a wall. It was gushing out before we arrived and will go on gushing after we've driven away. Abundance of life. Ceaseless cascade. It had something of the fairytale or magic of film. Like detached hands reaching out of walls in Jean Cocteau's *La Belle et la Bête*. But it also had the power of miniature. Like a snow-globe containing the Colossus at Rhodes the rush from this humble village spout seemed in little the perilous onslaught of the Falls of Dochart she and I confronted in deafened awe one winter's day at Killin.

In the crumbling of the director's expression to which she was ever blind was the thought of *whorl* in all its crazed circling: the well and the wall and the whirl of the end of the whorled. Poetry was the meaning of my mother's face. But it was stopped. As if the spring rushing up out of the earth falling in joyous spasms from the wall for centuries was in this wheeling reeling impossible instant plugged forever. Spring out of bounds. I experienced damage to my retina in a shower making love in the intense tumbling of hot water pressing my mouth in to my lover's expression of love as one speaks of making love but love is never made I caressed her in the falling water and suckled and entered licking every orifice and others I hadn't seen in the water swirling about my face kissing her mouth and all her mouths suddenly an extreme spike of pain in my eye and the retina injured as if unable to retain. That was the sensation now made flesh in a new and inconceivable manner. My mother was looking at me without seeing who I was and this tore off my sight. It was necessary to summon up the film crew around me as onlookers and witnesses: Wheel the camera round! Quick quick! Move in! Too late. Never a time. Witless witness. No one but the son no longer son in the trembling crazy corridor. How was it to be borne? As by a specialist memory tsunami the phantom team dispersed. Thrown back. Away. All wards off. Distribution company destroyed. Transfers metaphors translations all borne away in this brave new whorl. Off! In the spiralling maelstrom of my mother's un-look.

Bravery was the battle cry within. I was forty-five years old. I had to be brave. But who was I? As boys we were always braves. We were the native Americans standing for imagination justice truth. The desire to be brave came from her. Put on a brave face. But there was none. Nothing like this had ever happened before.

Fizzog

I don't associate my mother with the word *face*. She used to say *fizzog*. Hers by the end had something of the walnut intricacy of an Auden. *Fizzog* is at the edge of language. Off-centre off-stage. It lives and loves somewhere fuzzy. It is not concerned about spelling. *Fizzog phisog physog phizog*. It belongs to the air. The pleasure of sound. It's an onomatopizztake. It is fizz and sog. Vivacity and mire. The ghost of a vanishing *phiz*. 'Physiognomy' is reanimated. The dictionary calls *fizzog* 'humorous colloquialism'. It is not sufficient to bracket the word off from the domain of proper discourse. Take care: 'colloquialism'! The word must also be marked as if it were damaged goods ('humorous'). To be taken with a pinch of salt.

But what's a pinch of salt? Whenever my mother took salt to add to something at the stove she'd throw any excess over her left shoulder. She must have learned this from her mother. The mire of the mother of the mother. When I'm cooking and take too big a pinch of salt the impulse to do the same is the arc of a narrative in my body. Silhouette of the grandmother I never knew. I don't think of the bedevilments of Christian spillage at the Last Supper or acting out the evil eye but of my mother's and mother's mother's body in me. What's a pinch? It is all I'm trying to do. To remember the pinches. In pinches. To evoke my mother at a pinch. To pinch time. Sleight without slight. The squeezes and caresses of bringing back memories of my mother's hands. The deftness of my mother's thumb and forefinger pinching salt before arthritic seniority withered them.

My mother the cook: this was something about which she remained diffident all the *compos mentis* days of her life. At certain things she excelled: mashed potato and pancakes and apple pie and sponges and rice puddings. But she never seemed very comfortable cooking dinner. She preferred washing up afterwards. And better than washing up was drying up. Making all the cutlery and plates and pans disappear dried by hand with a fresh linen tea-towel back into the cupboard out of sight. She liked it when I made dinner. It might be chickpea curry or ratatouille or lentil stew or chilli *sans* carne or spaghetti with tomato sauce. Whatever it happened to be she always called it by the same name: *splodge*.

To class as 'humorous colloquialism' is a belittlement. An attempt to render peripheral. But my memory of my mother is inseparable from such locutions. Humorous colloquialisms are her very spirit and wit. *Fizzog* opens up another thinking of culture and society. Philosophers ponder the face. They hum and haw over the idea that it is the basis of ethics. They reflect on whether other creatures such as cat or snake or dog can be said to have a face or if the face is something unique to the human. In the World According to Humorous Colloquialism the word 'face' is replaced with 'fizzog'. No social or political exchange could take place without a sense of laughter and benign absurdity. All violence would become impossible. No defacement could be entertained. Facebook would be a laughable blast from the past.

Still I'm left with that horror. I do not wish to remember the instant but can never be done with it. With hindsight it was her dying look at me. A fortnight later she left the world. George Eliot speaks of a 'maternal transference of self' when a dying mother looks on her beloved son. How did we miss? Impossible first last time in which my mother looked without seeing me. No more not seeing ourselves as others see us. Maternal transference of fizzog into thin air. She shuffled her feet and turned away.

Dreamother

Since her death I have been visited with dreams in which my mother is still alive. Even the most nightmarish are marvels to be cherished. As old age approaches it seems to me that dreams of the return of the dead – especially of those we love – are among humankind's greatest achievements. People can travel to the moon but that seems a small matter compared with the experience of a world in which a beloved person passed away passes back. The matter of my mother. Restored to absolute liveliness without a trace of implausibility. Such dreams carry a joy that goes beyond any others. It is in the dream but it is also what the dream gives. A joy enduring. If only for a few seconds. It irrupts into the waking world and overturns it.

A single example: My mother and I are revisiting Oxford. The town I first visited with her – on a day trip from Cheam in 1975. We walked into the back quad of Exeter College to the loud unexpected starting-up of the Rolling Stones' 'Paint it Black' and I knew standing beside my mother that this was where I wanted to study. (I arrived there as an undergraduate the following autumn.) In the dream the city centre is not so much dreaming spires as rows of old flat-roofed buildings with small temples on top of them. A proliferation of elevated mini-Ashmoleans and Clarendon Buildings. We are looking at properties. Not in any definite way but we are driving down residential streets thinking of a place my wife and I might buy. And then I'm by myself again at home in Sussex and thinking with passionate resolve that I could and should move the family down to the West Country to be closer to her because she's fine now living by herself still doing the crossword in the mornings. She's bright and quite recovered from her Alzheimer's. Cheerful but frail. And then I come to.

Funereal

I also dream about my mother's funeral. One time for instance I was in some kind of 'funeral waiting area'. Holding my Uncle Pete's hand. I don't recall ever having done that in real life — when he was alive. Then I became aware that my father was in front of us. He'd started walking ahead. The route was awkward. There were various obstacles. The detritus of some social event from the previous night. A pint glass on a doorstep. Other items in a box. Clothes strewn. We proceeded with difficulty. Stopping and turning with no one to direct us. Then we were in the church itself. My father was sitting alone at the back. I told him he should go to the front. He seemed pleased at being reminded he could do this. But still he moved only one row forward. I sat down next to him. I saw that he hadn't shaved for several days. Unlike him: he was not a man for stubble. But at the same time he looked very well. Except that he was crying. Then I realised he was crying with joy. He was remembering early days with my mother. In the dream I knew this: I could read his mind. He was beaming through the tears. And now I saw with a swelling wave of happiness that it would be possible to ask him to reminisce. To tell me just a few of the marvellous memories he must have of my mother.

Then I woke up. Or the world woke up. The immediate feeling: bereftness. Bereft of my uncle bereft of his brother.

Funereal

My father bereft of my mother. Bereft of the memories he
had of her and about which it had never occurred to me
to ask. But also the faint irreversible crest: that feeling of
being in the wake of a world-changing wave.

Of another dream I jotted down:

> My mother's funeral. Somewhere in central London.
> One of my old school friends due. I haven't seen him in
> decades. One of the boys who used to come to our house
> in Cheam and spend his time in conversation with my
> mother. Like others he found in her both comfort and
> inspiration. Vital time out from a 'broken home' as it
> used to be called. But he and I became estranged. I'm not
> happy about the prospect of this reunion. But he doesn't
> show up. Then I'm in a rush. I'm using a wheelchair.
> Racing a busload of others along Embankment en route
> to the British Museum. I stop at some benches. There is a
> raised dais with various old folk sitting about and a young
> prankster who appears intent on winding them up. Here
> I remove my contact lenses. The lens solution is black.
> Everyone at the benches is going or returning to where
> I'm headed – the ancient Egyptian and related exhibits.
> Mummies.

A dream becomes memoir. It becomes the recording
of its memory. It also *becomes* in the sense of suiting:
memoir aspires to the dream. I should have annotated at
the time with more clarity and care. Sometimes a dream
is like a 'found object'. As in the one about the oversized
antiquated sewing machine trundling down the street. At
other times it is little more than a feeling of something
mysterious missed. Irrevocable. A night cavity. Like the
eerie dip in the ground in the field just behind my aunt and

uncle's farmhouse at North Berwick. So close to destroying the building. Caused by a Luftwaffe pilot offloading on his flight back to Germany after dropping bombs on Edinburgh. I am dismayed not so much by the obscurity of the dream as by my incompetence in recording it. As if by scribbling 'Mummies' at the end I had captured it all. The memory of a dream cannot be filed away for future consultation under the heading of a single word.

Coleridge remarks in one of his notebooks on 'the non-existence of Surprize in sleep' but the same cannot be said of the experience of writing down a dream. Writing down? Or up? Or across? The parallels with doing a crossword flicker into view. Surprises lie in wait everywhere. The dreamer accepts the desire for the dream to be remembered. It will be a memoir of the dream. The least pause in transcription can be fatal as Cleopatra. As faithful. Or as fateful. It is supposed to be a strict Platonic relationship. In other words a singular kind of non-relationship. But the dream is seductive. As alluring as salad days. It keeps showing its back above the element it lives in. The dream shows its appreciation of being remembered – with every word the waker writes. And with every word it asks: 'Not know me yet?' It invites pinching and being pinched. Pinching and desiring. Salt of the earth. The more the dreamer submits the greater the prize. The dream prises open and surprises without end.

Mummies. What is that conclusion about? It might be just a reference to the embalmed dead bodies in the British Museum. Or a misspelled exclamation (the sort my mother herself was capable of) identifying what belongs to my mother: *Mummy's!* (And thus a return to the beginning: *My mother's funeral...*) It might be a one-word telegram meant to condense all the different possible denotations and connotations that the dream evokes. Today or in the future. However construed the dream says: *the funeral never takes place just once.*

Why did I not speak at my mother's funeral? It was spring. The village churchyard was packed with daffodils. Far more people came than I'd ever expected. My father gave no tribute. It didn't occur to me to ask why not. Grief hard as a brick. Across the congregation there were pockets of shock at the size of the event. Several individuals expressed their amazement. Others their lack of it. *She was a popular woman your mother... A lot of people were very fond of her... Natural such a big turnout...* As the grave was being filled a heavy rain began to fall and it was necessary to retreat. Next morning as I set out on the journey back to the other end of the country there was once again bright spring sunshine. As I drove down the lane and approached the church I felt impelled to stop to look at the flowers on the grave. My four-year-old son exclaimed from the back-seat: *Oh no! We're not going to see Granny's funeral again?*

What would life be like if funerals could be repeated? Ghosts of the real in the funereal. *Groundhog Day* from the other side. Instead of working out how to steal a load of money or get someone to fall in love with you everyone would work again with increasing candour and articulacy to share the unbearable event. There would be a tribute from the father and the son and every other member of the family and in due course every person in the congregation who wanted to remember and share. Memories would return in steady ebbs and thought-pools one morning after another. People's capacities for eloquence would intensify. All the sweetness of remembrance would be compacted into this single afternoon day after day coming back. Everybody would go to bed shattered with exhaustion and next morning: *Awake!* Time to attend the funeral again. The congregation would become ever more mellifluous in singing. The renditions of 'Morning Has Broken' and 'Jerusalem' would grow each day more accomplished and affecting. An unknown lone piper would find his way into the scene and play 'Amazing Grace' on the hill beyond the church. Elsewhere a phonographic glass rendering of 'The Lea-Rig'. There would be rushes of loving laughter in the service at memories of the gifts of grace and playfulness of the woman brought back in tribute after tribute. Humorous colloquialisms would flare like fireworks along the pews. The vicar would become defenceless. Even though he never knew her. Come to her through the mourning of music laughter anecdotes and reminiscences he would find himself in a state of absolute euphoria stripped of all religion.

Trap

Keep your trap shut my mother liked to say. It's another of the idioms that distinguishes hers from the language of my father. He would never use such a phrase. He would never say anything to anyone else about their silence or their loquacity. For the majority of his life my father seemed devoted to keeping his trap shut. Did he think about speaking at his wife's funeral? Or did the idea never cross his mind? This is as mysterious to me as the idea that he never dreamt. Is it possible to go to bed every night for decades and never remember anything that occurred in the land of shut-eye? Or did he have dreams as vivid and powerful as anyone's but choose to keep his trap shut? He was one of the most reserved people on earth. He had an inner calm at times more discombobulating than any outward agitation could be.

The lane up to the cottage from the church was winding and single-track. There were just a few passing-places. My father knew very well where they were. It was not uncommon while driving up or down the lane to have to stop for a delivery van approaching too fast in the other direction. Sometimes there would be the makings of a confrontation. The other driver needed just to back up a few yards. Whereas my father knew that he himself would be required to reverse along a fair stretch including two blind bends in order to get to the nearest passing-place. So he would sit at the wheel placid as the strange Buddhist he was. If the man in the van did not take action the waiting game could last for some time. But then my father would get out of his car and stroll over to the other driver's window and deliver with great deliberation and numerous pauses a humble but magisterial maxwellian oration explaining that if in fact this fellow road-user would care to take the trouble to put his motor into reverse gear and back up a short distance he would very soon arrive at a space adjacent to the hedgerow quite satisfactory for the rather brief period of time required for my father to be able without further ado to galvanise his own vehicle into action and drive past. Such was my father's mild and gentle manner that he never encountered any opposition or unpleasantness in these situations.

I suspect that it was not so much the softness of his speech as the silences he injected into it. He would start a statement then stop. A word or phrase could come. Or not. Just as his usual response to any question was a maxwellian *Hmm* that might grow to inordinate length and lead anywhere or nowhere. The latent logic seemed to be that it would be better if he and indeed everyone else could just keep their trap shut. Michel de Montaigne writes somewhere: *I have never met a man who does not say more than he should rather than less.* Montaigne never met my father.

My mother by contrast was like Montaigne himself. An endless generator of speech. In herself and in others. An ever unpredictable borrower of the stories and experiences of others. The designation of mouth as trap is sublime. I don't know how many times I heard her use the phrase before I began to understand what she was saying. *Keep your trap shut* mingles in my memory with the Venus flytraps we tried to keep when we were young. A plant as challenging to tend as any animal. We tried positioning it on the windowsill for maximum warmth and sunlight. We tried not to feed it too often. We tried not to water it too much or too little. But this plant proved very resistant to cohabiting with us. It would wilt and die and we would have to acquire another. No doubt we should have let it keep its trap shut more often. But my brother and I were smitten by carnivorous curiosity. We wanted to feed it a fly whenever the thought came into our heads.

It would have been good advice to the old woman who swallowed one. The distinctive disagreeableness of a fly alighting in one's mouth. 'Keep your trap shut' recalls the old British wartime propaganda 'Careless talk costs lives'. And like so many of my mother's everyday sayings it continues to resonate. There are plenty of bad silences. There are compelling reasons why people should talk. But in their very volubility Montaigne and my mother have a point. What if we spent more time keeping our traps shut? What if – as we keep them shut – we think about what we are doing and try in a concerted way to do something with that? What if alongside or beyond the 'talking cure' we hearken more to the creative energy of a psychoanalyst's silence? Why is silence so rare? What are people so scared of? What about the value of silence in schools and universities? Why should there not be courses – in the sciences as well as the humanities – devoted to the benefits of keeping one's trap shut? I imagine Montaigne and my mother at work together compiling a list of 'Learning Outcomes'.

The word 'mouth' trips off the tongue. To have a mouth would seem an inalienable human right. But in the World According to Humorous Colloquialism no one would have such a thing. Everyone would have a *trap* and be encouraged to see it as that. You no sooner open than you've fallen into it. You trap yourself. You let yourself be programmed. You let language trap you.

In the late 1970s and early '80s I got interested in what was called 'theory'. And so too therefore did my mother. On occasion I would read aloud to her from an essay by Blanchot or Foucault or Derrida or Lacan. But more often I tried to explain what I thought they were talking about and why. Her nodding smile and blue eyes lighting up were essential to my making sense of it. 'Theory' always seemed an absurd name. These texts were about thinking and doing everything anew. Desire and identity. Language and literature. Education and society. I talked to her with heady enthusiasm one evening about Althusser's Ideological State Apparatuses: the idea that family and school and TV and church and so on are ways of controlling people – their identity and their thoughts. Their beliefs and behaviour. The concept of ISAs now seems almost quaint. Today's 'culture of surveillance' is so much richer and more varied. And while Foucault was with feverish and magnificent intensity making possible so many new kinds of 'history of the present' other forces were doing away with any need for 'society' altogether. *There's no such thing as society* as Margaret Thatcher would sum up in 1987. *There are individual men and women and there are families.* The ongoing catastrophe of global capitalism is the remorseless and grotesque expansion of such claims.

But in my mind's eye the 1980s are one long Wimbledon singles final: Margaret Thatcher vs. Kathleen McAdam. It is a very dilated drawn-out sultry stultifying day. The umpire is Creepy. An African gray parrot who belonged to my Uncle Pete in the Cotswolds.

Trap

He's only there for the seeds. And of course fair play. *Fault!* he cries. Creepy wants there to be tennis. My mother wants there to be tennis. *Second service.* But Milk Snatcher just seems intent on inflicting on the audience as much as possible of her voice. Her toxic self-conviction by gradual degrees makes the grass turn yellow. She tries non-stop to interfere with play. She shows no respect for Creepy. She patronises the ball boys. She vents venom on all sides. First and last on the enemies within herself. My mother responds with top-drawer stuff at every point. Quick-as-a-flash sumptuous colloquialisms with top-spin. Brilliant backspun sliced puns. Here a hilarious put-down backhand smash. There a delicious drop shot. Laughing-to-tears lobs. Breathtaking down-the-lines. A final passing shot. A communications ace. My mother plays lawn tennis in the world according to humorous colloquialism. The Iron Lady is dressed for the occasion but can't play tennis to save her life. Or anyone else's. She's the grocer's daughter who wants to play shop but is just trying to serve herself. She knows she is self-serving but she doesn't know which end of the racket to hold. Or what the racket is that's holding her. *Double fault!* cries the African gray. Purse up those plummy rotten lips. *Match point.* Keep your trap shut. *Quiet please!* Margaret Thatcher appears to have walked off with the trophy but everyone watching knows that whatever future of society there may be rests with the spirit and wit of Kathleen McAdam.

Autobiography

The innumerable evenings spent in peaceful Devon pubs. The names of the villages are a sort of music in themselves: Colyton Wilmington Sutton Barton Dalwood Axmouth. My mother would have a bitter lemon or a tonic water or a cup of coffee and I would have a pint and a half of beer or lager – the legal limit for me as the driver. And we'd smoke like chimneys. We'd talk about anything but be just as much at ease not speaking. Sometimes I'd have written some fiction and we'd find a discreet corner of the bar and I'd read aloud to her. In our pub-going there was an element of ritual in keeping with her father in his final years wearing his jacket and flat cap as he sloped off alone to The Harrow for a Guinness or two. I never thought of that at the time but she must have done so. My brother and her father and her mother and my father and others were also there with us in the pub. No: there's no such thing as 'individual men or women'. There are ghosts and dreams of listeners.

The critic Mary Jacobus has suggested that 'autobiography comes into play on the basis of a missing mother'. I encountered this idea just after my mother died. I was asked to give a lecture on Wordsworth's *The Prelude*. His autobiographical poem (sub-titled 'The Growth of a Poet's Mind') is supposed to be about his mother. Ann Cookson

Autobiography

Wordsworth died when William was seven years old. Of the thousands of lines of blank verse that make up *The Prelude* only two refer to her in an explicit way:

> Early died
> My honoured mother, she who was the heart
> And hinge of all our learnings and our loves.

When I'd read *The Prelude* in the past I had taken note of the heart and the love but not so much the hinge and the learning. While preparing my lecture on 'the growth of a poet's mind' I also came across something Adam Phillips says in his book about D. W. Winnicott: 'the mind is a mother, a process of self-care based on mothering'. In the weeks following my mother's death I felt a strong compulsion to write some 'story of my life'. I had no idea how to go about it. I was forty-five years old and had always thought the very idea of autobiography impossible. You couldn't write such a thing unless you'd come to the end of your life. How could I be contemplating an autobiography? Montaigne observes: 'If I have only one hour's work to do before I die, I am never sure I have enough time to finish it.' Death never comes on time. Neither does autobiography. The thing, as Jacobus puts it, *comes into play*. I had to write.

I based my autobiography on the formal constraint of 'three score and ten'. This Biblical summation of life was another of my mother's favoured idioms. (I was also conscious of some distant great uncle called Bindon Blood who had written a book of 'reminiscences' entitled *Four Score Years and Ten*.) The text would not exceed seventy pages. I would write by hand. I had more or less given up handwriting in the wake of acquiring my first computer (an Amstrad 8256) in the late 1980s. It was strange to return to handwriting. On some days it was bigger than on others. But as I drew nearer to page seventy it grew smaller and smaller. The Faustian pact of the packed page. I finished in early September 2004. I recall only three things about the whole manuscript. It ends with me running ecstatic down a street in Chicago with the love of my life. It is called 'Unhinged'. And despite all my great as well as small expectations it makes next to no reference to my mother.

When is a mother 'missing'? How much is the lag of years in writing about my mother related to her dementia? Wasn't she already a missing mother years before she died? Is it possible to separate the delay from what brought on the dementia in the first place? Had she not become a missing mother the night her younger son died in the early autumn of 1986?

Worlds not realised

Life speeds up as you get older. My forties flew by. My fifties went in a twinkling. Clichés help to describe what happens and encourage you to believe you can prepare for what is coming towards you. But I was not prepared for what has been happening over the three years since I started working on this book. In quite unexpected ways I have begun to see how much I missed. How much I hadn't thought. Or thought to feel. To adopt Wordsworth's words describing childhood: I am *moving about in worlds not realised*. The green chasms. The welling perspectives. The blind precipices. The gaping upside-down skies. The missing mother of my past.

I once remarked to a girlfriend that smells cannot be recalled. She started to remonstrate then halted. *Oh wow! You're right. That's so weird. It's as if God forgot*. We cannot remember smells but we can recognise them with ease. And they can be powerful triggers and encrypters of memory. When I smell wallflowers I remember my mother. When I smell sweet peas. When I smell honeysuckle. When I smell sandalwood. When I smell tarmacadam burning.

My mother's voice has been preserved nowhere. No stories no laughter no song. How can that be? No one can ever hear. When I think about this it seems as implausible as smells eluding recollection.

Yet a single recollected word or phrase can release new vistas. For instance her 'spending a penny'. Few people today any longer use this idiom. Call it colloquial or euphemistic. Think of it as humorous. Classify and categorise as wished. Take whimsical pleasure in knowing and informing others of its origin. None of that clarifies the singularity of my mother's speech. A question once again of her dazzling twilight irony. When we were children there were still pennies. Big round brown flat things. The older darker ones still had Queen Victoria's head on. To think of my mother saying *spend a penny* is to become enveloped in the sweet funniness of her voice. 'Spend a penny': it's priceless. My mother's priceless intonation. (Likewise with her playful fondness for referring to the urinary system as 'waterworks' or to the mechanics of one's 'undercarriage'.) And it makes the penny drop in quite other memory slots. She took us one washed-out winter's day to Chessington Zoo. It was wet and cold. There was a penny-slot machine of 'What the Butler Saw'. My brother and cousin Mike and I were given penny after penny to spend on this. And pennies now make pounds and pounds of the huge flesh of a prehistoric creature called an Indricotherium. One of the largest mammals that ever existed. In my memory it was taller than a giraffe. Gray-skinned and benign. A hornless herbivorous rhinoceros standing five metres tall. Down this memorial vista I can still picture this marvellous extinct gigantic giraffe-cum-horse. My mother and I saw it. We saw it together in one of the enclosures that rainy and windswept day at the zoo.

I have on occasion encountered my mother as an eerie apparition through others. Once when I was living in Scotland I happened to meet Doris Lessing. She knew nothing about me. Nothing about the importance of her books in my mother's life. It was a large-scale drinks reception just after Lessing had received an honorary degree. Someone introduced us and she gave me an intense look that lasted for several seconds. Then she said: *I've seen you before.* And she paused. I imagined some embarrassment was in the offing. She was mistaking me. Misremembering some other occasion. I would have to point out that we had in fact never met. Then she declared with a serious and knowing face: *In one of those pictures of Jacobean gentlemen hanging in the National Portrait Gallery.* I had no answer to this. The word *fizzog* sprang to mind and a desire to tell her about my mother's immersion one summer in all her books. I said nothing. But I felt something spook. Redolent of what Angela Carter somewhere calls maternal telepathy.

On another occasion I had a distant *tête-à-tête* with Edward Said in Cambridge. It was just inside the entrance to King's College. He was due to give a seminar later that afternoon. I planned to go along. I had never met him or heard him speak but his face was well-known to me. He was coming into the college and I was about to wander out across the road to spend a while at Heffers bookshop. There was no reason he should have stopped to look at me. But there was a strange suspended moment in which we both gazed at one another. Too far away to speak. I knew he was close to death. (His leukaemia was a matter of public knowledge.) He didn't know me from Adam. But in that exchange of looks something took place. It had to do with my mother. And – I supposed – with his.

And then a couple of years ago I sent an email to Hilary Mantel. Relating to a book or giving a talk. I'd read her *Giving Up the Ghost* by then. We've never met. I didn't expect a response. But she wrote back within moments.

With disarming warmth and generosity. In the line of address at the head of her message she left off the final 's' of my forename. She wrote back a few minutes later to apologise but the lovely smile-inducing error had been made. It has kept me company in the writing of this book.

If I had been born a girl I would have been called Nicola. My mother took great pleasure in recalling this fact. The small handful of letters she wrote me are all addressed to 'Nic'. I think of that as preserving the Nicola. Bringing in the unborn feminine. While she wrote few letters she left many notes. Such as 'Gone shopping' or 'Choc ice in the freezer' or 'Over at Minnie-ha-ha's [i.e. Marion's]'. Even such terse messages (signed 'M x' or 'Me x') were often addressed 'Darlin' Nic'. She also used to call me Sidney. Her little Sidney. Or Sydney. Spoken not written. The spelling as always neither here nor there. Creatures in a twilight zone.

Neither of us in those days was aware of the girl called Sydney in Elizabeth Bowen's *The Hotel* but it didn't seem to me insignificant that my mother liked to call me by an androgynous or at least gender-ambiguous name. I loved the idea of being a girl and imagined this was with my mother's full blessing. On the last day of primary school one girl in the class was allowed to dress up as a boy and one boy as a girl. I cannot remember if I was competing with other boys but I ended up being chosen. Boy-girl: the special one. My mother made me a little navy-blue dress for the occasion. I loved wearing it. I returned home from that final day of primary school and at last slipped it off and threw it on the bed in a transport of grief. Tears idle tears. Tears sidling up to tears for a life that was no more.

Machine

Like every other mother we knew at that time ours had an old hand-operated Singer sewing machine. An ordinary standard-size version of the surreal trundler in the dream of Peter Townend. Memories waft and turn in the anonymous sounds of machines as much as in the rhapsodies of Maria Callas on the radio or a blackbird in the park. In the evenings my mother would sew name-labels into our school clothes and mend socks and make this and that for herself. I loved being in the room when she was using the sewing machine. The feeling of quietness and night. The energy and tranquillity. The unfurling of movement then tiny jog and pause. I also associate my mother at the sewing machine with the rhythms of the carriages of the old railway train streaming north across England into Scotland in high summer.

And then we never had a washing machine or dryer at home. My mother drove to the launderette once a week. Sunday was best. And in my teens and twenties I loved to go with her. Sitting with her in the warmth facing the soft churning of soapy clothing in the long row of washing machines made for a kind of suspended animation somewhere between womb and poem. Being immersed with my mother warm and comfortable in the gentle dredgery of a deserted launderette on an otherwise eventless Sunday afternoon or evening was a magical interlude I never wanted to cease.

But there was one mechanical sound I loathed. The noise of the vacuum cleaner did something to my insides unlike anything else. Even in late adolescence its raring up anywhere in the house unleashed rage and nausea in me. It was always my mother at the helm. My father never raised a finger to clean anything in the house and nor (at least until their early twenties) did his sons. The noise of the hoover seemed always to be in dire excess of any hygienic benefits it could bestow. It mimicked a damaged and dangerous warplane. Forever unable to take off. Cut off from any runway. The filthy noise approached. Legs must be raised. Bodies must eject themselves from the scene. It was our mother and it was not our mother. She too seemed possessed as she pushed or let it sweep her on. She had no fondness for this heavy hot ill-designed contraption. It must have enraged and nauseated her even more than it did us. But I never considered this. I more or less held my breath for the moment of its surging away into another room.

We always had a dining room and the same mahogany dining table and six high-back chairs with upholstered bumpy velvet floral-patterned seats. When we lived in Surrey we ate lunch there every Sunday but in Devon the table and chairs already seemed ghosts of themselves. You passed through the cottage dining room to get to the kitchen. One of my clearest memories of that transitional space is coming home to see that my mother had been hoovering. The chairs were strewn about as if in the wake of a Mafia meeting. How I hated her hoovering. Was my childhood antipathy to the vacuum cleaner to do with separation anxiety? After all didn't it separate stuff off wherever it went? Make things disappear? Take our mother away from us? Indeed separate our mother from herself?

She had a fundamental wariness about the language of

psychology. As well as about its professional representatives. She would unravel 'separation anxiety' as a delighted kitten might a ball of wool. 'Separation anxiety' has nothing to do with what she called the common touch. It is a miserable machine-like phrase. It martyrs and murders the mother. It serves to stifle the affirmation of an inseparableness of the mother from anything and everything in life. She'd put the kibosh on such clinical claptrap without a second's hesitation.

She loved to say *kibosh*. She always pronounced the first syllable long: 'ki'. Rhyming with 'tie' and 'my'. It also sounded like a playful mispronunciation of the first letter of her name. K for Kate or Kathleen. And at the same time she invited you to hear in this word both nonsense (*bosh!*) and ancient surrealism (Hieronymus Bosch). *Kibosh* was part of her amorous armoury of humorous colloquialism. Of words' attire and word-satire. 'Claptrap' was another. 'Caboodle' another. Each an additional tiny piece to be maintained in the war of the worlds of language. Whether in tennis against Margaret Thatcher or in the sketching of a new language of psychotherapy.

The loops of sound in memory. Eight years after my mother's death my wife and I were visiting her grave and thought to see if the church itself was open. By a happy chance it was. We walked in to the most unexpected sound: the violence and incongruity of someone unseen hoovering. Out of the vestry emerged a woman as surprised to see us as I was to see her. An old neighbour from up the lane who looked as cheerful and ageless as ever. She turned off the vacuum cleaner and greeted us with great warmth and affection. Within seconds she was remembering my mother. *What a lovely woman she was — your mother. So kind. So good to talk to. Could have talked all day.* The years since her death giving way. Massive and irreversible as a landslip.

Mother tongue

We talk of a mother tongue as if this were an obvious and familiar possession. Everyone is supposed to have one. But it is never simple. It is the language of dream and flux. No one can own or master it. 'Cat got your tongue?' my mother liked to say. It never occurring to her that she was the cat. The pleasure of having words in our mouths is inseparable from the maternal. What we call the mother tongue is a licking loving tongue. To love the mother tongue is to know that this mother is a cat or an owl as well as human. It is to be exposed to the wet soft dry hard caresses of its flames. One evening at the white Formica-top table I read aloud to her an essay by E. M. Forster called 'Anonymity'. Forster suggests that literature is something that comes from letting down buckets into the underworld. A place of imagination. A place foreign to names and naming. I have called my mother *mother* in these pages. I have also recalled her so-called 'birth names'. And I have tried to query this language of the obvious and familiar. For it is not my mother's tongue. I continue to think of her as sheer creature of the imaginative underworld. Names have a deadly character. I associate my mother with life. With an implacable eluding of what fixes and freezes. With the unsettling and loosening of all death-driven convictions – from proper names to national identities. With what in words slips the lips and laughs and shows up again mole-like where you couldn't have envisaged.

'Too late she cries!' My mother was fond of this exclamation. It was never written and so never clear how far the 'too late' was to be lapped in quotation marks: '"Too late!" she cries.' Or where the lapping began or ended. 'She cries too late.' There is a saying of uncertain origin that dates from the nineteenth century: *'Too late!* she cried, as she waved her wooden leg.' But my mother never mentioned any prosthetic limb. And the cry for her was always in the present: it was *cries* not *cried*. With regard to some misfortune already happened or happening: 'Too late she cries!' It encapsulates her quickness. Too quick for words. She is and is not the she who cries. She has already given words the slip: too late she cries!

Another little pellet or earthwork she sometimes cast up: *ouijamiflip*. This was her quirky version of 'what's-it-called' or 'thingamajig'. I never saw the word transcribed. It wasn't a word in writing. It was still to be spelled. It was another instance of her inhabiting a language and a world beneath the surface. At once more spontaneous and more dreamy. A pre-word at odds with any proper. With Man. Authority. Stasis and rigidity.

An old friend from school and university days resolved at some point in the late 1980s to start calling my mother Gwendolen because (he said) she had 'a genial countenance' and 'a lovely complexion' with 'bright, blue eyes, a pretty face'. 'Gwendolen' is a nineteenth-century Welsh name from *gwen* (fair pure blessed white) and *dolen* (loop or bow or link in a chain). A lovely loopiness. My father on the other hand seemed to understand that she called for a name beyond names. In birthday and wedding anniversary cards he always referred to her as Mlalao. A word composed out of his love for her. A childlike hypocoristic that incorporated the letters of his own mother's first name: Lola. As teenagers my brother and I regarded *Mlalao* as risible. Later I came to think of it as almost unbearable in its poignancy. My father was not an expressive person – but there were moments when he tried to be.

Over a series of baking hot days one summer in Devon I read Samuel Beckett's *The Unnamable* aloud to my mother in the garden. Beyond names. Not capable of being named. Or in the original: *L'innomable*. In eccentric accord with the fizzles and fizzing up of memory this recalls another French word: *limonade*. The many glasses of home-made stuff she and I drank in accompaniment. Innumerable unnamable unquenchable. With clumps of ice and shreds of mint picked from where the plant was running riot all around the greenhouse on the other side of the stream. The back of the house had a wonderful view over the valley below. But we sat on the bench at the front. In a suntrap facing my mother's beloved flowerbeds. A great thronging of hot colours and scents and a small lawn that retained moisture even in the driest summers. Above that a mossy grass bank and hedgerow. Behind which the lane ran unseen. When the sun became too intense we put up a parasol. Reading *The Unnamable* aloud is the best route to experiencing its hilarity. And the unflagging purity of its rhythms. Smoking cigarettes and drinking lemonade I read and my mother listened and I listened to my mother listening as we leapt and limped with laughter through all its goings-on. Happy days tempered by the unspeakable. For this was in the great eerie interval. One summer in the middle of the period when my brother's cancer was in remission and we were all in abeyance waiting hoping despairing wondering would he come through seven years and be pronounced cured.

B-r-ring!

It's the same thing. That was the innocuous phrase some three years later that my mother enunciated over the phone when I was living in a run-down bedsit in south Oxford trying to survive in the deepening dark of the Thatcher years. I'd completed a PhD and had some teaching experience but university lecturing jobs were more or less non-existent. I was getting by on whatever I could find. A-level and Oxbridge entrance. Teaching English as a Foreign Language. Plus a solitary undergraduate. A sweet young man who came to my nasty little bedsit once a week for a tutorial in his chosen special subject: satire.

B-r-ring! It was early evening. My mother on the phone. She didn't waste words. *It's the same thing.* It took me a few moments to apprehend. My brother had got the results of his latest test. An all-clear would have moved him on to no further check-up for twelve months. But it was back. *It's the same thing.* I was leaning against the dilapidated marble fireplace. With a few gentle parting words my mother hung up. I was hysterical. My girlfriend was in the room. The bedsit had no space for privacy even if I'd tried to seek it. My eyes were streaming head flowing fingers clinging to the battered mantelpiece of the defunct fireplace as I said the same thing. *It's the same thing* I said over and over and over. My girlfriend was frightened. She didn't know what was happening.

My mother's words have lasted longer than the building she telephoned. I remember years later revisiting Oxford and happening to walk along this road to see: nothing. The bedsit and steep gloomy staircase that led up to it and to other bedsits and the Beer Shop that had stood below it: demolished. But the wall with its marble fireplace was still visible. Exposed. Scorched and blackened. From another time. Like something out of the Blitz. Or out of the crazed scrap of fiction I wrote soon after the phone call. A circular horror story called 'Telephoning Home'. There's a character who is peering into a brown paper bag containing the cans of soup and vegetables and so on that he is in the process of purchasing from his local corner shop and the shop-owner also peering into the bag remarks: *Uncanny how similar tins look innit?* A displaced stammering of what my mother said. The entire story in my ear mere embellishment over and over of those four words: *It's the same thing.*

The specific clinical name was never spoken. Alveolar soft part sarcoma. According to one consultant it was a cancer so rare he knew of only one other documented case. Somewhere in Russia. Nowadays its existence seems to be acknowledged all over the place. It affects children and – less often – young adults. It continues to have a very poor prognosis. And it has come to be known by its acronym: ASPS. 'Have I the aspic in my lips?' Cleopatra asks. Then she applies an asp to her breast in order to become a nurse and mother for the last time: 'With thy sharp teeth this knot intrinsicate / Of life at once untie... / ... Peace, peace! / Dost thou not see my baby at my breast, / That sucks the nurse asleep?' And then *Applying another asp to her arm* she drops. It's the most beautiful death in Shakespeare. Gentle as a lover's pinch. First the mouth then breast then arm. The course of my brother's fate in reverse. First the arm then lungs chest back brain and at last the tongue. Tripping a death-rattle too awful my mother locked upstairs in the bathroom howling inconsolable for the rest of life the rest of us men of stones. Tripping the last thing my mother did in the care home. The fall and cut to the head that precipitated the least Cleopatra-like parting on earth. *ASPS*: what oncological clown thought this acronym fitting?

When fitting it was my mother who took charge. Just before the onslaught of the final year a consultant at the hospital in Exeter laughed as he explained to my brother the reason for the fits: *The cancer's got to your brain*. It was she who stepped in as nurse at home when my brother had his seizures and shifted him on to his side to make sure he didn't swallow his tongue or his own vomit. As ever the one cleaning up. The one watching.

Whatever happens you mustn't end up *bitter and twisted*. This was a term of special force. At once half-humorous turn of everyday speech and classical rhetorical figure: hendiadys. Ancient Greek for 'two-through-one'. A twofer. Like *hearth and home* or *sound and fury* or *cheap and cheerful*. Bitterness is twisted up. In a bitter twist. Few verdicts were more damning than when my mother called someone bitter and twisted. Even after her younger son's excruciating years of suffering and godless exit she resisted any 'bitter and twisted'. The eighteenth-century philosopher Immanuel Kant speaks of the moral law within us akin to the starry heavens above our heads. 'Bitter and twisted' was my mother's phrase for those who recognised this law but ended up with their perspectives awry. Which is not to say she lived on in any simple quietism. She liked her kitchen to be spick and span (another hendiadys she was wont to use). Always clear. The little bone china ashtray in which she'd stubbed out a cigarette would be washed and in the drying rack before she lit up again. The simple white china cup washed up as soon as she'd drunk her coffee. An object remaining on the side in the kitchen for more than a few hours was exceptional. For instance the kaleidoscope. But at some moment she had written out the words of Dylan Thomas's 'Do not go gently into that good night' and on occasion would bring it out. A slip of paper in her lovely simple rounded handwriting leaning against the radio or Formica upstand. Then it would go undercover again. Into a kitchen drawer with her little scissors and binoculars and painkillers and handkerchiefs. Never far away: *do not go gently*. Still I've sometimes wondered if my mother's battle against 'bitter and twisted' (an aspect of her resistance to whatever fixes and freezes) wasn't what sent her mad.

Flowers

After the First World War her father moved to Canada. In recognition of his contribution to the war effort (as a horse vet) William McAdam was given thirty acres to farm just outside Winnipeg. He and Emily said farewell to family they would in all likelihood never see again and voyaged off for a new life. After a few years the harvest failed. They lost everything. By now with two young daughters (Peggy and Nettie) they migrated south to Chicago looking for work. My grandfather got a job in the construction industry. Building skyscrapers. That was when he discovered he suffered from vertigo. The family gave up. They returned to Drymen. His brother Watty was working in the field as my grandfather came into view. Watty looked up and saw it was his brother returning. He looked down again and went on working. The emotions were too much.

After my brother died that was how my mother worked in the green chasms of the garden. In the beds and on the banks. Hemmed in by her buddleias and hydrangeas. Amid roses orchids irises tiger lilies montbretia primroses daffodils narcissi pansies violets saxifrage lavender sunflowers begonias geraniums fuchsias and so many other flowers. All living. Thriving and other.

They had to be living. She hated cut flowers. Whenever a guest brought a bunch to the house my mother exclaimed: *How beautiful!* And then as if already undertaking a dying vigil she raced to put them in the nearest conceivable container of water.

Other Men's Flowers: this was the title of one of my mother's cherished books of poetry. A.P. Wavell's anthology was first published in the year her mother died. The title is from Montaigne: 'I have gathered a posie of other men's flowers and nothing but the thread that binds them is my own.' Other men's and other women's. The thread of the anthology (notes Wavell) is his own memory. So many hours and so many evenings passed in the quiet Devon cottage at the kitchen table reading poetry to my mother: Dante Wyatt Shakespeare Marlowe Donne Herbert Marvell Milton Cowper Gray Blake Wordsworth Coleridge Shelley Keats Byron Tennyson Brontë Whitman Dickinson Rimbaud the Rossettis the Brownings Fitzgerald Lear Baudelaire Rimbaud Hopkins Swinburne Dowson Owen Rosenberg Apollinaire Sorley Moore Eliot Lawrence H.D. Yeats Mayakovsky Brecht MacDiarmid Bunting Auden Neruda Douglas Stevens Bishop Mandelstam Plath Hughes Snyder Lowell Stevie Smith Patti Smith Larkin Heaney O'Hara Ashbery Allen Fisher Ponge Murray Prynne. Not to mention my own juvenile screed. She with her instant coffee. Me with my whisky. Others' poems.

She never wrote any herself – apart from the provoking little birthday poem for my uncle John. She listened to everything. Sitting with her milky coffee and smoking her low-tar cigarettes. Sometimes knitting at the same time. Getting up to empty the ashtray. Or to make herself another Nescafé. Or – much relished by my father – to remove from the oven a full-cream-milk rice pudding in its dark golden coat. Or (most months of the year) to fill or refill the hot-water bottle she loved to maintain in her lap.

Flowers

To me the meanest flower that blows can give
Thoughts that do often lie too deep for tears.

These are the final lines of Wordsworth's ode about childhood memory and the loss of imaginative vitality that is already traumatic to him in his mid-twenties. He means 'meanest' in the sense of most lowly and inferior. Petty and insignificant. A flower not even worthy of being named. But also a flower that means most by not being named. The most meaning flower. It's another man's flower. Or *floweret*. In an unfinished ode published a few years earlier Thomas Gray speaks of 'the meanest floweret of the vale'. All flowers are others'. Others' others. Other to them. Them other. The mother. It has to do with something *too deep for tears*. A thinking of and through the otherness of the mother. A melancholy that is also a power. What gives of mourning.

Handbag

There is a photograph of my mother and father some time in the early 1980s. By a weir somewhere around Oxford. I like its simplicity. The sun is shining. There are trees and water and a footbridge in the background. My parents are close to one another. They are together and smiling as I take the picture. They look happy even if this is during the great eerie interval.

For me now the punctum of this photograph is my mother's handbag. What a fabulous and bizarre object! She

took it with her everywhere. From our youth my brother and I had a kind of veneration for our mother's handbag. It wasn't identical across the years. She would every so often acquire another one and we would have to adjust: now it was black with silver clasps and now it was brown with brass. It was where we weren't allowed to go. But it was right in front of us. More than anything or anywhere else in our house this strange unliving creature was a site of secrecy and allure. It had something of the quality of the Tardis in *Doctor Who*. You could always be surprised by its capaciousness. It could always turn out to contain something you never thought could be in there. We would ask her to show us what was in her handbag and on occasion she would do so. Not in a comprehensive fashion. Emptying the contents out as if in a police search. But she would permit a brief gaze within. Or she would extract one item after another but always leave us with the distinct impression that there was more in reserve. Some further mystery concealed.

Most or all of the following would be present at any one time:

cigarettes
cigarette lighter
face make-up (a gold compact case with a swirl design)
lipstick
purse containing money and cards
embroidered handkerchief
comb or hairbrush
scrap of paper with poetry on (anything from
    Shakespeare to Dylan Thomas)
suckers (boiled sweets or mints)
chocolate (Cadbury's or Galaxy milk)

small pair of scissors
Anadin or Dispirin (for headaches)
hayfever tablets (seasonal)
ballpoint pen
shopping list

In our later teenage years my brother and I would raid our mother's handbag for a cigarette. Or for small sums of cash. But these thefts were open secrets. The fundamental mysteriousness of the handbag never went away. For me now it is like the car that Neil Young sings about in 'Long May You Run'. It is here in the photograph but nowhere in the world. And nowhere in her handbag did my mother keep photographs. This seems more peculiar in the retrospect light of several decades. Our house was never decorated or blazoned with family photos. My mother did not keep any either in her handbag or in any albums. Photographs were consigned to a chest-of-drawers where they lay unlooked at. Often for months or years at a time.

The instant of her death

The instant of her death that was not her death. I was around ten and she and I were walking together hand in hand along the seafront at North Berwick. We'd gone past the 'buddy' beach and the open air saltwater swimming pool and were wandering along the promenade to the east of it and she had promised me a '99 and the ice-cream van was just a hundred yards ahead and I became aware of someone shouting but only after the sound of glass breaking and my mother falling to the ground. The promenade was parallel to a road and the road to the edge of a golf course. The shout might be assembled after the event as a 'Fore!' At the time I had no knowledge of this word. It is like the warning questioned and mocked by twelve-year-old Maud in Elizabeth Bowen's *A World of Love*: 'Beware Low-flying Aircraft'. Someone shouts 'Fore!' and you are supposed to do what? Freeze? Dive sideways? Drop to the ground? Jump up in the air?

At first I thought my mother had gone to ground by her own volition. In my unconscious I suppose I assumed that the beginning of any event emerged from her. It took me some moments to realise what had happened. People were crowding around us in gasps and shock. My mother had been hit in the head by a golfball.

I don't recall now whether I thought she was dead already or was overwhelmed just in the aftermath by the reality of the possibility. Helen McAdam's 'Who's turned the lights out?' in 1938 evokes the instant of one's death as the abrupt and random ease of someone flicking a switch. Here was a man who had tried to turn my mother's lights out now striding across the road red-faced blustering speaking in a sort of crusty English accent of the sort affected by well-to-do Scottish and English gents alike not so much apologising as explaining *blah blah* he had given warning he had done all he could awfully sorry *blah* fluster *blah* bluster it was quite out of his hands.

My mother who might very well have been stone dead returned to an upright position. Dazed and disorientated but unharmed. The golf ball had struck full pelt on the side of her head. Smashing the glass in the right eye of her spectacles and sending them clean off her head but leaving her without physical injury. I'm not sure she even requested compensation for the cost of the shattered lens. Everyone just reeled away from this scene of everyday miracle speechless.

Book

What is a book? On a shelf at home I find 'a bundle of tales' by G.A. Henty entitled *Yarns on the Beach*. On the inside cover a presentation slip has been pasted in: 'Drymen School Board. Drymen Public School. Third Prize. Awarded to: William Macadam. For: Excellence in Attendance. During Session 1897–98.' Appended below this are the signatures of the chairman and headmaster.

A book is not like any other object in the world. But when it is supplemented with some striking inscription or annotation it becomes something different altogether. What might it have meant to my mother's father to have received this book at the age of seven? What kind of village school was it that made a 'third prize' for 'attendance' appropriate or necessary? No doubt having to walk three miles in all Scottish weathers to the school in question had some bearing on the matter. It is the only book I have that has any direct connection with Gugga. I treasure it because I loved him and because my mother treasured it. The poignancy of the inscription survives in a world of memory over which there is no dominie.

I take down my mother's copy of *The Poetical Works of William Blake*. It's an Oxford University Press book edited by John Sampson. On the inside cover up in the left corner she has written 'K.B. MacAdam. June 1948.' I am puzzled and delighted by her apparent misspelling of the name.

Her cousin Ian changed the spelling of his name by deed poll in 1939 from 'McAdam' to 'Macadam'. It is probable that the earlier family name was Macadam and shifted later to McAdam. (But every one of them was deep down – beneath the palimpsest – a MacGregor. As is evident from the old MacGregor tartan trousers that my mother and her sister imposed on me and my cousin Mike – captured in

a photograph taken in October 1960. I recall in the late 1980s visiting Balquhidder churchyard with my mother and her impish amusement at reading the inscription on Rob Roy's gravestone: 'MacGREGOR DESPITE THEM'.) Her 'K.B. MacAdam' is a further variant. The only one of her kind. She doesn't specify a day in June but it's hard not to suppose a birthday connection: she turned twenty-one that month. I am struck not just by the bareness of the inscription but also by the more or less pristine pages of her Blake – a poet in whose work she was a great mental traveller. She kept this volume unblemished. As if unread.

She was the same with certain items of china. The finest plates or jugs or decanters were never used. They were stowed in safety in the display cabinet in the dining room.

Then I pick up a pamphlet called *Beethoven's Op. 18 Quartets* by W.H. Hadow. It's one in a series called The Musical Pilgrim. The fly-leaf bears the inscription: 'For Kathleen with best wishes for Xmas 1952 from Percy'. It also bears the stamp and address of where Percy purchased it: W. and G. Foyle Ltd. Booksellers (119–126 Charing Cross Road). Who was Percy? I recall my mother mentioning the name. Was he a family friend? An admirer? A lover-to-be? Or a lover lost? As in the *Romeo and Juliet* darkness of the second quartet. Percy's pamphlet comes closest to my sense of a book as musical abyss. Hadow concludes his account of Beethoven's works:

> Though we learn the notes until we are letter-perfect, we shall never master their secret: every time that we come back to it we shall meet it with fuller comprehension, like the face of a familiar friend which grows more beloved with every day of added experience and converse.

One could listen to the six quartets and read what Hadow has to say about them over and over and never get a heartbeat closer to what this music or this pamphlet or Percy meant to my mother. I imagine a memoir of musical precipices. Through a filament a-spin. Beyond and before meaning. A thread to read. Impossible strand of sound in the solitary gray hair at the end of my 1967 india-paper Bible.

As if these pages were an uncanny jukebox. A jukebook. Out of it lifts in automation the ghostly vinyl beauty of John Lennon singing 'Across the Universe' and I am listening with my mother. I can hear in the dead singer ring-ging his voice in the chthonic depths of my mother's memory that only the thinnest sheet of musical madness separates me from being with her. At once a reassuring fantasy – that in 'Across the Universe' I am sharing something with no one alive but sharing nonetheless – and a terrifying thought – that in the simplicity of this music I have passed into madness. It's not about the past. It's about a music that overflows. Across the universe. A sisterhood of man. A nursery and nursehood. Of human and other lives.

Planet

Along with the garden went my mother's love of birds. The otherness of them. Away from the corner of the kitchen in which she would sit so long was the picture window at the sink. From there you looked out at a big gnarled willow beside the stream that flowed down the length of the garden. My mother had my father put up a bird-table and a couple of birdfeeders and she kept these replenished as she would her coffee cup or hot-water bottle. The window was at first a fatal menace. We had to dangle some glittering twirls of plastic to ward off birds from flying into it. But over the years the view out was a source of amazing pleasure and intrigue. Woodpeckers robins sparrows blue-tits coal-tits goldfinches greenfinches nuthatches and others. She would gaze out of the window at the birdlife around the willow for long periods. Sometimes it seemed as busy as a rush-hour railway station. Birds of all kinds on the feeders in the branches on the ground and alongside the stream. Then there would be lulls. Bad weather. A sparrowhawk in the neighbourhood. Or for no apparent reason at all. The lesser spotted woodpecker might *keek* and tap and grub in the top of the willow one morning then go unseen for several days. My mother was the watcher and replenisher.

Mother: A Memoir

The secret sharer. My fascination with birds is linked to my brother who loved them so. But it is from our mother that everything took wing.

When I was very young I had a recurring nightmare of a giant. The giant never appeared in person. It was rather the sound of its approach. A deep regular echoing of footsteps growing louder and closer. I would cry out before the giant reached me and my mother would come and lie next to me and calm me back to sleep. It seemed that the giant was the creature of my own heartbeat. If I lay on my right rather than my left side it stayed away. But there were odd moments throughout my boyhood and adolescence when in the midst of a humdrum day the rhythm would pick up again. If I concentrate and let myself go I can still pick it up. The step in the distance. Faint but distinct.

I lie in bed first thing in the morning with my right hand held up out of the bedcovers very close to my eyes. I remain in night-clouds. Slit-eyed. There's an altered perspective that recalls Swift's description of the woman's 'monstrous breast' in *Gulliver's Travels*. The hand at this proximity is unfamiliar. I see how I almost don't or can't see it at all. I set aside how weak my eyes have grown. Instead I see in this first electric light of day how old my hand has become. How lined and bumpy. Wrinkled and full of folds. Like the skin of a lizard. I move my left hand up out of the bedclothes and rest it on the first hand. I see my mother's hands.

Nowadays people film their babies being born. I know very little about my arrival. My mother once told me that a month beforehand she was cycling up the road to Hammersmith Hospital and a large black Bentley slowed down beside her. She received a stern ticking-off from the bigwig inside. A consultant driven by his chauffeur. No offer of a ride either then or in future – just a reprimand for continuing to be on her bicycle when so big with child.

I was a breech birth. Whenever I asked what that meant my mother just said: *You came out bottom-first*. She didn't elaborate. I didn't seek elaboration. More often than ever I think of the ripping apart of her body of which she told me nothing. The unimaginable pain. The how ever many stitches. Bottom-first? How could that be?

I loved walking with her. For instance near our house in Cheam in the area of open land we called the Cornfields. Or on Headley Heath. Dreamy place of nightjars. And one time an adder's skin just sloughed off beside the path. In Devon the innumerable wanderings up the lane from the cottage to what we called the Marshwood. Or down to the postbox by the church. All the rambles up and down West Country footpaths and along beaches with their incongruous signs to 'beware landslips'. And so many walks in Scotland. Curlews along the sea's edge early morning and sunset at North Berwick. A golden eagle over the Quiraing on the Isle of Skye. Skylarks over the heather on the Lammermuirs. I remember her windcheater and silk scarf and never-sturdy footwear. The easy rhythm of progressing and pausing. The way we shared our looking and listening. But most of all I remember when she took my arm. Or slipped her hand in mine.

This hand above the bedclothes. It has to do with a feeling of *jamais vu*. Something recognised but strange. As if never seen. A wrinkled limb in the electric light in the squinting coming to consciousness never seen till now.

Mother: A Memoir

If my mother indulged in spectral beckonings and reckonings she might blazon out:

> *Don't fix and freeze. See every day and more than ever the openings of memory. Live forwards but also backwards. Don't end up bitter and twisted. There is hope and love. And the unquenchable desire for justice. Ridicule self-importance and privilege wherever you encounter it. Live in a world without religion. Not governed by the ways in which one God creates the need for murder and destruction in the believers of another. There is a world that is more real. In which every man is also woman. In which a mother unconscious speaks. Quieter than words. Under everything. And birth is not an event in the past.*

But my mother is keeping her trap shut. She refuses to be a ghost. She is too elusive and playful for such posturing.

In my mind's eye I see marine iguanas. Black on black. Hard to distinguish from the rocks. Washed over by rough surf. Waiting for nobody. In the west beyond the west.

David Attenborough recounts how the ancestors of the only sea lizards on the planet were in all probability arboreal iguanas in the rainforests of Central America who lived on leaves from the trees high above the rivers and about eight million years ago a small number were washed out to sea on rafts of reeds and ended up hundreds of miles away on the volcanic black rocks of the Galapagos archipelago. I connect Attenborough with my mother. They were born about the same time. And as a nurse she was called out to the family on one or two occasions. She remembered them as charming people. Nothing snobby about them. No 'side'. My memory of her connection with the Attenboroughs is as vague but solid as an eight-million-year-old raft of reeds.

I feel my mother's hands. In the electric light by the bedside lying on my left side. Through eyes almost closed. Moving into consciousness. A mess of iguanas. With fore-legs like old people's hands. Distended. Gnarled. At once puffed out and flattened. In the hours of darkness they retreat under boulders or into crevices. In the day they sometimes pile on top of one another. Bundling (sleeping in one's clothes in the same bed as others): another word my mother loved.

Imagine Darwin's *jamais vu*. Encountering them in 1835 he considered these creatures an affront to his own sense of being. He found them hideous and disgusting. Dirty black. Serpentine. Sluggish. Imps of darkness he called them. He failed to grasp many things about them. He says: 'I never saw one even ten yards in-shore.' But females will withdraw inland up to two miles to lay their eggs. The great blue heron in silhouette like Dracula in his cloak is quite partial to snacking on a hatchling. So too is the Galapagos hawk (though mockingbirds can alert a mother to its proximity). In more recent decades their continued existence has become threatened in addition by the rats and feral dogs brought in with the many thousands of people now living on these islands. While the threat of devastating climate change submerges all.

Darwin also of course never observed marine iguanas underwater. The larger males can hold their breath for fifty minutes or more. As long as a session with a psycho-therapist. Long enough to read a remarkable poem with some care. Or get to the acnestis of a crossword. They swim down as deep as twenty metres to feed off the succulent fast-growing green algae flourishing on the volcanic sea floor. They criss-cross the slumbering green.

Imagine the *jamais vu* for the creatures themselves come to shore after the longest shipwreck in history. Here's to life on the rocks with a more or less non-viable diet of seaweed! *Amblyrhynchus cristatus*: from the Ancient Greek for 'blunt snout' and Latin for 'crested'. Over millions of years the nose has squashed up so that they can graze better on the rocks and into crevices. To negotiate the seaweed their teeth and claws have become sharper. To deal with the salt they have developed a gland to excrete it. They sneeze a lot. They accumulate crusty white deposits on the tops of their heads like demented coke addicts.

They are herbivores. Great mockers. Not inclined to violence. When one male confronts another in a bid to mate with a desired female he nods his head. The males may indulge in a little butting and head-wrestling but serious injuries are avoided. They bob and strut. They make as if to move. As if if. Bluff is key.

They are patience supreme. They bundle and warm up in the baking sun then scooch and scuttle once more into the depths. Off on their virtual suicide missions. Ancient mariners. Till huge waves wash them up again. Small miracles they ever manage to get back to their rock in one piece. They move through the lethal chilling water with the slow whip-like strength of their long tails. With their legs close to their sides they resemble people waddling with their hands tied. Like victims of a home invasion. Upside down. Or: they pulse upward through the water with arms tucked in as if already coffined. They graze as fast as they can before their muscles seize up. Their faces are of old age. Smashed up. Unidentifiable. They batten on and shear green algae like salad leaves off the volcanic underwater rocks. They cling as if in thoughtfulness as they eat. In my mind's eye I am in this dreamless cold swirling world. Holding my breath. Holding on. Out of my element. Amazed such an alien feeling can last so long. Watching with mother.

Acknowledgements

In the first place I would like to thank Jinan, closest and most distant reader, love of my life and constant source of inspiration, fortitude and sustenance in the writing of these pages.

In addition I would like to express my heartfelt gratitude to my cousin and lifelong friend, Michael Morgan. From the earliest stages of this book he has been invaluable in recalling and verifying details concerning my mother as well as other family and friends. In addition, he has kindly provided a number of the images that feature in this book. Indeed, he took the photograph that appears on the front cover. Among other archival material, Mike also furnished me with a copy of the genealogical research conducted by my mother's (and his mother's) cousin, the late Ian Macadam, regarding their Scottish ancestry.

Much of this memoir was drafted in Seattle, where I have – for about a month every summer, over a number of years – enjoyed the great hospitality and kindness of Lucy and Saleh Joudeh. In particular, they provided me with a writing-perch in their lovely home and gave me the quietness, space and time in which to piece together this little book. I am immensely grateful to them both.

In the summer of 2019 Robb and Rachael Hamilton generously allowed me to occupy their cottage on Whidbey Island for several days: it proved a memorably rich and productive phase in the writing process. My hearty thanks to them for this dream-like break.

This book bears witness, among other things, to the pleasures of having cousins. I feel very fortunate in having had such a bountiful share. I thank Heather Holt, David Royle,

Vincent Royle and Caroline Smith for all their warmth, generosity and good humour down the years. It is a great sadness to me that my cousin Vanessa did not live long enough to read this memoir. And I am sorry that three of my other cousins – Graham, Ian and Rosalind (my mother's elder sister Nettie's children) – do not show up in person in the foregoing pages. I hope it might be understood that this was no deliberate omission, but rather an effect of the ways in which a book also eludes its author and veers about with determinations of its own. My mother watched them all growing up and remained especially close to her niece, Rosie.

I could hardly have written this book without the loyalty and commitment of my editor at Myriad, Candida Lacey. Candida championed the project from its inception. After reading the first full draft, she then challenged me to double its length. It is a testament to her singular gifts as an editor that I found myself taking up this challenge with passion. I am enormously grateful for her many critical suggestions regarding this memoir, but also more generally for the ways in which she has stimulated my writing over the past decade.

I would also like to record my special thanks to Linda McQueen at Myriad. In thirty years or more of writing books, I have known no other copy-editor who combines such a formidable professional efficiency with a warmth and personal engagement that sends me back to my own words and phrases, punctuation and tone, and compels me to ponder them in newly critical and enlightened fashion.

I am greatly appreciative of the encouragement as well as helpful comments of friends who read this book in draft: Matthew Frost, Hannah Jordan, Gabriel Josipovici, Ute Keller, Rob Penhallurick and Carol Watts. Above all, I am indebted to the perspicacity, enthusiasm and support of my dear friend Peter Boxall – both for the many conversations we have had about this project and for his reading and detailed comments on more than one draft.

Additional thanks – for details that they might, I hope, readily recognise – to Michael Gasson, Jackie Hall, Heather Holt, Jennifer Kerr, Colin Mackrell, David Royle, Lindsay Smith, Nick Smith and Cristina Ulander.

For guidance on the photograph of the *Burke's Peerage* editorial office, my thanks to Emilie Pine and Richard Pine.

For guidance on murmurations of starlings around Bass Rock, my thanks to Ann and Tony Elger.

My thanks to Mary Jacobus for kind permission to quote from *Romanticism, Writing and Sexual Difference* (Clarendon Press, 1989), and to Adam Phillips for kind permission to quote from *Winnicott* (Fontana Modern Masters, 1988).

For his generous assistance with the digitisation of images for the book I am very grateful to my colleague at the University of Sussex, Stuart Robinson.

'Exam' was first published anonymously in the *Oxford Literary Review* (1995), then reprinted in Nicholas Royle, *The Uncanny* (Manchester University Press, 2003).

Finally, although my mother lived long enough only to know four of them, this book is dedicated to all of her wonderful grandchildren.

About the author

Nicholas Royle is Professor of English at the University of Sussex, where he established the MA in Creative and Critical Writing in 2002. He is the author of two novels, both published by Myriad – *Quilt* (2010) and *An English Guide to Birdwatching* (2017) – and many other books, including studies of Elizabeth Bowen, Hélène Cixous, Jacques Derrida, E. M. Forster and Shakespeare. His books about literature and critical theory are widely influential and have won considerable acclaim. They include *The Uncanny* (2003), *Veering: A Theory of Literature* (2011), and *An Introduction to Literature, Criticism and Theory* (fifth edition, 2016, with Andrew Bennett).

This is his first memoir.

Energy Medicine:

Healing from the Kingdoms of Nat

Sabina Pettitt, M.Ed., L.Ac.

Pacific Essences®
Victoria, B.C.
Canada

Printed in Canada

ISBN 0-9694083-3-1

Published by:
Pacific Essences®
Box 8317
Victoria, B.C.
V8W 3R9
CANADA

Tel 250 384-5560
Fax 250 595-7700

www.pacificessences.com
www.energymedicine.ca

We guarantee the quality of **Pacific Essences®** only when they bear our label and are purchased directly from us or from an authorized distributor.

MEDICAL DISCLAIMER
The material in this book is not intended to replace consultation with a qualified health professional.

Dedication

This book is dedicated to Dr. John G. LaPlante – chiropractor, naturopathic physician, and above all healer and fellow human being. Thank you for your love, inspiration, and nurturance of the healing seeds within me.

Acknowledgements

I thank the Nature Spirits of the Pacific Northwest coast for showing me the gifts they offer to the human kingdom and for allowing me to be the channel for, and caretaker of, their energy.

I especially thank the Sea Spirits for entrusting us with the first essences made from plant and animal life from the Ocean. We have much to learn from her depths.

I am grateful to my friend, Fiona Macleod, for co-founding **Pacific Essences®** with me. Without her initial enthusiasm and curiosity, **Pacific Essences®** may never have been born.

For final proofreading and editing I am most grateful to Lou Mitchell.

On a personal note I wish to acknowledge my family, my parents and my three brothers. They have given me unreserved love and support throughout my life, and for this I am deeply grateful.

I want to thank my husband, Michael, for his encouragement, love, and participation in all aspects of **Pacific Essences®** and especially the birth of the Sea Essences.

And I want to express heartfelt gratitude to Master Choa Kok Sui for seeing who I am and encouraging me to be even more of who I really am.

Finally, I want to thank all my clients. It is a privilege to participate in your healing journey.

Contents

Introduction

I have known Sabina Pettitt personally for almost a decade and have worked with the Pacific Essences since their inception in the early 1980's.

When I first met Sabina I was impressed by her easy way of connecting with people, warmed by her fiery spirit, entertained by her lively humor, and grateful for her open-hearted generosity, all of which come across in the words of this book.

I am also impressed with the depth of Sabina's commitment to her work, in all of its aspects. This commitment is most obvious to me in the way Sabina has developed the repertory of Pacific Essences over the years – and that is through a balanced, respectful, and deliberate interaction with the forces of nature. Sabina understands the potential for healing that exists between humans and nature, and the strength of her dedication to the task of developing and sharing this potential with others is evident in how well these essences have been researched, and in how well they are presented here.

I believe it is not enough to just make essences you hope will be relevant to the healing needs of sentient beings. These essences must be grounded into a structure and language that makes sense, that gives people a clear and practical way to incorporate them into their lives. Sabina has done this extremely well by presenting the healing qualities of her essences within the structure of the ancient system of Chinese medicine.

The brilliance of this approach is that it marries the potent healing power of the flowers and gems of the earth, and the plants and creatures of the sea, with a very organized system of restoring balance to all levels of the being.

I congratulate Sabina on this new edition of *Energy Medicine*. I know it will be inspiring and of practical value to all those who read it.

Steve Johnson
Alaskan Flower Essence Project
PO Box 1369, Homer, Alaska 99603
December 1998

Preface to the Second Edition

Welcome to the second edition of Energy Medicine – Healing from the Kingdoms of Nature.

You will notice some improvements in this text – notably the colour images of each of the 48 flowers and 24 sea plants and sea creatures along with a prayer or blessing for each one, and a revised and expanded repertory of correlations. All of these features will assist the practitioner in using the essences more effectively.

Since publication of the first edition in 1993, we have come to realize that this book is really an essential tool for the essence practitioner as well as for other health professionals who want to incorporate essences into their practices but don't quite know how to begin. We have been told repeatedly that the fact that our correlations and research are based on the energetics of traditional Chinese medicine is very helpful for incorporating them into other health practices. The chakra correlations are also a useful key, especially as Ayurvedic medicine becomes more familiar to the western mind and available to the western consumer.

Essentially this book is still about Pacific Essences. In fact, we have come to regard it as a basic handbook for the use of these essences. It provides information on how to access and to utilize the particular healing qualities of 48 flower essences and 24 sea essences. At a much deeper level we hope and trust that it will acquaint you, the reader, with a sense of appreciation for the formless beneath the form – Spirit which permeates all living things.

An Arbutus tree, a sea Anemone, or an Ox-Eye Daisy can never be the same after we have journeyed into its heart and returned with an awareness of its vitality and energetic structure. At the very least we may feel a kinship with other living forms on this planet that we all share. More than that we may discover that a particular plant or sea spirit speaks to some part of our being which has stayed unconscious as we went our way of worldly pursuits.

The book includes what essences are, how to make essences and how they interact with us to achieve health and well being, how to incorporate essences with other healing modalities and how to use them as a therapy by themselves. There are detailed descriptions and correlations for all of the flower and sea essences in the Pacific Essence collection, as well as a repertory for easy reference access to the most appropriate remedy for a particular mental or emotional state.

In the past 25 years there has been a huge shift in consciousness with regard to each of us individually taking responsibility for our health and well-being. The increased interest in vibrational medicine is in itself an indication that we are expanding our consciousness both individually and collectively and beginning to incorporate new modalities into our healing systems. But now, on the eve of the Millennium, I perceive that there is a growing appreciation and understanding that vibrational medicine is here to assist us in a much larger quest – our own expansion into the Light Beings which we truly are. And the plants and sea life who have waited patiently to engage in a dynamic and conscious relationship with human kind are bursting forth in a chorus of delight as we finally embrace the wisdom and potential innate in their kingdoms.

This book is for the lay person and the health professional. Hopefully it will capture the imagination of the non-professional while providing practical guidelines for the practitioner.

A Personal Note

Since the publication of the first edition many things have evolved in my life. I have travelled many miles especially in South America and Europe to teach about the essences and their contribution to health and well being. For these opportunities I am truly grateful, and for all the beings on the planet who are working/playing with these Nature Spirits who live in my world I bless you all. When I return from one of these teaching trips there is nothing more wonderful than touching down on Canadian soil and when I reach Victoria I am literally vibrating, almost at the speed of light, with delight and gratitude to be back with these Nature Spirits who have truly changed my life.

In the past five years I have renewed my commitment to teaching meditation by becoming a certified Primordial Sound Meditation teacher with Deepak Chopra. I am convinced that meditation is probably the most critical tool for all of us to create health and achieve personal growth and the knowledge of who we really are. Indeed Dr. Chopra is probably the most elegant thinker and eloquent speaker about health and healing on the planet today. His talks on quantum healing and the new physics have certainly helped me to grasp why these vibrations from nature have healing abilities and how they work.

In my personal journey, however, I am deeply indebted to Master Choa Kok Sui who has helped me to understand what it is that I'm really doing when I make an essence. I've always known that I'm merely the channel and delighted to play that role. But through my work/play with this truly great teacher I have experientially connected with who I really am. And things which I believed to be true I now know are real and that soon all of humanity will be able to appreciate the wonder of ourselves and the wonder of Nature. Master Choa's Twin Hearts meditation is an opportunity not only to connect with our own divine self but also to bless all the divinity manifest on earth. And his work with energy through Pranic healing and Arhatic yoga has definitely enhanced my abilities to attune with Nature spirits and to interpret their gifts.

Essences – Gifts From Other Realms

What is an Essence?

Imagine that each plant could express itself through sound. Then each different plant would express a different note, and we would recognize all Water Lilies by the similarity of the note they played whether they were growing in New Zealand, China, or Canada. But the note of a Delphinium would be heard as quite different from the note of a Water Lily, as would the note of a Rose. Of course, most of us do not hear the sound of plants, nor do we experience their vibrations, but we do recognize their different colours, shapes, and fragrances. A Skunk Cabbage and a Rose do not elicit the same response from our olfactory centre! Even visually the Skunk Cabbage presents itself as very masculine, while the Rose is usually perceived as feminine. It is all these unique qualities, from the gross physical differences to the subtle energy differences, which make up an essence.

Essence is the manifestation of Spirit in each physical form. It reveals itself as the unique vibration or frequency in all living things. It is the energetic pattern underlying the difference between a Nootka Rose and an Ox-Eye Daisy or between a Moon Snail and a Starfish. It is the Infinite embodied in the finite.

An essence is, by definition and by its very nature, the intrinsic value of something, its "being-ness."

Between formlessness and form there is a gap where the subtleties of differentiation occur. In this gap lies the blueprint for physical manifestation. It is like the DNA map for physical reality and contains the code for differentiation among all living things. It is where three dimensional reality interfaces with Spirit.

What we learn to recognize in the plant kingdom with our physical senses are the differences of shape, size, texture, colour, and fragrance. A scientist might be able to recognize the different chemical components of the plant and know how to extract and use these components for health, cosmetic, or even destructive purposes. This physical manifestation, or form, is known as the plant signature and provides valuable clues to the plant's purpose and uses.

Just as there are different layers of expression and beingness in humans, so too there are deeper aspects of each plant beneath the phenomenon of its physical expression in the world. This deeper and unseen aspect is called the noumenon and can only be contacted through intuition. When we open our hearts and minds to the plant we can journey through the doorway provided by the plant signature into uncharted territory. This is where we find the essence of the plant.

What is a flower essence? It is the energetic imprint of the life force of a particular plant. The carrier substance is water, the universal solvent, with a proportionate amount of brandy which acts as a preservative. Although all flower essences tend to look and smell the same, they all have different ways of interacting with the human body, mind, emotions, and spirit.

The energy pattern of the plant or sea creature is transferred to the water through the action of sunlight. The water becomes infused with the energy of the specific substance and can be used to correct imbalances in human energy fields.

When we make a flower essence we are literally entering the world of Spirit and "lifting" the vibration of that plant and storing it for future use. This is why essences are often referred to as vibrational remedies.

There is an aspect of flower essence work that can only be defined by analogy and metaphor. This sometimes makes the remedies seem less than tangible in a world of apparent cause and effect and where we now have tools to dissect the physical into the smallest of atomic components. Nonetheless, flower essences are fast becoming a valuable tool in complementary medicine, as we begin to appreciate that each human being is a multi-faceted, complex web of vibrating energy as well as a physical form.

How Essences Work

The simplest way to appreciate how flower essences work is to begin to think of ourselves as multi-dimensional beings in which there exist three distinct but intertwined energy bodies infused by Spirit or Life Force. These three bodies are the Emotional, the Mental, and of course, the Physical. When there is disharmony in any one of these bodies, the potential for illness exists. If the disharmony is sudden and severe as in trauma and shock, or becomes chronic and longstanding as in depression and despair, the Spirit or Life Force will begin to diminish.

Spirit takes form in each individual as a personal soul. It has a distinct energy body which indeed sustains the physical and who we think we are. Even though it is beyond sickness in the way that we have understood this in Western medicine, Spirit can also become sick. Spirit sickness can be recognized by symptoms of despair, loss of a sense of self, lack of enthusiasm, or feelings of being lost, isolated and alone.

An essence may be primarily physical, mental, emotional, or spiritual. When it enters the physical body (usually as drops under the tongue), it plays a pure harmonious frequency. The aspect which is out of harmony is drawn to this healthy frequency like a magnet and begins to vibrate in harmony with it.

Essentially this is the principle of resonance which most of us learned in high school physics. In the physics lab it was demonstrated by striking a tuning fork at one end of the room and noticing that a second tuning fork, at rest, at the other end of the room would begin to vibrate in harmony with the first one.

Each of the three bodies has an optimal level of functioning which then contributes to the overall functioning and harmony of the whole. The optimal level of functioning for each body varies from individual to individual but demonstrates a range of vibrational frequency which is universal.

In his book, *Vibrational Medicine,* Dr. Richard Gerber uses the analogy of a piano keyboard in which each body or aspect of the individual expresses an octave of notes. The physical body would be the range of the musical scale below middle C. The scale beginning at middle C represents the Emotional body. The next scale is the Mental body and the scale above this one represents the Spirit. Spirit is also all the notes of the piano in terms of its immortality but in each incarnation Spirit also resides in a particular range of musical notes. So health and well-being for one person might be all the E notes, while health and well-being for another person could be all the G notes.

At one level the role of essences is to introduce a pattern of harmony into a system where there is discord. At another level, essences can provide a frequency which is missing. For instance, a person may have learned, through some bitter experience, to shut down at the level of feeling. So the Emotional body may not be playing any notes on its particular scale. Taking a remedy which plays a range of frequency for the Emotional body will gently coax it towards a healthy vibration.

Essences work to change something which is out of balance or in a state of dis-ease in the multi-dimensional human. There is an innate intelligence in all of life which demonstrates a natural tendency towards orderliness. The Emotional body prefers calmness to extremes. The Mental body prefers a comfortable balance between logic and intuition. The Spirit prefers to find itself "at home" and only does so when the other three bodies are maintaining their own levels of balance and harmony.

Essences also serve to uncover or to expose the source and location of discord. There may be many layers to any particular problem. All the energy bodies are involved in some manner because they all interact with each other. Identifying and treating the root cause will harmonize the whole being. This can sometimes be done in one essence consultation depending upon the skill of the practitioner and the willingness of the client. More often than not, however, working with essences is a process of uncovering many layers, especially if the problem is long term in nature.

Using essences is a journey of self-discovery and self-healing. They not only provide a framework for connecting with all aspects of our own unique energy system, they also help us to attune with the larger energy system of "All That Is."

Essences and essence therapy are part of the newly emerging field of Energy Medicine in the Western world. This field incorporates information about the mind, the emotions, and the spirit, as well as the physical body when addressing illness and health. In itself Energy Medicine is not new and includes age-old traditions like acupuncture and homeopathy, but in the West our thinking has been strongly influenced by the Mind/Body dualism of Newtonian physics. As a result our medicine has been focused primarily on the functioning of the physical body. As we begin to appreciate ourselves as complex energetic patterns, we can develop a truly holistic model of health.

Flower Essences – Historical Perspective

Plants are fundamental to life on earth. They have been used since the beginning of time to provide both nourishment and shelter. They are essential to the survival of human life on the planet even at the simplest level of converting carbon dioxide to oxygen so that we can breathe.

All over the world flowers are part of major celebrations and cultural and religious rituals. All cultures and civilizations have used plants in some form or another for healing purposes. We have placed them in sick rooms and buried the dead with them. We have extracted herbal tinctures from roots and flowers, and these herbal remedies became the forerunners of modern Western drug therapy. When humans lived closer to nature we learned the gifts of healing offered in our environment. And in the sixteenth century, Paracelsus is credited with collecting the early morning dew from different plants and giving these drops to his patients therapeutically. But it is only in the twentieth century, a relatively small fragment of time in terms of human history, that we have harnessed the different plant energies in the form of liquid infusions, or essences, for healing purposes.

Flower essence therapy was brought to the attention of the Western world in the 1920s by Edward Bach, a British physician and homeopath. When he began his search for a holistic medicine he was convinced of two things:

1. The human body had the innate ability to heal itself, so he was looking for something which would activate this natural process.

2. Medicine should above all do no harm, which of course is part of the Hippocratic oath which all physicians swear when they become doctors.

Bach's 38 flower remedies have circulated the globe since then, and his methodology both for making the essence and for collecting research data has been duplicated by many other flower essence producers around the world.

By 1983 a morphogenic field around flower essences had been created. This is when six or seven developers from around the world, including Pacific Essences, began to publish information about the properties and gifts of flowers other than the 38 originally discovered by Bach.

Pacific Essences

Flower Essences from the Pacific Northwest

I learned about flower essences through my healing work with Dr. John LaPlante. Trained as a Naturopath and Chiropractor, he was one of the most gifted healers I have ever encountered. Dr. John, as he was lovingly called by his patients, always responded to the whole person. Flower remedies were virtually the only substance that he prescribed, which is one of the reasons he was such a remarkable healer. Usually the healing occurred as a result of the interaction between him and the patient in the moment. Occasionally he sent patients home with a flower remedy to stabilize and integrate the healing. Each remedy looked and tasted the same, but the symptoms which were dispelled were totally different. The only common denominator was that they impacted primarily on emotional states or attitudes.

In my personal study of healing modalities, essences were the first thing I encountered which acknowledged human beings as more than a body and a mind with different medical approaches for each. In a world of black and white, vibrational remedies offered a rainbow of healing for the whole person. So when we moved to Vancouver Island and I discovered a whole new plant life I began experimenting with making some of these into vibrational remedies. I had no idea that I was playing a part in a global undertaking, nor did I have any intention of creating an international company. I did however recapture a forgotten childhood memory of making healing potions for my dolls out of coloured chalk dust and flower petals and there was an air of magic and fun in my undertakings.

The Arbutus trees were among the first things I noticed on the West Coast. Nothing I have seen anywhere in the world compares to them. Their bark is like a thin reddish orange skin which peels off gradually over a seven year cycle, and leaves greenish yellow trunk and branches exposed. Arbutus trees are always in the process of change, and emanate the quality of wisdom. They are witnesses and hold much information about what has transpired on the West Coast. If I sat and meditated under an Arbutus tree, I often found myself transported to another time when there were no concrete buildings on the island and a state of greater harmony seemed to exist between humans and nature. In making the essence of Arbutus it turned out that one of the qualities that it promoted was wisdom and that it acted as a spiritual tonic which could reconnect our spirit with its Source.

When spring arrived and I saw the first wild flowers blooming, I began buying plant identification books and reading a little about how the native people had used these plants both for healing and for nourishment. Soon there was a cupboard full of little brown bottles with notes on how I felt when I made the acquaintance of the plant and made the essence. As I experimented with friends, family, and clients, it became clear that these remedies were valuable healing tools and that it was my task to make them available.

In 1983, Fiona Macleod and I formed Pacific Essences, and with the assistance of seen and unseen helpers, we proceeded to research the plant energies which attracted us. When we were satisfied that the information on each flower essence was consistent, we included it in a kit which could be sold publicly. This required both careful documentation and a certain amount of courage. Flower essences were not exactly the most popular or credible medicine of the time, and we had no idea that there were individuals just like us doing exactly the same task with flowers in Alaska, Australia, and France. By 1985 we had researched 24 wild flower remedies and 13 spring flowers, and I thought that our contribution to the field of vibrational medicine was complete. I had no idea that I was going to be given the task of acting as the channel for the first vibrational remedies from the ocean.

The First Sea Essences

In the summer of 1985, a friend was having yet another recurring bout with a rare form of skin cancer. She had tried almost every conventional and unconventional therapy, including laser surgery and photo-chemotherapy. She was on massive doses of painkillers and was experiencing major fear and frustration. We began to work with flower essences together. Although they seemed beneficial for a time, none of them provided the lasting effects we both desired.

One morning my husband, Michael, and I were walking along a sandy beach. We were simply enjoying the sand beneath our feet, the sea breezes on our skin, and the fullness of the ocean. Both of us simultaneously stopped in front of a Sand Dollar and knew that it was to be made into a remedy for our friend. Thus began the work with sea essences from the ocean, and a whole new realm of Energy Medicine began to unfold.

At this point we hadn't even considered the possibility of vibrational medicine from the ocean which surrounds us, and I certainly didn't have any idea how to make a sea essence. Gently guided by our inner direction we placed the Sand Dollar in a glass of sea water and brought it home to place under the pyramid in the sunshine. After diluting it down to the stock concentrate, we gave it to Corrie. There was an immediate shift in her symptom pattern and her need for analgesics. Most significant of all was her new willingness to discover how her own attitude might be a contributing factor to her illness and to take a serious look at what "benefits" she derived from this rare and very painful disease. She discovered that the rareness of the disease made her feel quite special and unique. There was also an element of excitement and high drama about being rushed to the hospital in the middle of the night for pain relief. These were all hard things to face, but at the point that she realized that she was almost totally dependent on drugs, she had the courage to do precisely that. It is now 11 years since Corrie was able to turn the corner with her disease. Apart from two minor recurrences, she is completely healthy and now satisfies her need for excitement by mothering two healthy children.

I am not suggesting that Sand Dollar is a cure for cancer. However, for Corrie, it was the right therapy at the right time and represented a remarkable turning point in her healing process.

The gift of the Sand Dollar is to assist us in seeing ourselves and our patterns with greater clarity. Everyone is unique. Every disease is unique, and each person will respond in a different manner, both to their symptoms and to possible therapies. It is never appropriate for the therapist to ask someone with a life-threatening disease what they are getting out of it. This can easily result in feelings of major guilt which will exacerbate the symptoms. Some people have never even considered the possibility that they might create their own reality, so to burden them with that notion when they are probably already experiencing intense fear about the physical diagnosis they have just received is not very likely to be therapeutic.

One of the things that was clear about the sea essences from the outset was that they offered a range of entirely new frequencies in the realm of vibrational medicine.

The sea essences are clearly about transformations in consciousness. They are for major breakthroughs, for being able to contact the basic rhythms of the universe when we are going through change and for moving into spaces of greater perspective. Our initial experiences suggested that the sea essences are best taken individually. However, with further research we discovered that blends could be equally therapeutic. Even blends that used Pacific flower and sea essences in the same combination, or blends that used sea essences and essences from some other lines have proven to be effective. However, one of the gifts of the first twelve sea essences is that each one is precisely calibrated with one of the twelve meridians of Chinese medicine. As an acupuncturist, I still find it more effective to use the essences in the simplest possible mode and to attempt to discover the key underlying causative factor before selecting the remedy. Each sea essence is very precise and very powerful. They are like the energy of the ocean which can be peaceful and calm one minute and turbulent and fierce the next. They act quickly and usually have quite noticeable results.

For instance the Mussel essence is for "releasing the burden of anger." Often when this remedy comes up for someone they will experience anger within the first 24 hours of taking the remedy. It usually feels like a major release, or healing crisis, and as they continue to take the prescribed dosage a new awareness of choice about anger dawns for the client. And this is the important shift, for often anger feels like one of those emotions about which we have no choice. How many people are voluntarily angry? Mussel seems to dissolve the powerlessness around the feelings of anger.

So what really makes Sea Essences different from the flower remedies? My experience to date suggests that the key factor is the very medium from which they come – Water, specifically salt water.

Water not only makes up 75% of the planet Earth, it also comprises 75% of the human body. It is the medium, or carrier substance, which we use for the vibrations of the flower and gem remedies.

Water is one of the five elements in traditional Chinese medicine and has been recognized by other medical systems as not only vital to human life, but also symbolic of character and personality types. In addition, water is a key symbol in both Tarot and Astrology.

In the Chinese medicine cosmology Water is related to reproduction, growth and maturation, including the development of Marrow or the brain, and Essence, which is the material basis for the Mind. Herein lies its first association with transformations of consciousness.

When we are aligned with our own inner consciousness we create our own reality rather than following someone else's myths. We are enabled to perform "right action," in tune with our own inner knowingness and direction.

In Chinese medicine, the emotional characteristic associated with Water is fear. Fear is the obstacle which blocks expression of our true selves. Have you ever noticed that when you are coming from a place of total harmony within, there are no obstacles to action?

At the level of spirit, Water is related to Chih, the psychic strength which leads us through obstacles to growth. As Lao Tsu said:

> *"Under heaven nothing is more soft and yielding than water.*
> *Yet for attacking the solid and strong, nothing is better;*
> *It has no equal."*

Archetypically it is the symbol for the unconscious.

The Sea Essences, by their very nature, expose the unconscious and strengthen consciousness to move forward in its own unique unfolding. They are dynamic and act quickly and help us to flow with inner strength and knowingness.

Perhaps the rigidity of our fears and unexamined myths and beliefs can only be transformed by the Yin qualities of Water, for by its very nature it demands and challenges us to "let go" into the direction of our own being. And isn't "letting go" into life our first act as we claim human form when we leave the safe watery amniotic fluid of our mother's womb and embrace life on earth?

Even as the first kit of twelve sea essences were released, we continued research on other possible sea essences. I began working with whale energy by making an essence from a whale's tooth from New Zealand. And I began attuning with Sea

Horse energy and trying to find out the best place to make an essence from one. The gift of the Sea Horse came from the Philippines, and even though the story of its making is in itself an epic tale, I did not know how right it was to make it here until we saw a TV special this year on Sea Horses and how they are becoming extinct. The only place in the world where a sanctuary for Sea Horses has been created is in the Philippines. And at the same time this is the only place where they are being harvested consciously.

The second kit of sea essences offers a range of frequencies which complement and go beyond the first kit. It contains more sea creatures, large mammals like dolphin, whale, and sea turtle. Connecting with these amazing beings in their natural habitat and getting close enough to them to make an essence was truly a blessed experience. As we began to research the potential of each of these essences it became clear that many of them have been given to us at this time because of their ability to help humans refine their nervous and electrical systems to expand into new dimensions of being. When we work with Diatom to repattern cellular memory or Sea Horse to fortify the life force within and to nourish the central nervous system, we begin to realize what a generous gift these essences really are.

Indeed, as we work with them and our own abilities mature, I am sure that these essences will lead us to increasing self understanding as well as a much deeper appreciation for what they offer the human realm at this time.

My personal journey with Pacific Essences has been a gradual awakening and has required immense trust. When I took my first flower remedy with Dr. John in the early 70's, it never even crossed my mind that I would make a flower essence, let alone discover sea essences and devote a huge part of my waking hours to educating people about the potential of Energy Medicine and Self Healing. On the eve of the Millennium the dragons of self-doubt are quelled, and in my heart I absolutely trust the joy, contentment, and heightened awareness I experience when working with these blessed energies from the Plant and Sea Kingdoms. And not a day passes that I do not give thanks for this work that has selected me in this life. Although Dr. John left the earth plane in 1986, I often hear him gently guiding me, as the sacred journey continues to unfold.

A New Model of Healing

The focus of Western medicine has been the physical body, and the irony of this is that most of what we know about the physical body and the way it functions has been learned through the examination of dead bodies! In the past one hundred years there has been some recognition of the mind through the work of Freud, Jung, and Reich. But even though we recognize mental dis-ease, it is seen as a separate category of medicine. Essentially, mind and body have been viewed as two distinct entities, and consequently we have a medical model which reflects this fundamental perception.

Our health system is full of specialists – specialists for the nervous system, the heart, the respiratory system, the reproductive and urogenital systems, and of course specialists for the mind and emotions. Sometimes there is overlap between systems, but essentially we are treated as fragments. We have begun to pay lip service to Mind/Body unity but only to the extent that if we are unable to find a physical cause for illness we deem it to be psychosomatic, i.e. illness induced by the mind.

At the heart of Western medicine, however, is the understanding that the physical body contains a variety of self-regulating mechanisms which serve to keep it alive and healthy. Known as homeostasis, it is the first principle described in any physiology text. Homeostasis is the complex system of checks and balances which maintain life, including the flight or fight mechanism in times of danger, the inflammation response to foreign invaders, detoxification of the blood via the liver, circulation of oxygen and nutrients to the cells via the blood, and control of hormone levels via the pituitary gland, not to mention the intricate and delicate balance maintained in every single cell in the human body. These are just a few of the specific mechanisms that occur 24 hours a day and none of them requires conscious control or intervention on our part. It is as if we all come wired from the factory with an auto pilot whose only motive is to keep us alive and in health.

When we become physically ill it is because some stress has disturbed this natural order. The goal of Western medicine is to restore homeostasis, but it has acknowledged only the physical. Moreover with the vast amount of medical specialties which exist today it is difficult to see how three or four different specialists, and sometimes more, working with their own isolated perceptions and skills, can put Humpty Dumpty back together again and restore homeostasis.

Other health systems have maintained their focus on the whole person. For instance, the Chinese see the universe, and humanity within it, as energy unfolding. The source of all phenomena is Qi (pronounced chee). Basically, Qi is the energy which permeates and penetrates all matter. It is the invisible framework for all of life. Invisible is the key word here, because in our Western system of thought we have ignored anything which we cannot see, touch, or quantify in some way. It is only spiritual thinkers like Teilhard de Chardin who dare talk about noumenon. Our thought system for health is characterized by explanation of cause and effect based on so-called empirical data.

The Chinese view of health can be summed up in one word: BALANCE. Although similar to the notion of homeostasis in Western medicine, this idea of harmony or balance embraces a much larger view of reality. In Western medicine, homeostasis relates only to the systems of the physical body, whereas the Chinese view of balance includes body, mind, emotions, and spirit within each individual, as well as balance in relation to the cyclical rhythms of Nature. I will address the Chinese view of health in more detail in the section on Meridians and Chinese medicine.

On the eve of the twenty-first century, we are also on the threshold of a new medicine in the West, a medicine which will truly acknowledge and heal the whole person. This medicine will acknowledge each individual as a growing, changing whole.

As previously mentioned, Energy Medicine assumes that there are at least four aspects to address – the Physical body, with which we often solely identify, and the Emotional, Mental and Spiritual components which are housed in the auric field. The aura, or auric field, is like a cocoon of vibrating energy which surrounds and permeates the physical. Not only is the physical body the densest field of vibrating energy, it is also the only field which most of us are able to see. It is the form in which we consciously recognize ourselves and each other.

The physical vehicle is the gross physical being, the most manifest and seemingly solid aspect of each of us. It is the body which begins at the union of sperm and egg and ends when the soul leaves the body at death. In between birth and death it is "the greatest miracle in the world." It has an innate intelligence which constantly seeks homeostasis, the body's natural tendency to maintain harmony or balance among its systems. This tendency is an involuntary response and happens automatically without our even thinking about it.

The physical body also stores information from the emotional and mental vehicles.

The Emotional body consists of feelings. Feelings seem to be with us from birth and probably even in utero. At this point they are like sense responses to our environment and to the people around us. At some point in the developmental process we learn labels for these sense responses. Even as a tiny babe we may find our feeling response to our wet diaper or to hunger described as anger or frustration. These are visceral kinds of feelings which occur in response to external stimuli and our comfort or discomfort with the experience. We also learn that some emotional responses bring us rewards while others bring us punishment. This is the socialization process. The socialization process is not necessarily conducive to emotional health. In fact, by its very nature it is someone else's agenda for appropriate responses and often leads to suppression and denial of one's true feelings. Suppression and denial are always unhealthy, and especially damaging when they are rooted in someone else's criteria for behaviour.

Emotions also arise from both the body and the mind. For instance, many healing systems associate anger with the liver. While excessive anger will eventually damage the liver, abuse of the physical function of the liver, as in excessive use of alcohol or recreational drugs, will result in feelings of anger. It is an intricate energy dance between the physical and emotional bodies.

Emotions are also related to the Mental body. If we are thinking harsh and critical thoughts about someone, these thoughts will give rise to accompanying feelings. By the same token when we are thinking happy, loving thoughts, the emotional body will be filled with happiness and love.

Many people believe that we even carry emotional imprints from previous lifetimes, and these also affect balance in the emotional body.

Homeostasis in the emotional body is not involuntary, and requires conscious direction. Without conscious guidance emotions are merely reactions and not responses. Whenever I was "gripped" by some emotional state, Dr. John would gently remind me that I had choice about how I was feeling. He said, "Emotions are like the tail wagging the dog when we hang on to them."

In the case of a person who is damaging his or her liver by excessive drinking, there is a choice available to not drink. In the case of the person who is filled with critical thoughts, there is a choice available to think differently. The cellular memories from previous incarnations can also be filtered through consciousness. When we bring these memories to conscious awareness, we can choose to incorporate the patterns into the current life or to release and discard them if they no longer serve us. Once we are able to recognize these patterns, we can then begin to rearrange them and to choose different responses which are more supportive to our own unique life path.

The Mental body is made up of thoughts and beliefs. It is a framework for feeling and action. Like the Emotional body it is initially programmed by the socialization process. We are taught what to value, how to see ourselves, and what goals to set for ourselves. Usually there comes a point in life when we have to "sort it out for ourselves." We discover that we can choose new ideas and create new belief systems which are more "in tune" with our individual essential nature. Jung called this the process of individuation and implied that eventually claiming our individual selves and fulfilling our soul's purpose is what human incarnation is all about.

Spirit is the formless behind the form. It is Life Force, Qi, the God within. It is the part in each of us that is universal, the ground of being. It is our Source, our true nature. The paradox is that our Spirit is also unique, for as Spirit emerges from the formless through the gap of infinite potential, it brings with it the eternal history of each being and the personal blueprint for further evolution. Some have referred to this aspect of being human as the Soul and others refer to it as the Self. Whatever

the name, Spirit is the essence beneath the illusion of solid reality.
We know it is there and at the same time we cannot see it, feel it, or quantify it.
It permeates the other three bodies. It is the aspect of each of us which does not
begin at birth nor end at death. It cannot be drugged, or cut out, or invaded by
medicine. It is also the part of ourselves which is least understood and for the
most part has been ignored in our Western society, particularly in the fields of
health and education. In the twentieth century in the Western world, Spirit has
usually fallen under the domain of "religious structures" which have seen it as
separate from the rest of the being. All too often these structures have attempted
to nurture Spirit with empty rituals and practices rooted in guilt and fear.

Along with the emergence of Energy Medicine however, there is also a new
interest in Shamanism and the healing practices of aboriginal cultures, all of which
acknowledge and directly contact Spirit in order to effect healing.

The Chinese have always talked about Spirit inhabiting the physical, primarily
through the Heart channel. All mental and nervous disorders are apparently
related to Spirit not being "at home" in the physical. Spirit is not "at home" when
any one of the other three vehicles becomes stressed, misaligned, ignored,
suppressed, or denied. The potential for dis-ease occurs when we are dis-
integrated, when we are "out of integrity" with our very Being.

So a new model for health must incorporate medicine for the whole person. It
must provide acknowledgement and sustenance for all four aspects of being
human in order to heal the whole person.

The physical body itself is like a projection of the other three aspects. The actual
physical vehicle is the last place where dis-ease and/or dys-function show up.
Prior to the appearance of physical symptoms there is some disruption of harmony
in the emotional or mental energy fields. When the disharmony becomes
excessive, the Spirit itself can become sick.

Spirit chooses a physical vehicle and the emotional and mental challenges for any
particular lifetime. When the Spirit is actually in the midst of its script it can forget
its eternal identity and can become overwhelmed, lost, and homesick. This is Spirit
sickness and it bleeds through the auric layers into the other bodies.

Emotionally, we can suppress and deny feelings according to social programming
or we can be emotionally reactive. Both of these options represent the potential
for disharmony and dis-ease.

When we buy into "mass consciousness" and have not learned to think for
ourselves in alignment with our own inner being, we create the potential for dis-
ease at the Mental level.

The popular opinion is that health is maintained by providing the physical body with
proper nutrition, exercise, and shelter. However this model does not take into account

the other aspects of who we are – the emotional, mental, and spiritual selves.

As we begin to relinquish the Newtonian model of mind and body as separate, there are more and more stories of how dis-ease at an emotional or mental level creates life-threatening illnesses. One of my favourites is from Dr. Bernie Siegel, the Oncologist, who writes about his exceptional patients. In his book, *Love, Medicine, and Miracles*, he tells the story of a young patient who has cancer, and Bernie eventually realizes that the disease is somehow rooted in the patient's hatred towards his mother. One day Bernie asks him if he is willing to forgive his mother. The patient replies: "I'd rather die than forgive her." And he dies.

A new model of health implies recognition of the whole being and carefully attuning to the disharmony and being willing to heal the dis-ease at its energetic source.

In a new model of healing we need to have tools to dissolve crystallized thought and feeling patterns and to promote the return to multi-dimensional homeostasis.

This is where flower essences and vibrational medicine are so effective. They have the potential to repattern the different bodies to harmonious frequency because each essence is a pure harmonious frequency of the original physical form.

Healing for the twenty-first century must at least take into account these four aspects of embodiment. It is no longer sufficient to be experts in the functioning of the physical body. We are multi-dimensional and our medicine must also be multi-dimensional. It is homeostasis of the whole person.

In this new model, health is these four aspects functioning together harmoniously to create a vibrating web of wholeness for each individual.

Thus repetitive thought patterns and emotional reactions become indicators of dis-ease. The challenge of homeostasis of the whole person is that it is not involuntary. Each aspect may have an inner knowing of wellness, but only the physical can self-correct.

Homeostasis in the whole person requires conscious intervention in the form of choice. Choosing means allowing ourselves to become more and more conscious of the subtle interplay among these four aspects and making changes accordingly. When we are willing to accept this responsibility, we can begin to notice repetitive and crystallized patterns which do not serve us in terms of our health and well-being. We may notice that every time we get really angry, and then hang onto the feeling in the form of resentment, we experience a corresponding pain under our right rib cage. We may discover that every time we speak ill of another person we develop a sore throat. We may find that certain colours, sounds, and even people have either an uplifting or disturbing effect on us. Then we can make a conscious choice to change the emotional response or the thought pattern. We can even choose to eliminate the triggers in our lives which do not contribute to our well-being. When we are willing to live more consciously in this way, essences can be immensely valuable in making the necessary changes.

Maps of Energy and What They Mean

The two oldest recorded healing systems both viewed human beings in a decidedly holistic way which included body, mind, emotions, and spirit. One of these is the Ayurvedic tradition which dates back to the fifth century bc in India. The other is the system of traditional Chinese medicine which dates back to the third century bc in China. Both these systems mapped energetic pathways in the human body and accessed these to effect healing.

The Seven Chakras

One of the ways that the three Energy Bodies connect with one another and with Spirit is via the chakras. Chakras are energy centres which are described by clairvoyants as spinning wheels of light along the midline, but just outside, of the physical body. The identification of chakras stems from the Ayurvedic tradition of India, where working with their energy is not only a path of spiritual development but also a means for maintaining health. It is believed that the life force enters via the crown chakra on the top of the head and disperses into a full spectrum of colours as it activates each of the other six chakras and their corresponding physical organs.

Chakras distribute the life force to the Mental, Emotional, and Physical bodies. They also serve as energy conduits among the three bodies. The chakras form part of the energy template which allows subtle, high-frequency energies of the spiritual realm to be translated into physical matter. A chakra becomes dysfunctional when the area of the Mental, Emotional, or Physical bodies to which it is connected is blocked by crystallized energy patterns. Then the chakra is not able to efficiently translate life force energy to the level of cellular function. Crystallization of energy occurs when patterns become fixed due to the length of time they are held or to the intensity of the experience which initiated the tension.

Although I now personally work with eleven major chakras as a result of my work with Master Choa Kok Sui, traditionally we have learned that there are seven major chakras in the human body, all strategically located close to a major nerve plexus and/or endocrine gland. Each chakra is an energy junction where Prana, Qi, or the universal life force, can be absorbed into the physical body. Each chakra has a mental and emotional component as well as its physical correspondence. The following describes some of the important features of each of the seven major chakras.

The first, or Root chakra, is located at the base of the spine where the coccyx is situated in the physical. It relates primarily to the survival instinct and basic needs of security, food, and shelter. This is the predominant energy centre at birth. As we mature, the Root chakra serves to keep us grounded and connected to the earth. The Root chakra is related to the adrenal glands, which secrete adrenaline, the hormone which fuels our "fight or flight" response in times of danger. In our post-industrial world where there is very little real physical danger to contend with, it is the energy centre which is most taxed by the stress of day-to-day life.

The second chakra is called the Sacral chakra and is located at the sacral nerve plexus in the lower spine. This centre governs sexuality and creativity. It provides us with the inspiration to create in terms of both the continuity of the species as well as mentally and kinesthetically. Sexual energy is extremely powerful and can be used in many other channels besides procreation. Great salespeople use this energy, as do artists, writers, and dancers. The challenge of the Sacral chakra is to use the power wisely and not manipulatively.

The third chakra is located in the Solar Plexus and is the seat of emotions. It contains astral patterns from both past lives and earlier periods in this life. It is the energy centre from which our ego and personal identity is developed. The challenges of the Solar Plexus chakra are resolving karma and processing emotions. This is the centre where we can transform emotional reactions (unconscious) to emotional responses (conscious). Unconscious emotions leave their residue in this centre and create energy blockages.

In some spiritual texts the first three chakras have been interpreted as relating to man's lower nature while the upper three have been seen as relating to man's higher potential. In terms of health it is vital that all seven chakras are functioning optimally.

The fourth centre, which is the Heart chakra, serves as a vital conduit between the lower three chakras and the upper three. Located in the centre of the chest, the Heart chakra is associated with the qualities of compassion and love. Here the concerns about personal survival and identity are transmuted to the non-judgmental focus of compassion for both ourselves and others. When looking at the world through the window of an open heart there is only love. Often we can see this quality of unconditional love in very young children who radiate innocence and in older people who are able to embrace life experience with equanimity and acceptance.

The fifth chakra is the Throat, and its gifts are communication and self-expression. It is closely linked to the second chakra, the centre for creativity and sexuality. A balanced Throat centre will use the power of the Sacral chakra to join with others in a loving and creative manner.

The Third Eye, located in the centre of the forehead, is the sixth chakra which conveys the gifts of higher sensing – clairvoyance, clairaudience, and clairsentience – and leads to insight. Its related endocrine gland is the pineal gland. Imbalances in this centre will lead to depression and dissatisfaction with life experiences.

The seventh chakra is located at the top of the head and is called the Crown chakra. It is the avenue to "All That Is." The potential here is for unified consciousness where there is no ego separation or boundaries. (See Table I)

These subtle energy centres play an important role in the transportation of essences to the energy body where it is needed.

When a vibrational remedy enters either under the tongue or through the skin, the physical aspects of the essence flow into the bloodstream. The energy of the essence is attracted to the subtle energetic pathways of the body and the chakra with which it resonates. The chakras are like electrical junction boxes or switches which channel the energy of the essence to the energy body which needs it. The essence proceeds to different parts of the energy body via the meridians mapped by Chinese medicine.

The Meridians of Traditional Chinese Medicine

Chinese medicine describes fourteen major energy pathways, or channels, through which the Qi, or vital force, circulates to all areas of the Body/Mind.

Qi moves out of formless into form and circulates through the dynamic tension created by the polarity of yin and yang. Thus for every yin channel there is a yang partner and vice versa.

The first two channels run along the centre line of the front and back of the body. These are called the Conception Vessel in the front and the Governing Vessel in the back. These two channels act as reservoirs of Qi energy to sustain the other twelve channels. They also play a fundamental role in linking up the seven major chakras.

The other twelve meridians are named after the physical organ to which they relate and work together to maintain life and health. It is apparent that the Chinese have always viewed the human being in a holistic way. The acupuncture points on each meridian have very carefully delineated attributes which access body, mind, emotion or spirit. Dis-ease is attributed to energy deficiency or excess in any one channel or any one of the four energy aspects which would automatically disturb the harmony of the whole being. Each channel also has a two-hour period of peak functioning in the 24 hour clock and an element to which it relates. Perhaps the easiest way to see the cosmology of Chinese medicine in the human being is through the metaphor of the five elements which contain all of the twelve channels and function together to create and to control each other.

Fire is the element which contains the channels of Heart, Small Intestine, Heart Protector and Triple Warmer. It is the only element which embraces four channels. Heart and Heart Protector are Yin channels, and Small Intestine and Triple Warmer are Yang. Heart and Small Intestine are directly related to the physical organs of the same name. The Heart is seen as the king, the supreme ruler, and provides order for the entire domain of the Body/Mind.

Small Intestine is the Alchemist. It sorts out the pure from the impure physically and also helps us to sort out our thoughts and feelings.

The closest physical correspondence for Heart Protector is the pericardium sac which surrounds the heart. More than this, however, the Heart Protector, as its name implies, acts to protect the heart against injury and insult emotionally, psychically, and spiritually.

In the ancient Chinese texts the Triple Warmer was often represented by three fires located in the lower abdomen, the solar plexus, and the chest. It is interesting that these three fires also correspond to the second, third and fourth chakras respectively. Although the Triple Warmer has no particular physical organ correspondence, it is involved with elimination and reproduction, digestion and absorption, and circulation and respiration. The three fires are the energy required to perform these vital body functions, and the Triple Warmer channel acts as a network to maintain harmony among all these physical activities. As its name implies, it serves to regulate body heat/energy.

An unhealthy Fire element may manifest as blood and circulatory disorders, sexual dysfunction, body heat irregularities, and a build-up of toxins in the system.

The Fire element radiates light and warmth. Its energy provides the impetus for communication and relationship and sets up the yearning for happiness which leads to love, and can lead to agape. It is the seat of compassion. When the Fire element is healthy it is vital and intense. It is the animating force of the five elements. Without the Fire the other elements could not exist in the physical body. The emotion of Fire is joy and its sound is laughter. In the balanced Fire element there is a spontaneous bubbling up of delight. More than any of the other elements, Fire gives rise to enthusiasm – from the Greek "en theos" in God, and is the path to at-one-ment or unity with Spirit. The Fire element houses the Shen, which is the spirit of the Mind. When Fire is deficient and passion for life is lacking, depression results and Shen is not at home in the Body/Mind. There may be a blank look in the eyes and the person may have difficulty with sleep or with concentration and memory. Fire creates Earth.

The Earth element contains the yin channel of the Spleen and the yang channel of the Stomach. The Spleen acts as the transport manager and distributes Qi, blood, and nutrients throughout the system. It is like the mother who nurtures us both physically and emotionally.

The Stomach channel is in charge of rotting and ripening and prepares food for digestion. It also plays a role in the digestion of thoughts and feelings.

People with an unhealthy Earth element may become obsessive and preoccupied with the mental realm because they are not grounded in the physical. They may suffer from digestion problems or eating disorders.

The Earth element is like the fertile ground of being. It is our connection to the earth plane and to the physical body which our Spirit inhabits. When we are nurtured physically, emotionally, mentally, and spiritually we allow ourselves the full experience of our incarnation. The feeling which corresponds to the Earth element is sympathy or empathy – we are all "strangers in a strange land" at some level. The sound of Earth is singing.

The spirit of Earth is I, the quest for nourishment, support, and understanding in our embodiment. It is from the Earth element that Metal arises.

The Metal element contains the yin meridian of Lung and the yang meridian of Large Intestine. Both of these channels are concerned with bodily purity.

The Lung channel governs respiration and takes charge of rhythmic order in the body in the form of breathing and other rhythms like that of the cranial sacral pulse. It receives pure Qi from heaven and distributes it via the blood to all the cells in the body.

The Large Intestine channel is the great eliminator. It carries away impurities from the body, mind, and spirit and leaves us pure and brilliant.

An unhealthy Metal element may manifest as breathing problems such as asthma, bronchitis, and laryngitis or as bowel problems like constipation or diarrhea. All of these physical difficulties have corresponding emotional and mental challenges such as being unable to let go of the past or of being unable to take in and assimilate new life-supporting experiences.

The Metal element is cold, rigid, and hard, but it is also the source of precious metals – the minerals and chemical elements which are vital to healthy functioning. The Metal element seeks spiritual truth and purity.

The sound of Metal is weeping and the emotion is grief. The spirit of the Metal element is Po – our animal soul and the realm of desires. It embodies the same challenges as the eighth house in astrology – money, sex, death, and power. The Metal element creates Water.

The Water element contains the meridians of Kidney and Bladder. Kidney is yin and is the controller of all the water balance in the body. It is the storehouse of the vital essence and from it flows the stream of ancestral energy. It provides the blueprint for physical embodiment – the sperm, the egg, and DNA.

Bladder is the yang channel and it controls the storage of water. It stores the body fluids and maintains adequate reservoirs of water and fluids in the body.

An unhealthy Water element may manifest as energy problems, back pain, urogenital disorders, problems with the nervous system such as Multiple Sclerosis and Parkinson's disease, infertility, tooth and bone disease, and lack of will power.

The Water element is cold, deep, transparent, and transporting. It is cleansing and purifying and also persistent. There is no force in nature more powerful for wearing away hard matter like rocks. Its sound is groaning and its emotion is fear. The Water element governs the will, our will to sustain life. Its spirit is Chih which is the seat of our willpower. Water creates Wood.

The Wood element contains the channels of Liver and Gall Bladder. The yin meridian of Liver is like a general in the army who excels in strategic planning. It is a vital channel of detoxification for the Body/Mind and provides clarity and order for the other channels.

Gall Bladder is the yang partner in the Wood element. It is responsible for decision making and wise judgement for the Body/Mind.

When the Wood element is unhealthy there may be muscle and tendon problems, vision disturbances, epilepsy, and menstrual difficulties. There may also be anger, complaining and indecisiveness.

The Wood element connects heaven and earth, like a tree firmly rooted in the ground with its branches rising toward heaven. Trees are strong and enduring as well as flexible and bending. The Wood element is the source of creativity and is connected to birth and renewal. It is the activator of the DNA blueprint found in the Water element. The sound of Wood is shouting and its emotion is anger. The spirit of Wood is Hun, the force of creative expression. The Chinese say the Hun is the only spirit which we carry with us from lifetime to lifetime. It is the motivating force for the optimal creative expression of the soul in each lifetime. (See Table II)

The preceding is only a minute sketch of the landscape of Chinese medicine and some of the clues to look for when working with the essences. The following case notes may help to focus this material more clearly.

Some Case Studies To Illustrate These Connections

Fire

A female aged forty-five came to me for acupuncture. She was under a great deal of stress. She had recently moved to this city and had invested a lot of time, money, and energy in establishing her life and work here. The weekend prior to her appointment she had returned to see her ex-partner and discovered that he was extremely depressed, to the point of being unable to work. She believed that the only way she could live with herself was to return to him and to help him through this difficult time in his life, even though it would mean giving up her own dreams and plans. Her cheeks were very flushed. She spoke very quickly and she complained of stiffness in her joints and feeling emotionally tense. When I took her pulses her Heart pulse was significantly depleted.

I inserted needles in some points on the Wood channels for emotional tension and physical rigidity, but the Heart pulse still remained deficient.

I placed a drop of Jellyfish essence on the heart-related acupuncture point in her ear. It seemed as if a cloud of tension lifted from her solar plexus. Her body became relaxed and her Heart pulse strengthened.

TABLE I

Chakra	First – Root	Second – Sacral	Third – Solar Plexus
Hindu Name	Muladhara	Svadhisthana	Manipura
Location	Base of the spine	Pelvis	Above the Navel
Colour	Red	Orange	Yellow
Issues and Concerns	Survival, Security, Basic physical needs. Foundation	Sexual Energy, Expression of Self through Sexuality and Creativity	Development of ego and identity in the world, Resolving challenges and Karmic issues
Meridian Association	Bladder, Large Intestine	Spleen, Kidney	Liver, Gall Bladder, Stomach, Small Intestine
Endocrine Gland	Adrenals	Gonads	Pancreas, Liver
Planets	Earth, Saturn	Moon, Pluto	Mars, Sun
Function	Survival	Sexuality	Power & Will

Fourth – Heart	Fifth – Throat	Sixth – Third Eye	Seventh – Crown
Anahata	Visuddha	Ajna	Sahasrara
Centre of the Chest	Hollow of the Throat	Centre of the Brow	Top of the Skull
Green / Pink	Blue	Indigo	Violet
Love, Compassion, Devotion, Acceptance, Non-Judgment	Self-expression, Communication, Knowledge	Spiritual perception, Calirvoyance, Clairsentience, Insight	Spiritual awakening Unified consciousness, Union with the Divine
Heart, Heart Protector	Lung, Stomach	Conception Vessel, Governing Vessel	Penetrating Vessel Girdling Vessel
Thymus	Thyroid	Pineal	Pituitary
Venus	Mercury	Jupiter, Neptune	Uranus
Love, Community	Communication	Intuition	Grace

Earth

A woman aged thirty-six came for essences and acupuncture. She was in a new relationship. Although she was happy, she was having some difficulty dealing with her partner's children. She had begun overeating (an old pattern) and was gaining excess weight rapidly. She felt unnoticed and uncared for when the children were around.

We did some acupuncture on her Spleen channel, and I gave her the Urchin remedy. She reported a shift to normal eating patterns and began to heal the other areas in her life where she felt misunderstood and unaccepted.

Metal

A woman aged fifty-five came for acupressure. Her mother had recently died and she felt sad and exhausted. She had developed a continual cough and this brought up fears about her own aging and dying. She was having lots of dreams about her childhood and her relationship with her mother. Her upper back (associated area for the lungs) was very tense and she was extremely constipated. Most of the points on her Lung channel were painful.

I immediately thought of Purple Crocus and Starfish, both of which are grief remedies. When muscle tested she responded with a lock to Starfish. When a muscle locks, or is strengthened, it is indicative that the person's internal bio-computer is welcoming the remedy. I will say more about muscle testing in the section on Selecting the Remedy.

I believe that Starfish was the essence of choice for this particular woman because she had a strong affinity for the ocean and found it very calming and soothing. A lot of her physical and emotional pain seemed related to her inability to let go of the old form of the relationship with her mother. She wanted to learn a new way of being with her mother even though her mother was no longer physically available. Within a few days of taking the Starfish essence her elimination changed and she began writing a journal. The journal became a powerful vehicle for healing her relationship with her mother because as she was writing many previously unconscious memories surfaced.

Water

A woman aged forty-three came for essences. She complained of lung congestion, pain in her right ovary, and swelling in her legs. She had dark rings under her eyes and spoke in a groaning monotone. When asked what she was doing in her life, she described herself as "in transition" and felt as if she didn't know what the next step was for her. My sense was that she had a great deal of fear around taking this next step. She also had a history of bone disorders which had once been diagnosed as cancer. In addition, after the birth of her second child she had experienced kidney failure.

We came up with a combination of Blue Camas, Candystick, and Death Camas. Each one of these essences impacts on the Kidney channel.

The lung congestion and swelling in her legs disappeared the next day. When I saw her the following week the dark rings under her eyes were gone and she reported that she had begun to do the channelled writing which she believed was her next step.

Wood

A man aged forty-one came with pain under his right rib cage which was always worse at night between waking and sleeping. He was never able to fall asleep before 1 or 2 A.M. (peak time of functioning for the Liver channel). He had a brown discoloration in the whites of his eyes. He complained of mood swings, irritability, and mental confusion which led to indecisiveness. These symptoms had begun when he was working in a factory with some highly toxic glue. He was tired all the time.

We came up with two remedies for him. The first one was Mussel to be used as a bath therapy for the anger and irritability. The second was a combination of Arbutus, Chickweed, and Pipsissewa to be taken orally.

The first night he took the essences he had a dream in which he was killed with a spear being driven into his back and through to his liver. He awakened sweating and screaming. The next day he felt very relaxed and experienced increased mental clarity. The pain in his liver area had also disappeared.

And Other Stories

A woman aged thirty-seven injured her lower back lifting a heavy object in an awkward position. After a week of physiotherapy with limited results she began doing bath therapy with a combination of Candystick for pelvic alignment and Salmonberry for spinal alignment. There was an immediate relaxation of the muscle spasms and the effect of physiotherapy treatments was greatly enhanced.

A man aged forty-three presented with asthma and hypoglycemia. He had been in the war in Vietnam and still carried much tension from this experience.

He complained of dizziness and blackouts if he didn't eat something every couple of hours.

The remedy which came up for him was a combination of Barnacle and Surfgrass. Subsequently we learned that Barnacle seemed to help him to sort out his feelings about the war experience and to attune with his feminine aspect which had been totally suppressed at that time. Surfgrass served to dissolve the raw fear around survival during the war experience. The asthma disappeared temporarily, and the hypoglycemia and accompanying symptoms have not reappeared.

A young woman aged nineteen came to my clinic with the eating disorder of bulemia. She ate and ate and then forced herself to vomit. She felt unloved and unwanted by her parents. It appeared that eating was her way of attempting to nourish herself, but it also created self-hate. She felt really locked into this self-abusive pattern. We did some acupuncture on the Spleen channel and I gave her the sea Anemone essence which is related primarily to the Liver channel. I perceived that her Earth element was not strong enough to support her Wood and that the excessive eating was also an attempt to block her creative expression. I asked her to draw some pictures before her next appointment. When she returned ten days later she had had no episodes of bulemia and the drawings were truly amazing. It was as if all the drawings had been done through the vision of her Third Eye. Taking the Anemone essence marked a complete turn-around in her eating disorder pattern and to date she has not had another episode of forcing herself to vomit

A woman aged fifty, who appeared otherwise healthy, was having difficulty driving home at night without falling asleep at the wheel of her car. Periodically it was so bad that she had to pull over to the side of the road and nap for half an hour. I asked her if she was sleeping well at night.

She said that she never went to bed before midnight or 1 A.M. and woke at 6 A.M. She did not have any difficulty falling asleep but stayed up late "to get things done." It occurred to me that she was quite compulsive about "doing" and that it was from "doing" things that she derived much of her self-worth. I immediately thought of Polyanthus, a remedy par excellence for self-worth. She stopped falling asleep at the wheel of her car that very first night. Since then she has had no recurrences.

Preparing and Prescribing Remedies

How We Make Essences

The process of making an essence is filled with joy, delight, and Mystery for me. To begin with, it involves finding the right plant, which has led me to places that I might otherwise never have discovered. I deliberately choose areas that are in the heart of nature, off the beaten track, and away from energy interference patterns from cars, high voltage wires, and people. This ensures the purity of the plant's vibration.

After spending some time attuning with the plant energy and noting how and where it is growing, I ask permission from the Plant Spirit to pick some blooms and carefully select the ones which appear to contain the highest life force. At Pacific Essences we usually include full-blown flowers and buds and add a couple of leaves to incorporate all of the plant energy manifestation.

After gently picking the parts of the plant to be used and placing them in a crystal bowl filled with water, they are left in the sun close to the plant for at least one hour or sometimes longer. Sometimes the bowl is brought home with the plants and water in it and set under our pyramid. In both cases I find that as the sun is potentizing the water with the plant energy, it is a good time to receive information about the healing potential of the plant. For instance, I may note something about its shape, colour, or texture which gives me further clues to the plant signature. It is also a good time to do a plant journeying process where I invite the Plant Spirit to communicate its purpose to me.

When this part of the process is complete, I thank the Plant Spirits and take the water, which now holds the vibration of the plant, and mix it with equal parts of alcohol. This is the Mother Essence. The flowers and any additional flower water are placed under a tree in the garden as an offering back to the Earth.

To make stock concentrates we take seven drops from the Mother tincture and add them to a dilution of 40% alcohol and 60% water.

The general rule for making dosage bottles is to take two drops from the stock bottle and add it to a dilution of 25% alcohol and 75% water. However, we have also found it extremely effective to take into account the plant signature when making dosage bottles. For instance, for Blue Camas we might put six drops of stock in the dosage bottle or for Periwinkle we might put five drops of stock in the dosage formula.

TABLE II – Meridians of Traditional Chinese Medicine

	FIRE	EARTH
Yin Meridian	Heart Heart Protector	Spleen
Yang Meridian	Small Intestine Triple Warmer	Stomach
Season	Summer	Indian Summer
Climate	Hot	Humid
Taste	Bitter	Sweet
Sense Organ	Tongue	Mouth
Emotion	Joy	Sympathy / Worry
Sound Expression	Laughter	Singing
Tissue	Blood Vessel	Flesh, Fat
Body Fluid	Sweat	Saliva
Manner in time of change or excitement	Grief, Sadness	Belching
Faculty (Intrinsic Quality)	Inspiration	Intellect
Movement of Qi	Meditation, Deep Thinking	Embracing, Holding
Peak Function	Ht 11 am-1 pm HP 7-9 pm Sm. Int. 1-3 pm TW 9-11 pm	Spleen 9-11 am Stomach 7-9 am
Smell	Scorched	Fragrant
Dreams	Fires, Deserts	Food, Lethargy, Music
Direction	South	Centre
Colour	Red	Yellow
Chinese Word	Fluo	T'u

METAL	WATER	WOOD
Lung	Kidney	Liver
Large Intestine	Bladder	Gall Bladder
Autumn	Winter	Spring
Dry	Cold	Wind
Pungent	Salty	Sour
Nose	Ears	Eyes
Grief	Fear	Anger
Weeping	Groaning	Shouting
Skin, Body hair	Bone, Teeth	Ligament, Muscle
Mucus	Urine	Tears
Cough	Trembling	Spiritual Control
Vitality of Qi	Will	Spiritual
Yawning	Set up to Rush	Vacillation
Lung 3-5 am	Kidney 5-7 pm	Liver 1-3 am
Rotten	Putrid	Rancid
Flying, Sad, White Objects	Water	Rooted, Immobile
West	North	East
White	Black, Blue	Green
Chin	Shui	Mu

At Pacific Essences we always use pure spring water for all stages of the process except for the sea essences. Spring water is lively and pure. It contains the energies of both heaven and earth and is affected by both the sun and the moon. It tumbles over rocks and contains minerals which are natural to both the earth and the human body. It is vital and alive.

It is clear to me that the quality of the water is a critical factor in producing essences of the highest vibration. The water is the carrier of the etheric imprint. We do not use distilled water because we do not find that it carries a sufficiently high frequency.

It has been reported by practitioners that boiled water is a good option for making dosage bottles when a pure source of natural water is not available. We ourselves have used boiled water when clients have an alcohol intolerance. In this case we take two drops from the stock concentrate and fill the one-ounce dosage bottle with the boiled water. We then recommend that the bottle be kept refrigerated to prevent the water from becoming mouldy.

I have also heard that some practitioners make dosage bottles with apple cider vinegar or vegetable glycerine instead of brandy for those with alcohol sensitivities.

Brandy has been an important part of the process, since the first flower essences were made in this manner by Dr. Edward Bach. It is used as a preservative for the water which may otherwise become tainted in some way. Moreover, essences made with brandy have an indefinite shelf life if properly stored.

With the sea essences we use only ocean water for the first stage of the process when potentizing it with the energy of the sun. At the stock and dosage levels of dilution we use spring water.

It is also important to note that when making the sea essences, *nothing is harmed in the process*. The first question I am always asked about the sea essences is: how did you make the whale, or the dolphin? What size glass bowl did you use? And the truth is that all the sea creatures are made in the location in which they are found.

I can't even begin to describe what it's like to be swimming with a pod of Spinner dolphins with a container strapped to my wrist so that I can collect the water. The sensation is somewhat like being carried on a gentle cloud of energy.

Selecting the Remedy

The first time that someone arrives for a flower essence consultation I spend a fair amount of time asking questions and attempting to find out as much as I can about who they are, why they have come to see me, and why they are attracted to vibrational medicine as a form of therapy. I find that it is really important to keep patient records so that I can follow their progress. Keeping accurate and complete records is also valuable for patients to help them to recognize changes that are occurring. I have discovered that it is often difficult to see the changes in ourselves when we are engaged in treatment, especially if we are in either a chronic or a crystallized pattern. Good records allow both the patient and the practitioner to acknowledge alleviation of symptoms and new perspectives on the problem.

The following questions are designed to elicit information which will be useful to me when using Chinese Medicine as a framework for selecting the remedy.

Table III – Client Assessment Questions

Name:

Address:

Age: Birthdate: (time and place if you want to do astrological work)

Why are you here? (get them to indicate all their symptoms in detail and note if they are primarily physical, mental, emotional, or spiritual)

When did these symptoms begin?

Take a brief history of past health and note surgeries, accidents, etc.

With whom do you live? (often this question can give some clues as to what their relationship stresses are)

What kind of work do you do? (pay special attention to their tone of voice and level of animation when describing their work activity – does it sound as if they are just working for the pay cheque? Are they "following their bliss"? Do they seem to be a workaholic?)

How do you relax? (Do they play? What's fun for them? Are these activities primarily social or do they tend to be loners?)

What is your favourite colour?

Do you crave any particular food?

What time of day do you have the most energy? – the least energy?

Have you experienced any major emotional traumas or stress in your life? In the past year? In the past five years? (things like death of a loved one, divorce, money problems, chronic illness, job change?)

How do you respond to stress?

If you were going to die in six months, what would you do for the next six months? (This question has interesting possibilities. You might want to note their immediate reaction to it – the look on their face, alteration in breathing pattern, etc. Then listen carefully to their verbal response. It might include a radical departure from their description of themselves and their life as it is right now. You can also get some clues as to how they really see themselves – i.e., Who do they think they are?)

Give me three positive words which describe you?

Give me three negative words which describe you?

These questions are not designed to be used as a questionnaire to be filled out by the client. It is important to sit down and really listen to what's going on for the person. It is also important to carefully observe the person from the time he walks into your room.

What does the person look like? What colour is she wearing? If she is dressed all in black and then tells you that her favourite colour is pink it would be useful to record both pieces of information and to note the discrepancy. How do they greet you? Do they appear timid and shy or open and gregarious? Do they make eye contact effortlessly? What is the tone of their voice? What is the strength of their handshake if they shake hands?

Notice where in their physical body they appear to be carrying their tension and body armour. Shoulders which are hunched forward may be protecting the heart. A backward tilted sacrum may indicate an imbalance in the second chakra and difficulty with sexuality. Listen to the quality of their voice. Are they whining or shouting? Talking fast or slow? Loud or soft? Note any incongruence between verbal language and body language. These are all valuable clues to unravelling the human energy system before you and choosing the optimal remedy.

I hope this doesn't sound too clinical on paper. I find the initial interview an incredible opportunity to join with the person in front of me. I also believe that the healing begins right here at the first contact between practitioner and client.

It is critical that the client feels heard and understood. Many people come to complementary health practices after they have been through a lot of previous experience of being unheard and undiagnosed in other systems. What they seek is a safe place and a fellow traveller with whom to begin the healing journey.

As the practitioner I am deeply moved by the mystery unfolding before me. I am honoured by the trust placed in me and in the essences. I find myself wanting to give back to the client that same honour and trust.

Choosing the most appropriate essence or combination of essences is really a process of attunement just like making the remedy in the first place. Sometimes a client comes with particular essences in mind because they are already familiar with the literature, and they feel as if they know what they need. In this case I always encourage the client's inner wisdom. At the same time, if I feel that I can assist them in identifying an underlying cause, I suggest that we test for other remedies.

Sometimes the symptoms match a particular essence. For instance, someone with low back pain might benefit from Candystick and Salmonberry, since both of these have proven to be very powerful physical remedies. This particular combination has been effectively used orally and as a bath therapy. (The latter involves putting ten drops of the stock concentrate in a bath full of water and soaking in it.) If, however, the low back pain is primarily due to fear of "not having enough," the appropriate remedy might be Polyanthus, a remedy which works more on the attitudinal issues of self-worth and self-esteem. Our major goal in selecting the remedy is to uncover the root cause, not merely to alleviate symptoms.

One client of mine always chooses all her remedies at home with her own attunement process; then I just make up the dosage bottles for her. She has been guided to use as many as seventeen essences in one combination. Even though this is most unusual, we have been able repeatedly to confirm her inner wisdom through kinesiology. It is interesting to note that this patient actually has seventeen identifiable personalities, and I've often wondered when she comes up with a combination of so many essences if there is one essence for each different personality.

While I would not normally make up a combination that included so many different variables, I believe that an important component of a new model of health includes encouraging clients to take responsibility for their own well-being and that my work is to support them in that process.

When I am the one selecting the essence, I tend to give people single remedies so that they can work through one thing at a time. If a combination does seem appropriate, at the most I might mix four or five essences together. I have found that the Sea essences in particular work best as single remedies. This may, in part, be due to their direct action which tends to bring issues to consciousness. It may also relate to the fact that in the first Kit of twelve essences there is one essence which resonates with each of the twelve channels of traditional Chinese medicine.

During the interview I may have noted some particular expression or words or a recurrent theme which matches the action of a particular essence. If so, I will take out these remedies and ask the person to hold them while I use Applied Kinesiology – muscle testing – to confirm the match. The use of Kinesiology is a way for the person to directly experience whether the remedy strengthens him or her.

Kinesiology or muscle testing is a clinical method of accessing information in the human bio-computer. The basic principle is that we all know at a body level what substances, feelings, thoughts, and environmental circumstances are life and health supporting to us. This is a subconscious response and is measured by testing the strength of various muscles in the body.

The simplest form of muscle testing involves asking the person to hold a particular essence in one hand while you test their ability to hold their thumb and index finger together on the other hand. If the essence strengthens them it will be virtually impossible for you to separate the thumb and index finger. This is called a muscle lock. I usually ask the person to think about their problem while we do the muscle test because it provides a focus for the test. Generally, thinking about the problem automatically weakens the muscle and adding the appropriate remedy to the energy circuit will strengthen the muscle. Sometimes I add another remedy which has not been indicated and ask the person to hold it along with the ones that have already tested positively. If the essence is not useful for the person the muscle will weaken. Removing the inappropriate remedy will once again produce the lock. This is important experience for clients especially if they are unfamiliar with essence therapy. At a conscious level it provides confirmation, and at a subconscious level it anchors the effectiveness of the remedy.

Another way to apply Kinesiology is to use the muscle that is related to a particular meridian of Chinese medicine. This system, called *Touch for Health*, demonstrates which energetic system is affected by a particular problem.
By muscle testing the gross physical anatomy we can determine where the problem reflects in the energy system by noting which muscle/meridian complex is weakened by the problem. First you check all the relevant muscles to determine which are weak in relation to the issue. Then test the weak muscles again with the client holding the corresponding essence. (See Table IV)

TABLE IV – Applied Kinesiology

MERIDIAN	MUSCLE
Central	Supraspinatus
Governing	Teres Major
Stomach	Pectoralis Major
Spleen	Latissimus Dorsi
Heart	Subscapularis
Small	Intestine Quadriceps
Bladder	Peroneus
Kidney	Psoas
Circulation Sex	Gluteus Medius
Triple Warmer	Teres Minor
Gall Bladder	Anterior Deltoid
Liver	Pectoralis Major Sternal
Lung	Anterior Serratus
Large Intestine	Fascia Lata

If you are a competent Touch for Health Practitioner this is an excellent method for direct access to inner wisdom of the Body/Mind. It can be used both for diagnosis and for confirmation of a treatment plan.

Another method I use to select the remedy is to dowse with a pendulum. This is a good method to use when the client doesn't seem to know what's wrong. I place one hand on the person's body and with my other hand hold the pendulum over a box of essences, and when it is moving in a clockwise direction I ask the patient to put their hand, palm up, between the pendulum and the essences. If the pendulum continues to spin clockwise, and possibly even faster and with greater amplitude, we know that there is an essence in the box that will help. If, however, the pendulum begins to move in a counterclockwise direction, we select another box of essences, and begin again. When we have identified all the boxes that contain a possible essence we go through each essence one by one with the client touching each bottle and getting a pendulum reading for each. When we have all the remedies that have been dowsed we use the finger lock muscle test to confirm the combination. Having confirmed the remedy selection, the client and I read the essence correlations to see how they fit. Often this is an experience of true insight, and reading the description of the selected essence serves to shed more light on the underlying issue for the client and the practitioner.

What is critical for practitioners in selecting the optimal remedy is to use a system with which they are comfortable and with which they have some considerable skill. We have experimented with a number of different techniques simultaneously. For instance, one person dowsed with a pendulum, the client himself used his own sensing device – i.e., he ran his hand over the bottles about three inches away from them and noted energy field shifts, while I matched symptoms. We all arrived at exactly the same essence.

Ayurvedic medicine, Chinese medicine, Kinesiology, dowsing, and energy field readings can all be used effectively to select an essence. So can Astrology, Tarot card readings, and consulting the I Ching. These are all frameworks for attuning with the client and keys to unlocking the doorway to the problem. Whatever framework is used, I believe that it is of the utmost importance to look for what is not obvious about a patient's energy pattern in any dis-ease. The process of selecting a remedy is not about putting the client and their symptoms into a neatly labelled category. In other words, look and listen for the phenomena which the person in front of you is presenting rather than trying to match their symptoms with a known pattern of disease or an astrological transit.

My experience confirms that there can be no wrong remedy; however, there are more or less effective ones for any given problem. The most effective remedy will be drawn like a magnet to the area of disharmony and gently guide the whole person back to balance. If the Body/Mind does not need a particular essence, it will not be absorbed into the energy system. This is known as the self-adjusting feature of essences. It is as if a tuning fork is struck in a room where there is no other tuning fork. There is nothing to vibrate in sympathy with the first pitch. What the Body/Mind doesn't need it doesn't use.

In *The Pattern of Health*, the author, Aubrey Westlake, describes a radionic device on which all the Bach flower remedies were placed along with a blood spot from the patient. The patient, who was not even physically present, absorbed only those essences which were necessary to alleviate the condition.

While I think that the self-adjusting feature of essences can give the practitioner confidence when they are beginning to work with flower essences, I also think that it is important to become highly skilled in a particular modality to select the essences.

The critical factor when working with essences is to use a system of selection with which you are thoroughly comfortable and familiar. When you have discovered your own medium and feel totally aligned with it, it will be easy to attune with the unfolding of phenomena.

Correlations and Research on Flower and Sea Essences

The following section includes expanded descriptions of all of the flower and sea essences in the Pacific Essence collection at this time. I have tried to incorporate the relevant data which we have accumulated over the years without making the description too lengthy.

In our initial stages of research we attuned with the plant and attempted to intuitively understand its signature. We took the essence before going to bed and asked for a dream about the Plant Spirit. Occasionally we just took the essence and asked our Higher Selves for information. This was a process of conscious journeying. Sometimes we just took the essence and noted where we felt the energy in our bodies. Did it produce an emotional shift? Did we suddenly note that we were on a flight of fantasy? Was there any noticeable difference in physical sensations in the body?

For instance when we did the research on Candystick, one of the people in the group had just had an abortion. She had been experiencing a great deal of cramping and congestion in the uterus, not to mention the sadness she felt about terminating the pregnancy. On taking Candystick essence the fullness in her pelvis immediately shifted and her uterus felt alive and healthy again. Essences often have a strong, noticeable impact like this. Later, other essences were used to alleviate the emotional trauma.

After we completed our initial work with each plant, we researched its herbal uses. With the native wild flowers we paid particular attention to how they were used by the local aboriginal people for nourishment or healing. When we had decided that Nootka Rose was for "expressing love of life, laughter, and joy," we subsequently learned that the West Coast Indians had buried their dead with Nootka Rose to ensure a safe and happy journey into the next life. This was a delightful confirmation of intuition.

As my own knowledge of energy systems in the body expanded, I also wanted to discover which energy system each essence would directly affect. As a Touch for Health instructor, I was able to access this information through the physical body via the muscles and meridians, so I confirmed our initial intuitive findings with this method to my own satisfaction. However, the part of me that had been programmed to believe in the Western scientific model wanted some further independent testing. I discovered that there were energy-sensing devices available which could access this data. We asked Dr. Michael Adams, founder and president of the North American Auriculartherapy Foundation, to test all the flower and sea essences. He used a combination of ear acupuncture points and an instrument called the Vega to determine which chakras and meridians were affected by each essence.

I found the results of this testing extremely supportive in that Michael confirmed 95% of our results. However, I also recognized that no matter how many different methods we used to prove that a given essence was related to a particular meridian, there would always be exceptions. It is precisely these exceptions, or phenomena, which I personally believe cannot be discounted if we are to embrace a holistic health model and acknowledge the unique energetic configuration of each individual.

For instance, a young man came to my clinic and it was apparent to me through hearing his story, taking his pulses, and muscle testing that the channel which was most affected by his dis-ease was the Heart. So I went through the repertoire and tested him for all the essences which impact on the Heart, and he did not demonstrate a strong response to any of them. Then something which he said about how he felt when he was jilted by his girlfriend came back to me, and I decided to test Polyanthus which repeatedly shows up as being related to Lung and Large Intestine, and addresses the issue of self-worth. The muscle locked, both in his fingers and in the Heart related muscle, subscapularis. I gave him a drop of the essence under his tongue, and his Heart pulse, which had been deficient and thready, became full and regular. If I had only worked from the apparent information, I may never have discovered the precise remedy that could help this young man. In this particular case, Polyanthus turned out to be what I call the "root" remedy, in that it went straight to the source of his problem. Within a few weeks this man had recovered his sense of purpose, and his inner changes quickly became reflected in his outer life as well.

Information needs to be used creatively. I always experience more effective results when I am open to phenomena, not only the phenomenon of the person in front of me but also the possibility of discovering something new about the essences.

The field of vibrational medicine is not static and unchanging. In fact, one of the many joys entailed in this work is the constant potential for deeper insight. For example, we have used Candystick repeatedly and effectively for physical trauma in the pelvic area and lower back. And please note that this remedy is equally effective for men as well as women. However, it was only last year that we learned how this remedy works at a much deeper soul level. We received an interesting story from a woman who had never felt loved by her mother. While taking the Candystick essence she realized for the first time the depth of her mother's love. In fact she had spent 15 years in therapy attempting to resolve this feeling of being unloved by her mother, but it wasn't until she began working with this essence that she was able to really experience this love. Her mother had been a war bride and had the possibility of a very successful career, which she set side in order to give birth to this child. When she was 15 she remembers screaming at her mother: "I wish I had never been born." At which point, her mother turned around and slapped her. When she took the Candystick, all this conflict with her mother was remembered including this incident at age 15. What she understood was how much her mother had really wanted her in order to give up this other path. And finally after many years, she really understands about the choices that both she and her mother made in this life.

I truly believe that we all have the potential to access information about essences through many different modalities. All that is required initially is an element of innocence and trust. Then with some focused effort the journey seems to unfold by itself.

Balancer™

Another door that opened during the work with Dr. Adams was the discovery of the Balancer. The subject involved in the research was showing signs of stress and exhaustion when we were testing the Spring flowers. Although Michael kept clearing his energy fields, there was a distinct pattern of "overwhelm" beginning to manifest. As we were testing the Spring Flowers, Michael had noted that three of them together impacted on all the channels and chakras. So when we stopped for the day, he made a combination of these three essences and gave some to the subject. I wish I had had a camera to take before and after pictures. A man who had looked deflated and tired was transformed before our eyes. It was as if he had stepped under the cool revitalizing energy of a waterfall and emerged refreshed.

We began giving this combination to people who were experiencing severe stress, such as anxiety attacks, shock and grief from a sudden bereavement, or emotional, physical or mental exhaustion. The effects have been so remarkable that Pacific Essences now sells it as a special combination essence called the Balancer. It repeatedly offers harmony in the midst of turmoil no matter what the apparent cause.

Its action is immediate, safe, and effective. A powerful adjunct to any holistic health first aid kit, the Balancer can be used in any situation of psychic, emotional, or physical "overload." You can take 3 - 4 drops as required until the stress is diffused.

Heart Spirit®

The Heart Spirit essence was discovered by a patient who really wanted to heal all his old heart wounds. He requested from his essence practitioner that they create a combination comprised of all the essences in the original repertory that resonated with the heart chakra, the heart meridian, and the heart protector meridian. This resulted in a combination of: Death Camas, Easter Lily, Fireweed, Harvest Lily, Hooker's Onion, Grass Widow, Lily of the Valley, Nootka Rose, Ox-Eye Daisy, Periwinkle, Purple Magnolia, Salal, Snowberry, Twin Flower, and Windflower in the flowers and Barnacle, Jellyfish, Pink Seaweed, Sea Palm, and Surfgrass in the sea essences.

The results in this young man's life were so significant that both he and his practitioner began experimenting with this combination for others. He took the combination at a rate of 10 drops every 10 - 15 minutes. I encourage patients to experiment with the dosage that feels comfortable for them.

The Heart Spirit essence dissolves old heart pain and encourages us to truly embrace the "spirit of the heart."

In traditional Chinese medicine the "spirit of the heart," or Shen, is often translated as "God." Heart Spirit inspires the individual using it to embrace their divinity and to radiate Light.

The spirit of the heart is Love, Light, Laughter, Joy. It is Peace, Allowing, Embracing, Acceptance. It is Comfort, Ease, and Enthusiasm.

Heart Spirit kindles a space/time in our consciousness where we are able to respond from our hearts with generosity and ease.

Usually people notice a difference quite quickly when taking the Heart Spirit essence. And this shift is quickly noted by others in their lives, so that they find people commenting that they seem more relaxed, happier, more at ease, etc.

The primary effect of this essence is to raise the vibrational frequency of the heart centre to its highest range. It promotes self worth and lends new meaning to the dignity of being human. It allows us to interact with each other with grace, ease, and compassion. It is much needed on the earth plane at this time.

All our essences can be taken orally right out of the bottle, diluted in a glass of water, and/or used as a bath therapy.

The following correlations are based on a combination of inner wisdom, independent testing, and personal reports from people who have used the essences during the past 15 years. This is where we are now. I trust that as we continue to work with these essences the plants and sea creatures will reveal even more ways in which we can utilize their energy for our healing and growth and will also communicate to us how we can live more in attunement with the laws of Nature.

Sea Essences and The Channels of Chinese Medicine

LUNG .... Sand Dollar, Sea Horse

LARGE INTESTINE .... Starfish

STOMACH .... Hermit Crab, Sea Lettuce, Sea Palm, Sponge

SPLEEN .... Dolphin, Sea Turtle, Urchin

HEART .... Diatoms, Dolphin, Jellyfish

SMALL INTESTINE .... Barnacle, Sea Lettuce

BLADDER .... Brown Kelp, Sponge

KIDNEY .... Coral, Surfgrass

HEART PROTECTOR .... Pink Seaweed, Sea Turtle

TRIPLE WARMER .... Moon Snail, Rainbow Kelp

GALL BLADDER .... Mussel, "Staghorn" Algae

LIVER .... Anemone, Chiton

CONCEPTION VESSEL .... Whale

GOVERNING VESSEL .... Sea Horse, Whale

Flower Essences and The Channels of Chinese Medicine

LUNG .... Arbutus, Bluebell, Death Camas, Fairy Bell, Grape Hyacinth, Indian Pipe, Polyanthus, Purple Crocus, Vanilla Leaf

LARGE INTESTINE .... Camellia, Grass Widow, Polyanthus, Vanilla Leaf

STOMACH .... Grape Hyacinth, Grass Widow, Narcissus, Red Huckleberry, Wallflower, Windflower

SPLEEN .... Goatsbeard, Pipsissewa, Silver Birch, Viburnum, Wallflower

HEART .... Fireweed, Lily of the Valley, Periwinkle, Salal

SMALL INTESTINE .... Goatsbeard, Salal

BLADDER .... Blue Camas, Candystick, Easter Lily, Fuchsia, Salmonberry, Snowberry, Snowdrop, Yellow Pond Lily

KIDNEY .... Bluebell, Blue Camas, Candystick, Death Camas, Douglas Aster, Easter Lily, Fuchsia, Ox-Eye Daisy, Pipsissewa, Snowberry, Snowdrop

HEART PROTECTOR .... Alum Root, Harvest Lily, Ox-Eye Daisy, Purple Magnolia

TRIPLE WARMER .... Harvest Lily, Orange Honeysuckle, Poplar, Viburnum

GALL BLADDER .... Chickweed, Forsythia, Pearly Everlasting, Plantain, Poison Hemlock, Red Huckleberry, Twin Flower, Weigela

LIVER .... Arbutus, Blue Lupin, Pearly Everlasting, Plantain, Pipsissewa, Twin Flower, Weigela

CONCEPTION VESSEL .... Indian Pipe, Hooker's Onion

GOVERNING VESSEL .... Douglas Aster, Nootka Rose

Sea Essences and Chakras

Root .... Brown Kelp, Sea Horse, "Staghorn" Algae

Sacral .... Dolphin, Moon Snail, Mussel, Pink Seaweed, Sea Horse

Solar Plexus .... Anemone, Coral, Dolphin, Pink Seaweed, Sea Lettuce, Urchin

Heart .... Barnacle, Diatoms, Dolphin, Sea Palm, Sea Turtle, Surfgrass

Throat .... Chiton, Coral, Dolphin, Hermit Crab, Jellyfish, Sand Dollar,

Third Eye .... Dolphin, Rainbow Kelp, Whale

Crown .... Brown Kelp, Dolphin, Sponge, Starfish, Urchin, Whale

Navel .... Rainbow Kelp

Flower Essences and Chakras

Root .... Blue Lupin, Chickweed, Indian Pipe, Narcissus, Polyanthus, Snowdrop, Twin Flower

Sacral .... Candystick, Death Camas, Fuchsia, Narcissus, Orange Honeysuckle, Periwinkle, Plantain

Solar Plexus .... Blue Camas, Camellia, Harvest Lily, Orange Honeysuckle, Pipsissewa, Purple Magnolia, Red Huckleberry, Snowdrop, Wallflower

Heart .... Alum Root, Death Camas, Douglas Aster, Easter Lily, Fireweed, Grass Widow, Salal, Silver Birch, Snowberry, Twin Flower, Windflower

Throat .... Bluebell, Blue Camas, Candystick, Chickweed, Lily of the Valley, Pipsissewa, Poplar, Purple Crocus, Weigela, Windflower, Yellow Pond Lily

Third Eye .... Easter Lily, Fairy Bell, Goatsbeard, Grape Hyacinth, Ox-Eye Daisy, Pearly Everlasting, Salmonberry, Vanilla Leaf, Viburnum, Weigela

Crown .... Arbutus, Easter Lily, Forsythia, Harvest Lily, Periwinkle, Plantain, Poison Hemlock, Purple Magnolia, Snowdrop, Vanilla Leaf

Navel .... Pearly Everlasting

Back Neck .... Poplar

***All Chakras .... Hooker's Onion, Nootka Rose

Flower Essences

Alum Root

heuchera micrantha

the power of the small; manifestation of "god-ness"; ability to move in a pattern without having to do it "your" way; willingness to choose "to be"

Signature: Delicate sprays of tiny pinkish-white flowers on long stalks with heart shaped basal leaves grow on stream banks and in rock crevices.

A magnificent remedy for resolving and dissolving the power struggles that often manifest in relationship. When we are able to express ourselves in an uncomplicated and trusting manner all things are resolved with ease. This essence eliminates projections and helps us to come from our inner "light" being. Moves us from a place of judgment about the other to a place of good-natured and easy-going acceptance. Light always dispels the darkness.

This is an uplifting remedy which allows us to stay in our god-ness. When we are as tenacious about our personal commitment to evolution as this gentle little flower is to blossoming on rocky outcrops, then indeed we will be "enlightened".

Chakra: Heart

Meridian: Heart Protector

Key Words: Grace, Trust, Light-hearted, Beauty

Challenges: Power struggles, Conflict

Affirmation: I can respond to all conflict with grace and ease.

Alum Root – *Trust*

Let us celebrate life. Let us celebrate being –
being who you are with trust and gentleness
will lead you to enlightenment.

Arbutus

arbutus menziesii

spiritual tonic; enhances qualities of depth and integrity

Signature: A signature of the northwest coast, Arbutus trees grow 30 - 70 feet tall. They have bright reddish brown bark which peels off little by little in a 7-year cycle, a poignant reminder of the cyclical and changing nature of life. Flowers are white elongated clusters and carry a unique, and not unappealing, fragrance. The berries are edible. Boiled and mashed with honey, they taste a little like applesauce.

Arbutus helps us to experience ourselves as embodiment of Spirit. It alleviates the feeling of sadness which can occur when we feel limited by physical reality. It allows us to experience ourselves as Spirit unfolding.

This is the remedy to take when we feel lost and homesick, when all our efforts seem futile and we feel like orphans far away from our true home.

Physically, Arbutus affects Lungs which are always depleted by sadness. This is a remedy for being able to hang on tightly and let go lightly, embracing life experience and simultaneously recognizing that our lives are a fragment of a much larger, magnificent tapestry. The breath flows in and out without conscious direction. We can navigate the course of our lives with similar ease. There is a part of each of us that remembers who we really are and can access that connection to our Source. It is said that Hun, the spirit of the Wood element in Chinese medicine, is the only spirit that returns with us to successive incarnations. When the Liver is healthy, we are able to follow the impulse of our individual growth towards wholeness.

Emotionally it helps us to move through homesickness, the inner longing of the soul to find its true home.

Chakra:	Crown
Meridians:	Lung, Liver
Key Word:	Spirit
Challenges:	Homesickness, Longing, Abandonment
Affirmations:	I joyfully express Spirit. I appreciate the wisdom of life.

Arbutus – *Integrity*

You are in a state of integrity and inner alignment
only when you are connected to Spirit.

Bluebell

endymion non scriptus

for giving up constraints; opening the channels of communication

Signature: Clusters of tiny violet blue, bell-shaped flowers grow on stems of 8 - 24 inches. Their faces are hidden inside the bells and the flowers themselves seem disproportionately small in relation to the height of the stems. It is as if part of the plant wants to be seen and the flowers themselves want to go unnoticed.

Fear prevents us from expressing ourselves: fear of being noticed, fear of being ridiculed, fear of being punished. Very early in life we learned to behave in ways for which we were rewarded, and we carry these cell memories into adult life where they stifle our ability to align with and to express our inner being.

Bluebell helps us to release old programs and to engage in what really fulfills us. It allows us to step out from the imagined comfort of being in the crowd and to express our own uniqueness. It fortifies our courage to "follow our bliss."

The violet blue colour of Bluebell resonates with the Throat chakra, the centre of self-expression. It is effective for emotionally caused speech disorders and autistic behaviour patterns. It combats shyness and that feeling of discomfort that arises when we feel unable to make ourselves understood or when we are afraid of being judged.

At a physical level this remedy affects problems related to deficient energy in the Lung and Kidney channels. It boosts low energy and combats fatigue. It promotes the ability to breathe during panic or anxiety attacks. It strengthens the will and alleviates fear, especially fear of being seen and self-expression.

Chakra:	Throat
Meridians:	Lung, Kidney
Key Words:	Openness, Communication, Self-expression
Challenges:	Limitation, Shyness, Tongue-tied, Uncomfortable, Fatigue
Affirmation:	I am willing and able to express myself.

Bluebell – *Expression*

Let me raise my face to the sun. Let me sing the song of
my unique beauty throughout the universe.

I am small and I sing my song unceasingly for I am here to
offer you the ability to rejoice in expressing your own
unique face of the divine.

Blue Camas
camassia quamash

for acceptance and objectivity; balances the intuitive and the rational; unifies the right and left brain

Signature: Light to deep blue-violet, star shaped flowers growing 1 - 20 inches in height. The star has long been a symbol of the union of Spirit and Matter. In this regard the ability to access both inner knowing through the right brain and logic and rationality through the left brain is an important aspect of full human potential.

West Coast Indians pit-roasted the bulbs and also boiled them to make syrup. It was a major source of food for some of the Plains tribes.

Blue Camas is for the really creative person who tends to be a little impractical and for the down-to-earth practical person who is unable to access intuition. When we are unable to fully utilize both hemispheres of the brain it is like trying to fly with only one wing. In order to live fully we need to feel able to move effortlessly between logic and intuition.

The Solar Plexus chakra stores memory from previous incarnations. It is the seat of the ego and personal identity in this life. So a person may hold an unconscious memory of being burned at the stake for using inner wisdom in a previous life and choose in this life to be an IBM executive. The residual primal fear stored in the third chakra/Solar Plexus prevents them from feeling comfortable with intuition. Blue Camas does not necessarily release the fear, but it does prevent it from interfering with access to the whole brain. For instance, it allows the IBM executive to be a watercolour painter after work.

At a physical level this remedy works well with dyslexia and other learning disabilities, including the inability to learn from experience.

Chakras: Solar Plexus, Throat

Meridians: Kidney, Bladder

Key Words: Conscious, Balance, Perspective

Challenges: Learning disabilities, Inability to learn from experience

Affirmation: I am creative and practical.

Blue Camas – *Integration*

You have the potential of all opposites within your one self.
You are saint and sinner, good and bad, dark and light.
You are feminine and masculine, yang and yin.

Let me show you how to delight in the full expression
of all these aspects of yourself.

Blue Lupin
lupinus rivularis

for clear and precise thinking

Signature: Purple or blue "pea flowers" on spikes growing 2 - 5 feet on hollow stems. Each little flower is shaped like the organ of the Liver. From its Latin name, lupus, meaning wolf, it was once believed to act like a wolf by devouring all the nutrients from the soil. In fact, Blue Lupins are usually found in very poor soil, like roadside ditches. Blue Lupin essence has the power to devour and to transmute toxins via the Liver channel, and this may be a more accurate description of its value.

This remedy links the pineal gland, the organ of spiritual perception, with the pituitary gland, the organ of metabolic control and balance. The optimal functioning of these two glands is essential for eliminating confusion and remembering who we are.

Blue Lupin can help to alleviate feelings of depression which arise from not being able "to see the forest for the trees" and helps us to focus our attention. It simplifies issues.

Blue Lupin impacts on the Liver channel, which is often referred to as the organ of detoxification and helps to maintain clarity and purity within the physical system. The emotion of the Liver is anger, which is just another energy in motion. When we hang on to anger it becomes frustration, depression, and even despair. Blue Lupin works to purify the emotional body of anger residue so that we can fully access our mental potential.

With Blue Lupin, the Body/Mind templates are clear and the physical survival energy of the Root chakra is transformed to the spiritual survival of the soul.

Primarily working at a mental level this essence will also impact upon the physical discomforts of toxin-related headaches and digestive disorders.

Chakra:	Root
Meridian:	Liver
Key Words:	Clarity, Focus
Challenges:	Confusion, Frustration, Despair
Affirmations:	I can see clearly. I can think clearly.

Blue Lupin – *Focus*

I grace your roadside ditches with my tall purplish cones,
standing stately and proud. My leaves are like
fireworks exploding green.

Let me remember that while I reach towards heaven my task
on earth is to live my purpose.

I offer you clarity of thought and purity of emotions.
I offer you the ability to focus and to see clearly.

Camellia
camellia sasanqua

catalyst for opening to new attitudes which reflect one's true inner nature

Signature: The buds begin with a delicate pink tip emerging from a tightly packed calyx of thick protective sepals. As the spring sunshine warms the buds they open into large composite blooms. When they are fully open you can see many delicate, fringe-like stamens – the heart of the flower, representing a full opening to life experience.

Camellia is an essence of expansion beyond self-inflicted limitations. It allows us to express the unique aspect of the vital force within us and to align with our own inner power. We can release old thought and behaviour patterns which do not serve us well.

Via the Solar Plexus chakra, Camellia releases cell memory of earlier experiences in this life. As a child we may have felt shamed by our inability to do something or by doing something which we were told was bad. This guilt and shame is stored in the Solar plexus chakra where it can run interference in current life experience. Camellia helps us to respond to present experience with grace-fulness. It assists the Large Intestine channel to eliminate old feelings, thoughts, and attitudes about ourselves. It accesses self-trust and creates attitudinal shifts. By dissolving our protective armour we can transform into flexibility and openness.

Chakra:	Solar Plexus
Meridian:	Large Intestine
Key Words:	Vision, Openness, Self-expression
Challenges:	Guilt, Shame, Closed to new experience
Affirmations:	I am true to myself. I am open to life experience.

Camellia – Opening

My gift for you is opening. Opening to life. Opening to
possibilities. Opening to new thoughts and feelings.
If I don't open, my buds harden and break off.

When I allow myself to be loved by the sun and the rain the
life coursing through my veins bursts forth in a perfect
expression of my inner self.

Guilt and shame keep you stuck in the past. Step forward
into the Light of your being and allow us to see you.

Candystick
allotropa virgata

physical tonic; releases pelvic tension and promotes pelvic alignment

Signature: *Candystick may be mistaken for fungus because it has no chlorophyll and grows sporadically in the deep shade of coniferous forests on red and white striped stalks. It produces tiny white or pink flowers on large red ovaries on the upper stalk of the plant. Its narrow, white leaves which point heavenward signify the ability of the soul to weather and to transcend the "dark night of the soul."*

Releases any blocked energy around abortion, miscarriage, birth and sexuality. It helps to transform self-anger and frustration at these times and to honour the self despite the trauma. It allows one to gain perspective.

In the case of abortion it is about learning to live with and being willing to honour our own choice.

In the case of miscarriage it is about being willing to honour the free will of the unborn soul.

At a much deeper level Candystick is about honouring the mystery of life – phenomena unfolding. It links the energies of the sacral and throat chakras both of which are connected to freedom of individual expression.

Physically, Candystick is useful for any injuries to the sacrum or pelvic girdle. For women it is helpful for any insult to the reproductive system – surgery, miscarriage, abortion.

Chakras:	Sacral, Throat
Meridian:	Kidney, Bladder
Key Word:	Survival
Challenge:	Free Will
Affirmations:	I am willing to take responsibility for my choices.
	I accept the free will of other beings.

Candystick – *Purpose*

Each soul has its own unique path. Find your own.

Use the signals of comfort and discomfort from your
Body/Mind to let Spirit communicate with you.
Then follow this inner guidance.

Chickweed
stellaria media

acknowledging and experiencing timelessness; being fully present and able to respond

Signature: The genus name comes from the small, white, star-shaped flower growing 4 - 16 inches tall on straggly succulent stems. The tiny white flowers are like beacons of light to guide consciousness. The common name is derived from its use as bird feed. The crushed plant has been used in poultices for arthritic joints; homeopathically it is used for the treatment of rheumatism.

This remedy is about harnessing all resources and being fully present without any thought of what has come before or what might transpire in the future. It allows us to be in the cosmic flow and to respond impeccably, as if each action has impact on the whole.

Chickweed nourishes the Throat chakra and allows us to express ourselves freely and easily. It supports the Gall Bladder channel to release tension and to give up its need for control. We can lighten up and experience the magic of this instant!

This is an excellent remedy for releasing grievances from the past and for "taking no thought" for the future. It helps us to see ourselves and our world as if this moment is the only time there is.

Chickweed is most helpful for health practitioners, therapists and counsellors who need to be able to be present and available for their clients. It is also effective when one is stuck in any kind of emotional drama or thought process.

Primarily a mental and spiritual essence, we have also received reports that it has been used effectively for losing weight. Excess weight can often represent a kind of stuckness, and carrying the baggage from old emotional hurts.

Chakras:	Throat, Root
Meridian:	Gall Bladder
Key Words:	Present, Available, Response-ability
Challenges:	Bitterness, Resentment, Unavailable
Affirmations:	I am able to respond to life as it unfolds before me. I am available and present.

Chickweed – *Present*

Lighten up. Let go.

Remember how absolutely "present" you were the first time
you saw stars twinkling in the sky.

Death Camas
zygadenus venenosus

spiritual rebirth; awareness of spiritual connection with all of life

Signature: Very different from the showy Blue Camas, Death Camas presents umbrella clusters of small white flowers on top of a leafless stalk. The flower heads are very bold in appearance, representing the boldness and courage required to face new challenges.

The bulbs are almost identical to those of Blue Camas, and early settlers and Indians were sometimes poisoned from eating them by mistake.

When it feels as if the whole world is crumbling, this remedy reminds us of the eternal thread which holds all of life together – the endless dance of the ebb and flow of energy. "What appears to be the end of the world to the caterpillar, the master calls a butterfly." (Bach)

This is a remedy for beginning new jobs, new relationships, starting any new adventure, or ending any of these. It alleviates stress and worry in times of transition and enables us to appreciate the experience as an opportunity to shed another skin that we have outgrown. It embodies courage and fearlessness which leads us to ecstasy and transformation.

Death Camas is the Tower in Tarot symbolism. The Tower represents sudden and unexpected change, giving us an opportunity for purification at all levels.

Death Camas is also especially helpful when we deliberately choose to do a process of self-cleansing – fasting, examination of beliefs, etc.

Chakras:	Sacral, Heart
Meridians:	Lung, Kidney
Key Words:	Rebirthing, Beginnings, Ecstasy, Transformation
Challenges:	New beginnings, Change
Affirmations:	I am in tune with the Infinite.
	I go with the flow.

Death Camas – *Rebirth*

The tree is in the seed manifest in the tree.

The energy of spring comes to fullness in summer,
retreats in autumn and sleeps in winter.

Every moment is a new beginning.

Douglas Aster
aster subspicatus

endless expansion while maintaining centre; savouring life experience; living fully and consciously; promotes courage and adaptability

Signature: Emerging from rocky outcroppings along the shoreline of the Pacific Ocean this small purple flower gladdens our hearts from July to October. It flourishes in very thin soil and literally looks as if it is growing in the rock. It manifests immense tenacity and a secure sense of self. Its purple rays emanate from a golden disk in its centre. In its natural habitat it braves all the elements with ease.

We can only feel expansive and manifest our inner shaman when we are connected to our source. Then whatever turbulence we encounter is easily weathered. This flower reminds us to savour experience and helps us to find our centre/source/god-ness within, for this is our true nature. Its strength is its adaptability.

This essence helps us to attune more easily with our senses and sensory experience without losing ourselves in the process of participating in life to the fullest. It heightens perception so that we are able to appreciate the celestial energies underlying physical manifestations. When we experience life at this level, our hearts are filled with gratitude.

Douglas Aster also helps us to stay centred in the face of many demands.

Chakra:	Heart
Meridian:	Kidney, Governing Vessel
Key Words:	Expansion, Generosity, Adaptability
Challenges:	Attachment, Ego, Clinging
Affirmation:	From the centre of my being I radiate generosity and love.

Douglas Aster – *Radiance*

What joy there is in expansion.
What delight in self expression.

I am a channel for the Light of heaven.

Drink of my essence and replenish your life force/source.

Easter Lily

erythronium oreganum

encourages free expression of self; eliminates social masks

Signature: The plant has solitary white, lily-like flowers which bloom on a graceful stem with two beautiful mottled leaves. The exquisitely curled white petals remind one of the flying nun and at a deeper level symbolize purity and freedom. Matthew Wood, homeopath and herbalist, recognizes this remedy as very helpful for premenstrual syndrome.

Easter Lily helps to integrate the different aspects of our personalities, allowing us to express ourselves openly and honestly.

Its connection to the Crown chakra makes it particularly effective as a tool for getting past the roles we assume in order to make ourselves more attractive to others. When we express our inner being from the Heart centre or serve as a channel for universal energy through the Crown chakra, the power of that energy alignment is so strong that we become as light shining away the darkness of illusion.

Connected to the Water element in Chinese medicine, Easter Lily affects both the Kidney and Bladder channels. The Water element is in charge of vital energy reserves in the Body/Mind and controls our ability to adapt to stress. Water always finds a course around obstacles in its path. It flows.

The Kidney channel stores the vital essence which is the energy matrix necessary for the formation of Qi. Easter Lily helps us to discover and to express the "pearl in the oyster," the "diamond in the lump of coal."

For women, Easter Lily has proved to be highly effective for Premenstrual Syndrome and other gynecological imbalances.

Chakras:	Heart, Third Eye, Crown
Meridians:	Kidney, Bladder
Key Words:	Truth, Purity, Integrity, Honesty
Challenges:	Duplicity, Dishonesty, Illusion
Affirmations:	I am who I am. I am that I am.

Easter Lily *– Authenticity*

As a butterfly emerges from its cocoon,
I emerge from the dark, wet winter soil.

I show you a pair of mottled leaves and then a single stem
which supports my bowed, white head.

As I feel my space in this outer world, I open my petals.
With a little more encouragement from the sun,
I lift my face to the world and let you see all of me.

Let me show you how to express the truth
and beauty of who you are.

Fairy Bell
disporum smithii

lighthearted release from murky thoughts; expands willingness to follow one's guidance; eases depression

Signature: *Growing in moist and shaded areas these cream-coloured cylindrical bells chime their soundless melody in the forest darkness. The plant itself grows low to the ground and the bell-like flowers emerge from beneath the leaves and face the earth. In the fall the flowers are replaced by orange-red berries.*

This is a gentle remedy to assist us to find the light when the mental darkness seems overwhelming and endless. It thaws frozen feelings and frozen body patterns.

It can help through the pain of a healing crisis emotionally and physically, sometimes providing a mild sedative effect.

It puts an end to ambiguity, especially any ambiguity about wanting to be here on the earth plane and in physical form. Physically it frees the lungs and eases the breathing.

It dispels any resistance to growth and reminds us that when we are in touch with our true nature every breath is a prayer. It can be used to assist a newborn to take its first breath and allows the rest of us to breathe into and through our feelings, especially dark feelings like despair.

The plant signature reminds us that guidance is always available and only our own resistance prevents us from accessing inner wisdom.

Chakra:	Third Eye
Meridian:	Lung
Key Words:	Lightness of being
Challenges:	Ambiguity, Resistance, Depression
Affirmation:	I am at ease. This too shall pass.

Fairy Bell – *Vulnerability*

Let me show you the incredible lightness of being.
Let me light your way. Let me guide you with my bells.
Let me lead you on the path of Light.

Discard your heavy feelings. Discard your murky thoughts.
Come with me and dance the steps of life.

Fireweed
epilobium angustifolium

realization of the abundance of love both within and without

Signature: A tall herbaceous plant with brilliant magenta flowers which grow in elongated clusters at the top of tall, erect, leafy stems. Metaphysically, magenta is the colour associated with emotional balance. The tender young shoots make an excellent vegetable and the dried leaves make a delicious tea. Beekeepers often set their hives in Fireweed patches to make honey.

With its connection to the Fire element and the Heart chakra, Fireweed dissolves fear and makes way for love.

Emotional experience is recorded on the Heart. In Chinese medicine, the Heart is the home of Shen, or consciousness. When our heart is broken or damaged from excessive emotional insult, the Spirit does not feel at home, and becomes restless. It can even temporarily vacate the body, as in cases of severe shock. Fireweed eases the Heart and gently coaxes the Shen back into embodiment. It allows us to experience love as a vital force in our lives and dissolves feelings of separation from self and others.

Physically this remedy improves circulation. It softens muscles and fascia in the chest and upper back.

Emotionally it allow us to embrace each relationship as a new experience without residue from previous ones.

After a forest has been clear cut and slash burned, Fireweed is the first plant to grow. One can see a purple magenta haze over the ugly burned stumps. This is Mother Earth's way of loving herself back to health.

Chakra:	Heart
Meridian:	Heart
Key Words:	Love, Loving, Lovable
Challenges:	Coldness, Uncaring, Inability to feel, Emotional wounds
Affirmation:	I am loving and lovable.

Fireweed – *Compassion / Service*

I cover the earth with a blanket of magenta haze.
I offer Mother Earth my love to heal her scarred surface.

I offer my fragrance to the honey bees.

I give and receive love and awaken the
loving potential within you.

Forsythia
forsythia suspensa

provides motivation towards transformation of old, useless patterns of behaviour – eg. habits, addictions, thoughts; helps to break addictions

Signature: *The flowers are bright yellow with 4 petals connected at the base. They bloom on leafless bushes in the early spring, the time of new beginnings.*

In herbalism yellow flowers are often used to detoxify the Liver which bears the greatest burden in the physical when we are addicted to a substance. The sturdy branches, on which the flowers are the first sign of new life, represent the strength of will required to change patterns.

Forsythia is the remedy for addictive mental, emotional, and physical patterns – those which fill us with self-loathing and yet we feel powerless to change. It grants us the ability to find our way out of the darkness and into light.

Forsythia helps us to respond intuitively and spontaneously with what really is "right action" for us. It is a catalyst for change.

Physically it can be used effectively for breaking alcohol, drug, and tobacco addictions.

Mentally it can release repetitive thought patterns which no longer serve us.

Emotionally it affords us the opportunity to release dysfunctional relationship patterns and long held grievances.

Chakra:	Crown
Meridian:	Gall Bladder
Key Words:	Transformation, Motivation
Challenge:	Self-destruction
Affirmations:	I am willing to change. I have the inner resources and energy required to change.

Forsythia – *Motivation / Transformation*

Allow the golden yellow of my blossoms to bathe you
in the Light of transformation.

Let me strengthen your willingness to move forward
to your perfect expression of Self.

Fuchsia
fuchsia

re-creation; letting go of dysfunctional patterns; being the change we wish to see in the world

Signature: *These multi-coloured plant spirits are like twirling, swirling ballerinas, always appearing to be moving even on a day with no wind. Ranging in a full spectrum of shades of white, red, pink, and purple, they gladden the heart and delight the eye. The flower emerges like a tear drop that breaks open into 4 outer petals which curl back and reveal a complete inner flower.*

Dancing coloured lights expressing their delight in just "being." This remedy helps the slow, phlegmatic type to "lighten up" and move. It helps the fast, busy, over-doing type to slow down, "chill out" and relax. Fuchsia is a remedy of balance. Helps to peel the layers of programming of "acceptable" behaviour patterns, and allows us to begin to attune with and to step with our own inner rhythms. It is a remedy for recognizing the little voice of the super ego - all the "oughts" and "shoulds" and being able to turn into what I really want. Behaviour shifts, and there is a measure of satisfaction and joy in being that cannot be experienced until we experience this level of self-actualization.

A constitutional remedy for the Water element it tonifies and nourishes both the Kidney and Bladder channels.

Chakra:	Sacral
Meridian:	Kidney, Bladder
Key Words:	Balance, Self-actualization
Challenges:	Procrastination, Sloth and Torpor
Affirmation:	I am the change I wish to see in the world.

Fuchsia – *Re-creation*

You think you're stuck with the script you have?

You think the past is etched in stone?

Wake up! Wake up!

You are the author. You are the director. You are the actor.

And in each moment you have the ability to create it,
all of it, exactly as you want/desire.

Let me help you re-create your journey.

Goatsbeard
aruncus sylvester

accesses the power to visualize oneself in a state of deep relaxation

Signature: Large filmy clouds of tiny white flowers cascade from a tall bush. The blooms give the impression of a gentle waterfall of rejuvenating energy.

Goatsbeard enables us to see ourselves as calm and relaxed in stressful situations. It activates the thymus gland to deal with stress effectively. This is the remedy of non-action, of resolving tension by creating a state of inner alignment before taking action.

Goatsbeard reminds us that desires can be fulfilled only when we are willing to balance mental, physical and emotional by pausing in peace. Only then can we be fully able to respond to whatever life presents to us. Rest before activity brings greater fulfilment from the action.

Primarily a remedy for the Mental aspect, it is also related to the Small Intestine meridian in Chinese medicine and assists with the assimilation of experience. Its connection with the Spleen strengthens the immune system and promotes the production of white blood cells.

Physically it will be helpful with any stress-related disorder by permitting us to relax and to rejuvenate our body chemistry.

For people who are using visualization as a primary tool in self-healing, this remedy is of great assistance in the centring process.

Chakra:	Third Eye
Meridians:	Small Intestine, Spleen
Key Words:	Fantasy, Meditation, Creative Visualization
Challenges:	Tension, Tightness, Holding
Affirmation:	I feel tension and stress dissolving.

Goatsbeard – *Rejuvenation*

Let me bathe you with my healing white cascade of flowers.

Let me nourish your wei qi. Let me support your immunity.

I am the energy of the goat – sure footed and determined.
I give you the ability of the cat –
to sink down into the ground of being where harmony prevails.

Grape Hyacinth
muscari racemosum

for times of external shock, despair, stress – allows the individual to step back from the situation while harnessing inner resources to meet the challenge.

Signature: *Stalwart little warriors are armed in elongated clusters of deep blue to indigo flowers which appear somewhat like the chain mail armour of the knights of the middle ages. The indigo colour is especially harmonious for the Third Eye centre.*

This is the remedy which comes up at times of any stress or trauma to the system, either emotional or physical. It allows for some space to re-integrate the systems before responding to the situation at hand.

Often the first place we experience stress physically is in the "gut." Grape Hyacinth harmonizes the Stomach. Via the Lung channel, it assists us to keep breathing in times of stress instead of holding our breath and cutting off the life force.

It can be used with bumps, bruises, accidents, shocks, and any emotional trauma.

Through its connection to the pineal gland, Grape Hyacinth dissolves feelings of despair – that place of utter hopelessness when we feel totally disconnected from our centre. Because of its connection to this gland it is also effective for some forms of depression.

Chakra:	Third Eye
Meridians:	Stomach, Lung
Key Words:	Balance, Perspective
Challenges:	Shock, Trauma, Despair
Affirmation:	I am balanced and whole.

Grape Hyacinth – *Balance / Perspective*

Shocks and traumas –
just part of the earth journey
to keep you on your toes
and remind you of your true Nature.

Grass Widow
sisyrinchium douglasii

releases old beliefs and limiting patterns

Signature: Magenta bowl-shaped flowers blooming from clumps of narrow sword-like leaves. The leaves symbolize the mental incisiveness necessary to be aligned with our own inner wisdom. The colour symbolizes emotional balance.

Primarily a mental remedy, Grass Widow assists us to question our beliefs and to be able to change them if they are not working for us. If we are not radiant and at peace with ourselves, this essence assists in identifying the underlying belief pattern and strengthens the will to release it. This includes beliefs about ourselves and others.

Grass Widow relates to the challenges of the structures we have chosen in this life – family, work, religion, etc. The choice can be to detach from the structures which are not in alignment with our greater purpose.

Mentally it relates to the indigestibility of unevaluated beliefs and physically to digestion problems especially those related to food intolerances.

Emotionally it relates to the fear around letting go of the illusion of comfortable discomfort if we find ourselves in a belief system which does not have the support of mass consciousness.

Chakra:	Heart
Meridians:	Stomach, Large Intestine
Key Word:	Freedom
Challenge:	Fear of being judged by others
Affirmations:	I release limitation. I am unlimited.

Grass Widow – *Freedom*

Expand your mind.

Examine your beliefs.

Push against the edges of your reality.

It's self-created, you know.

Harvest lily
brodiaea coronaris

supportive to group energy; supports the ability to see another's point of view

Signature: Violet, funnel-shaped flowers with three white non-fertile stamens shaped like fans in their centres. There are as many as seven flowers on one stem. They remain erect and open towards heaven throughout the growing season. The violet colour indicates its resonance with the Crown chakra, and the three white stamens symbolize our ability to connect with universal Light.

West Coast Indians used to dig the corms and eat them raw or cooked.

This is a remedy of expansion and awakening. It helps the individual to move beyond ego boundaries and to begin to appreciate "other" as the same Self. Here the potential for true community exists. Real community can only evolve from that place of "Namaste" – a Sanskrit word meaning "I acknowledge that place in you where we are both the same."

Harvest Lily works with the Fire element in Chinese medicine and especially the Triple Warmer and Heart Protector meridians. Both of these channels have to do with relationship. It is useful for resolving tensions in interpersonal relationships. When an individual feels harmonious and balanced, that energy radiates out into the group.

Emotionally, it provides an energy matrix for the unification of group energy. It is particularly helpful when two opposing groups are involved in negotiating a win/win outcome.

This remedy can be generally applied to disorders of reproduction and elimination, digestion and absorption, or respiratory and cardiac problems if their source is an imbalance in Fire.

Chakras:	Solar Plexus, Crown
Meridians:	Triple Warmer, Heart Protector
Key Words:	Community, Relationship
Challenges:	Social interaction
Affirmations:	I radiate my beauty and vitality. I recognize the beauty and vitality in others.

Harvest Lily *– Resolution*

Let me show you community, where many can be nourished
from the same source and still express their individuality.
I emerge through the tangles of dried summer grass.
There are many me's connected to the one vine.

Let me teach you how to see each other as a reflection of
your self so that without compromise or sacrifice
you can reach attunement and agreement.

Hooker's Onion
allium cernuum

for feeling light-hearted and refreshed; nurtures creativity

Signature: Pink and white flower clusters nodding gently from tall, thin stems. There is a quality of lightness and freedom of expression about these delicate blooms.

The bulb carries a strong onion smell and was used for food by coastal Indians who taught early explorers to use it for its curative powers against scurvy.

Primarily a remedy for Spirit, Hooker's Onion has direct impact on all seven major chakras, gently unfolding the full potential of each energy centre to work in harmony together. It creates a vital and harmonious link between heaven and earth.

Years ago when I asked for a dream with this essence, I was visited by the Hooker's Onion Deva. She was clothed in shimmering pink and silver and moved like a light beam in the forest. She led me to a hallway where there were many doors. Each door was labelled with the particular creative venture to which it would lead. She said: *"You are only limited by your thoughts of limitation. Leave these dense thoughts at the door and enter with expectation and joy."*

I awoke feeling nurtured and inspired. Hooker's Onion acts as a catalyst for creative expression and lightens the heart. It helps to dissolve writer's block.

This remedy also has the potential to release birth traumas. It dissolves the fear for both mother and child as physical separation occurs and helps to maintain the real connection at the level of Spirit. It is effective for post-partum depression. It resolves the emotional attachment – the "my child" syndrome – that inhibits a full and rewarding relationship between parents and children.

Chakras:	all 7 major chakras
Meridians:	all 12 meridians
Key Words:	Light, Freedom, Inspiration, Creativity, Spontaneity
Challenges:	Overwhelmed, Frustrated, Stuck, Dense, Heavy
Affirmations:	I am Light. I am a clear channel for Light and Creativity.

Hooker's Onion – Inspiration

When my luminescent sac cracks open
I am released from heaviness.

My tiny pink flowers are light and free.
I am deeply connected to Spirit.

Let me inspire you. Let me breathe new life
into your heart and mind.

Let me help you to free your creativity.

Indian Pipe
monotropa uniflora

reconciliation with others and making peace with self; reverence for all of life

Signature: White translucent stems and pipe-bowl shaped flowers characterize this small saprophyte which grows in the dark gloom of the forest. Clearly identifiable as a single plant these ethereal beings are always found in community. Native people used Indian Pipe to make poultices for wounds that would not heal.

In Indian Pipe we find the ability to "stand alone in closeness," so that we can be fully in relationship and community while maintaining and expressing our own unique qualities of being. It fosters self-respect and respect for others. It resolves the inner voices that endlessly cloud the beauty of our true inner being. It counteracts negative self talk and banishes feelings of worthlessness, so that we can easily find and live our life purpose.

For native peoples pipes were a representation of drawing in Spirit to earthly matters. Smoking the peace pipe after battle with one's enemies was an invitation to Spirit to bless the new relationship.

Indian Pipe is a constitutional remedy for the Metal element, helping us to express ourselves in the world and to recognize and to claim what is valuable.

Chakra:	Root
Meridian:	Lung, Conception Vessel
Key Words:	Reconciliation, Reverence
Challenges:	Illusion, Separation
Affirmation:	We are all one.

Indian Pipe – *Reverence*

Think of me when you need/want to create sacred space.

Even when physical space is limited,
you can hold a space in your consciousness.

Let me teach you how to honour yourself and
each other in this manner.

Let me show you the sanctity of the earth and all life on it.

Lily of the Valley
convallaria majalis

allows for freedom of choice by discovering the simplest mode of behaviour

Signature: The tiny white bells look so real that you can almost hear their soothing chimes. The gentle fragrance calms the mind and transports us to a place of unconditional love.

Lily of the Valley brings us back to that state of child-like innocence and wisdom where we only know how to respond with loving behaviour. It puts us in touch with that place within ourselves that existed before our lives were complicated by "shoulds" and all the other layers of conditioning we learned in order to survive and to get love and approval.

Lily of the Valley is an emotional tonic which helps us to see "through the eyes of a child." It connects us with the inner radiance and vitality in the heart centre. It helps us to listen with the ears of the heart and gives us the courage to express ourselves with clarity, trust, simplicity and ease.

People who live their lives bound by convention and seeking social approval can benefit from Lily of the Valley. Through its gentle energy each person can access their own unique essence within.

In eastern Europe, Lily of the Valley is used as a cardiac tonic and contains some of the same chemical constituents as Foxglove which produces digitalis.

Chakra:	Throat
Meridian:	Heart
Key Words:	Simplicity, Innocence
Challenges:	Sophistication, Over-Control, Rigidity
Affirmations:	I embrace life with an open heart.
	I embrace my own uniqueness.

Lily of the Valley – *Simplicity / Innocence*

Remember when you had no expectations?

Remember when one day ran into the next in flowing time?

Remember when the rhythm of your life was every moment
a unique unfolding?

Through connecting with me you can re-connect with that
time/space, which was not time/space, rhythm.

Moved from inner Spirit and experiencing BLISS.

Narcissus
narcissus pseudo-narcissus

for identification and resolution of conflicts by going to the centre of the problem/fear. From there the issue(s) can be faced by determining what is essential and nurturing to the Self.

Signature: Seven creamy white petals open to show a golden orange fluted cup in the centre. In traditional Tarot cards, the suit of Cups represent feelings and emotions. Narcissus looks as if it is smiling at the world, gracefully digesting experience. Its keynote however is its sweet perfume which can permeate a whole house bringing calmness and peace of mind.

Narcissus is the slayer of internal dragons, the little voices of fear which surface when life experiences seem to be a cycle of endless challenges. It helps us to digest experiences and use them for further growth. It calms that feeling of "butterflies in the Stomach." In Chinese medicine the Earth element requires support through nourishment. In the healthy Stomach channel the energy flows downwards from heaven to earth. When this flow is disrupted due to undigested ideas or emotions, there is a tendency for the energy flow to reverse and disturb the mind. This imbalance manifests as a preoccupation with details and obsessive thinking.

Narcissus affects the Root chakra, our connection to the earth and our impulse for survival. It assists us to feel really grounded.

Physically, Narcissus promotes digestion and helps with digestive disorders – excess stomach acid, ulcers, gas, and belching.

Mentally it alleviates worry.

Chakras:	Root, Sacral
Meridian:	Stomach
Key Words:	Safety, Nurturing
Challenges:	Worry, Anxiety
Affirmation:	I am safe.

Narcissus – *Nurturing*

Drink from my cup of life.

Bathe your soul in my creamy softness.

Breathe my scent and kindle the fire of Spirit within you.

Nootka Rose
rosa nutkana

expressing love of life, laughter, and joy

Signature: *Pale pink flowers growing on a thorny shrub. The gentle smell of roses permeates the forests where they grow. The rose hips are a good natural source of vitamin C and may also be used to make jams and jellies.*

Native Indians of the West Coast used to bury their dead with Nootka Rose to ensure a safe and happy journey into the next life.

Nootka Rose is the embodiment of Spirit. It centres us in the Heart chakra, promotes laughter and joy, and dissolves bitterness and resentment.

This is a spiritual remedy. It is a reminder that the life of the soul does not begin with physical birth, nor end with physical death. It is the remedy to take when the thorns of life experience are too sharp. It allows us to embrace life even when we have sustained major trauma to the physical, emotional, or mental. It is an excellent remedy for those who have experienced "spiritual crisis" – abuse, abandonment, psychic, emotional, or physical assault. It helps to reintegrate the psyche after such assault and can heal fragmentation even years after the experience. Even if the cause is self-abuse, as in the use of recreational drugs or alcohol, the effects are the same. It is for all those experiences where the Soul does not feel safe in the physical vehicle. Emotionally it balances the Heart Protector to make way for love in the heart itself.

Chakras:	all 7 major chakras
Meridians:	all 12 meridians
Key Words:	Enthusiasm (en theos – in God)
Challenges:	Weariness, Abuse, Abandonment
Affirmations:	I am an aspect of the Divine.
	I am a spark of the Infinite.

Nootka Rose – *Love*

Let me take your cares from you.
Let me show you that the thorns of life are part of the whole.
I offer my beauty and fragrance along with my thorns.
Life is like the rose –
the thorns which you experience are a gift.
You can choose to keep your wounds open and bleeding
or you can move forward into the Light.

Orange Honeysuckle
lonicera ciliosa

evokes peaceful creativity

Signature: Bright orange clusters of tubular flowers growing from two cup-shaped leaves on bushes 8 to 25 feet tall.

The keynote of this flower is its brilliant orange colour which is the colour to stimulate digestion. It is a powerful tonic for digestive disorders.

Orange is also the colour which harmonizes the Sacral chakra. This second chakra governs power and creativity, not only in the act of physical pro-creation but also the direction and expression of that energy into other creative channels. In this regard Orange Honeysuckle is effective for women going through menopause who have directed a lot of energy into birthing and raising their families. When their children leave home they often feel lost and have no outlet for the expression of this energy. It is also useful for teenagers where the volatility and turmoil of puberty can be channelled towards life-supporting creative expression. It is not about life changes per se, but about changes where energy has been directed in one way and that particular form of expression is no longer available. Often this results in a crisis of personal identity and accompanying tension in the physical body. Orange Honeysuckle helps us to tap into that place of inner body wisdom and to redirect the energy accordingly.

At the emotional level, it releases blocks to the creative force and thereby diffuses the frustration, or even anger, which arises when creative expression is thwarted.

It can transform sexual energy to be directed in other creative channels and can help to release us from the bondage of desires.

Chakras:	Sacral, Solar Plexus
Meridian:	Triple Warmer
Key Words:	Creative Expression, Inner direction
Challenges:	Identity, Lost, Anger
Affirmations:	I am creative.
	I find rest and calm in the full expression of my creativity.

Orange Honeysuckle – *Creativity*

Let my orange blooms revitalize you.

I am like the fallopian tubes releasing an egg to be fertilized.

Let me release the potential of the egg into the fertile ground of your being. When you are at a point of transition in your life, allow me to help you direct your energy towards creative expression.

Ox-Eye Daisy
chrysanthemum leucanthemum

total perspective; for being centred

Signature: The flower presents as a golden disk with slender white rays encircling it. The petals reach out towards more expansive vision. Somewhat resembling an eye, it is a perfect mandala, a symbol for focusing.

This is the remedy for vision and the visionary. It helps to move out of positions of being overfocused and allows us to tune into a larger perspective. When we can access the "big picture" we are able to put things together in a new way – synthesis/alchemy. Ox-Eye Daisy helps us to synthesize the elements of our lives in new and creative ways.

The golden yellow centre is a safe place from which to view all of life while maintaining a connection with our own inner being.

Related to the Kidney meridian and the Third Eye chakra, it dissolves the energy blocks of fear which prevent us from seeing clearly.

Physically it impacts on the eyes and ears and helps to develop better vision. It is the remedy of choice when we are really striving to see something in a new light, to gain perspective and understanding.

Chakra:	Third Eye
Meridians:	Heart Protector, Kidney
Key Word:	Perspective
Challenges:	Over-focused, Not being able to see the forest for the trees
Affirmation:	I am able to see things differently.

***Ox-Eye Daisy** – Perspective*

I sit on a golden cushion in the heart of the flower.
I can see in all directions and from every point in the circle.
I am a perfect mandala and I offer you the ability
to see all of life unfolding.

Meditate with me and find the peaceful centre where
you too can tap into infinite possibilities.

Pearly Everlasting
anaphalis margaritacea

commitment and lasting devotion; opening to the mysteries of life; transformation through service

Signature: Clusters of tiny white flowers with tight yellow centres bloom atop a long stem. The flowers appear dry and indeed need little water and last a very long time even after being cut.

White is the colour of Spirit and indeed these tiny white blooms bring the potential for lasting devotion to any relationship. When we are connected at a soul level it is easy to remain beautiful in the eyes of the beloved.

This flower essence helps us to deepen our connection with the other. The purifying fire of anger becomes a powerful ally which can be used to create transformation. Another remedy which helps us to stay connected to source and to bring the earth plane "stuff" into perspective.

Don't throw the baby out with the bathwater. Remember the Source to which we are all connected and from which we all emerge.

In the West we have many beliefs about relationship based upon our value of personal freedom. In the East where marriages are often arranged, the primary goal is to be devoted to each other and to care for each other, no matter what.

This remedy can be especially helpful to those who feel unwilling and/or unable to make a deep and lasting commitment in relationship.

Chakra:	Third Eye, Navel
Meridian:	Liver, Gall Bladder
Key Words:	Commitment, Devotion, Service
Challenges:	Perspective, Anger
Affirmation:	I am committed to this process of growing together in love and harmony.

Pearly Everlasting – *Devotion*

Many forms. One Self.

Do you think that you could love another more
easily than this one?

The next one will offer the same challenges.
They are a reflection of you.

Be devoted to your Self in form – within and without.

Periwinkle
vinca major

provides an opportunity to be responsible for depression and thereby dispel it; for clear memory

Signature: *Periwinkle blooms in the shade on a shiny, bright green ground cover plant. The flowers have five violet blue petals and when open reveal a pentagon in the centre. The colour is especially harmonizing for the Crown chakra, and the five petals and five sided pentagon symbolize freedom and change. Its need for very little sun shows that it maintains its integrity from within.*

Periwinkle lifts the dark cloud of depression regardless of what apparently caused it. It moves us to the place of inner knowing, our place of deepest wisdom, where we remember who we are. In Chinese medicine the Heart houses the Spirit. Depression and other mental/emotional challenges often show up as an energy imbalance in the Heart channel. When the condition is severe there is a sense that "nobody's home."

At the physical level Periwinkle affects hypertension, hemorrhaging, and nervous disorders especially anxiety states. It calms the mind. It is also used for SAD (seasonal affective disorder) which is a type of depression caused by insufficient sunlight to stimulate the production of a hormone called melatonin during the winter months.

As a herbal tincture it improves memory and as an essence provides clear memory. It is useful for past life regression work and easier dream recall.

As a herb it has been used in Africa to treat diabetes.

Chakras:	Sacral, Crown
Meridian:	Heart
Key Words:	Remembering, Centred
Challenges:	Confusion, Forgetfulness, Despair, Depression
Affirmations:	I am uplifted.
	I remember who I am.

Periwinkle – *Remembering*

You can remember who you are.

You are eternal, unchanging and magnificent.

You are a child of Father/Mother God made
in the image of them.

Let me help you to lift this dark cloud which oppresses you.
Let me help you to sing the song of your exquisite
being-ness once more.

Pipsissewa
chimaphila umbellata

decision-maker; clears ambivalence

Signature: *Pink bowl-shaped flowers with 5 petals growing on rocky soil in coniferous forests. The genus name originates from the Greek chima – winter and phila – loving, and refers to its evergreen nature.*

As a herbal decoction it was used by native peoples to dissolve stones in the kidney and gall bladder.

Pipsissewa helps to release the worry and confusion around the choices we need to make in order to get on with our lives. Often we get caught up in "ifs" and lose sight of our goal. Mental activity can begin to sound like a broken record as we get caught up in emotional drama around decision making. The corollary of making choices is that we cannot be a victim, for we have charted our own course. Choosing is a responsible act.

Pipsissewa also helps to resolve the frustration around having made a choice which seems not to turn out the way we thought it would. Instead of wasting energy bewailing where we find ourselves, the essence will help move us to the point of power in the present where we can make a new choice.

Physically it impacts upon the brain and awakens that area involved in choice. It also impacts on dis-ease stemming from deficient energy in the Spleen, Liver, and Kidney channels.

Chakras:	Solar Plexus, Throat
Meridians:	Spleen, Liver, Kidney
Key Word:	Decisive
Challenge:	Indecisiveness
Affirmations:	I am able to choose.
	I can trust my energy and follow my heart.

Pipsissewa – Choices

When you are at the fork in the road,
invite me into your heart and mind.
I can assist you to choose the right path for you.
There is really only one choice.
If you follow the path that leads to peace of mind and comfort
in your heart, it will always be the right choice for you.

Plantain

plantago major

releases mental blocks and draws off negativity

Signature: *Tiny greenish white flowers on a spiky stem. Green is the colour of healing and oxygenation and white is the colour of purity and elevated consciousness.*

Plantain poultices from the leaves are used herbally to draw poison out through the skin.

This essence works on an etheric level in a similar manner to the way in which the plant works at a physical level. Plantain helps us to release bitterness and resentment, which over time produces calcification and rigidity in the Body/Mind. It actually dissolves the negative thought patterns which keep us stuck and which can eventually lead to emotional and physical disorders if left unchecked.

Acting through the Liver meridian, it helps us to recognize and to release unhelpful thoughts as they come into consciousness. It is especially useful when we have repetitive thoughts and we feel we have no control over them. At the emotional level it dissolves the frustration and resentment that often arise when we are critical and judgmental.

Through its connection with the Crown chakra it enables us to bring the vision of Unity consciousness to bear on all the events and people in our lives, including ourselves.

Physically this remedy is most effective for blood and liver disorders. It works effectively on any condition of physical toxicity resulting from mental or emotional poisons, like migraine headaches and indigestion.

Chakras:	Sacral, Crown
Meridians:	Liver, Gall Bladder
Key Words:	Purification, Cleansing
Challenges:	Poisonous thought and attitudes, Resentment
Affirmations:	I release all obstacles to growth and healing.
	I release thoughts which are not life supporting to myself or others.

Plantain *– Purification*

Let me dissolve the hard thoughts and feelings which you
hold against yourself and your fellow beings.

Let me wash away everything which prevents you
from being the Light you are.

Poison Hemlock
conium maculatum

for letting go; for moving through transition periods without getting stuck

Signature: *Clusters of greenish white florets growing in umbels on top of 6 - 10 foot hollow stalks which are marked with elongated purple spots. The highly toxic yellow oil is concentrated in the roots and fruit, but even blowing on the hollow stalk has resulted in rapid impact on the central nervous system causing convulsions and death.*

Note: Due to its highly poisonous nature, the Mother essence is diluted to a 6C homeopathic potency to ensure that no physical residue remains in the remedy.

This essence dissolves the emotional, mental and physical paralysis which can arise in periods of transition and major change. It is especially effective if we somehow believe that the change is being initiated from outside ourselves, and therefore something over which we have no control. Paralysis is one way to avoid the present, to deny experience, and to relinquish our power.

Physically it acts on holding patterns in the body – constipation, fluid retention, overweight, and any kind of paralysis in the physical structure or the nervous system. It is effective for stalled labour in the birthing process.

Emotionally it helps us to release rigid feelings and to convert the energy of fear into excitement so that we can use the energy to move forward.

Mentally, Poison Hemlock allows us to release ingrained thought patterns – i.e., repetitive and often quite unconscious thoughts which do not serve us in the moment.

Chakra:	Crown
Meridian:	Gall Bladder
Key Words:	Releasing, Faith
Challenge:	Holding on to old structures and beliefs
Affirmation:	I let go.

Poison Hemlock *– Releasing*

Examine your beliefs. Assess your emotions.

Wherever there is a historical pattern,
be willing to throw it out and see anew.

Polyanthus
primula X polyanthus

dissolves blocks to abundance consciousness; transforms attitudes of scarcity into ones of worthiness and willingness to receive.

Signature: Polyanthus comes in a multitude of colours and blooms in the winter when everything else is still asleep. The flowers are like a hidden store of precious gems offset by the hard coldness of the brown soil. Their tiny golden yellow centres symbolize wealth. The leaves resemble the bronchioles of the Lungs.

Polyanthus helps us to dissolve the blocks which we have to claiming our true heritage. Entering via the Root chakra and spiralling upwards to the Crown, it is a reminder that the kingdom of heaven is within, now, and not some future desirable state. It creates abundance consciousness, attracts abundance, and treats unworthiness at whatever level it is manifesting. It also reminds us to recognize and to be grateful for the existing abundance in our lives – i.e., we may have vibrant physical health but be totally focused on our lack of financial resources. Gratitude for whatever abundance we already have is a way of opening to abundance in other areas of our lives.

Polyanthus is a member of the Primrose family which has long been used herbally as an expectorant in bronchitis and other respiratory infections.

In Chinese medicine this essence balances the energy within the Metal element. It supports the Lungs and Large Intestine to perform their function of purification for the Body/Mind by breathing in the pure Qi from heaven and eliminating waste. Physically it affects the respiratory and elimination systems.

Chakra:	Root
Meridians:	Large Intestine, Lung
Key Word:	Abundance
Challenges:	Unworthiness
Affirmations:	I am willing to receive. I deserve to receive.

Polyanthus – *Self-worth*

I offer you the gift of valuing who you are.
When you are firmly rooted in your worth you
are able to give and to receive with ease.
Too long have humans believed that it is
more blessed to give than to receive.

One cannot happen without the other.
Everything you give returns to you.
And you will only be able to receive blessings
if you are willing to see yourself as worthy of them.

Poplar
Populus tremuloides

for contacting Spirit; for ability to transmit healing energies; to improve choice-making; attunes to the gentleness of nature

Signature: *Beautiful shimmering trees, 20 to 60 feet tall with roundish shaped leaves with serrated edges. The leaves are green on top and silver below. They turn yellow and brilliant gold in the fall. Commonly called Quaking Aspen because the slightest breeze causes the foliage to quiver.*

This particular essence is made from a group of seven trees right on the edge of the water. The trees create an amazing energy field, and when you stand in the middle of it your whole body is enlivened. Standing in the middle of these "seven beings" is sacred space.

Poplar trees are giants which pull us into the gentleness of nature. Their leaves are shimmering green and silver – green for healing and silver for receiving higher spiritual energies, and then gold in the fall for transmitting these healing forces. The sound of these leaves as the wind whispers through them is a call to Spirit. It is a call to Nature. It is a gentle reminder of our "sameness" with, and connection to, Nature.

As the remedy connects with the Triple Warmer channel, it harmonizes the flow of energy in a spiralling upward movement from Tan Den and Ming Men, through the Heart centre and up through the Crown and tunes the physical instrument to a higher frequency.

Chakra: Throat, Back Neck

Meridian: Triple Warmer

Key Words: Healing, Innocence, Yielding

Challenges: Separation

Affirmation: I allow myself to be moved by Spirit.

Poplar – *Innocence*

I offer you the ability to be moved in Spirit.

I offer you the healing energies of Spirit.

Let my ability to be moved by Spirit,
to be renewed in Spirit,
to channel Spirit be an inspiration to you.

Yield to the energy of Spirit as it
courses through your Body/Mind.

Flow with this energy and be connected to all that is.

Purple Crocus
crocus tomasinianus

for resolving tension generated from grief and loss

Signature: The buds are the deep purple colour of mourning. The petals, tightly folded in upon themselves, symbolize the inward journey which grief provokes. When the petals open, a bright golden yellow centre is revealed, symbolizing the wealth of all experience and the possibility of accessing another part of our hearts and spirits if we are willing to embrace the experience.

This essence enhances our ability to attune with all aspects of pain and grief and to release the tension and restriction around these experiences.

Primarily an emotional remedy, it helps us to feel the energy of loss and allows us to respond from exactly who we are and where we are rather than from cultural conditioning. There is no appropriate manner by which to express grief. It just is. Embracing the "is-ness" of it allows us to experience the depths of our own being.

Purple Crocus enters via the Throat chakra to the emotional body and impacts on physical tension especially in the upper back and shoulders. It helps to release the heaviness and tension related to loss and allows us to experience grief and emptiness without resistance. As such it is effective for those who, after a loss, turn their own blocked energy against themselves and could create life threatening diseases. It assists the Lungs, the channel related to grief in Chinese medicine, to do their job of providing life-giving energy to the whole physical body.

Chakra:	Throat
Meridian:	Lung
Key Word:	Feeling
Challenges:	Grief, Deep sadness
Affirmation:	I allow myself to be exactly where I am.

Purple Crocus *– Feeling Embraced*

Let me fold my petals around your aching heart.

Let me nurture you in the womb of my flower.

And now in the safety of my embrace
allow yourself to embrace your pain.
Feel it to the depths of your being.
Grief is a rite of passage.
Feel it and move forward.

Purple Magnolia
magnolia soulangeana

promotes intimacy and non-separateness; enhances all the senses

Signature: Although it is named Purple Magnolia, the actual colour is closer to magenta which is a powerful emotional balancer. It blooms on trees which grow up to 25 feet high and 20 feet wide. The buds themselves are quite phallic and open into blossoms which are round and fertile looking. In this manner it embodies qualities of both male and female. The blooms are quite fragile and when full blown even the slightest wind will cause all the petals to drop leaving only the sexual parts of the flower exposed.

Purple Magnolia elevates sexuality to its full potential for intimacy and non-separateness. At another level it heightens our experience of all our senses and allows us the awareness and appreciation of wind and sun and rain and the scent of flowers and the earth. It eliminates our preoccupation with thoughts and allows us to experience feeling and sensation without labelling.

Primarily a remedy for the spirit, it physically affects the sensory systems, especially smell, touch, and feeling.

In Chinese medicine the Heart Protector is also called the Circulation Sex channel and is responsible for maintaining balanced sexual function. In this regard Purple Magnolia can be used as effectively for those who "crave" sexual activity as for those who withdraw from intimacy.

Chakras:	Solar Plexus, Crown
Meridian:	Heart Protector
Key Words:	Opening, Intimacy
Challenges:	Coldness, Frigidity, Withdrawal from life
Affirmation:	I celebrate life.

Purple Magnolia – Sensuality

Let my senses quiver and vibrate with the delight of the earth.

Let my eyes see and my ears hear and my hands feel.

Let me smell the fragrance of the earth.

Let me see the beauty of the earth.

Let me feel the texture of the earth.

Let me celebrate the joy of being fully embodied.

Let me sing a song of gratitude for life itself.

Red Huckleberry
vaccinium parvifolium

to experience the power of introspection; allowing ourselves to be nourished by taking time to digest; storehouse of intelligence, discretion, and spiritual wisdom; regeneration

Signature: Small shrubs growing in coniferous forests often emerging from the dead stumps of other decaying trees. The tiny red berries were used by native people for food and medicinally as a gargle for sore throats.

These tiny red berries are like little beacons of light that illumine a path through the dark forest. Obviously providing food both for humans and animals, they nourish both the body and the soul.

This essence helps us to claim the power of going within, of introspection, of hibernation. Gives us the ability to withdraw from "the madding crowd," the rush and "busy-ness" of our daily lives, all the things that we think are so important. Often it takes some sudden, unexpected shock to move us to this deep inner place. Red Huckleberry helps us to go within with ease, and reminds us of the power of nourishment and regeneration contained in hibernation.

This essence helps us to attune to the cycles of nature both on the planet and within our physical bodies. It's okay, and even desirable, to get more rest in the dark winter months. One of the reasons that people suffer from dis-ease like SAD is because they insist upon doing the same level of activity in the winter as they do in the summer.

Chakra:	Solar Plexus
Meridian:	Gall Bladder, Stomach
Key Words:	Introspection, Digestion, Nourishment
Challenges:	Being not Doing
Affirmation:	It is safe to retreat and go within.

Red Huckleberry – *Introspection*

Let me show you the value of going within.

Let me show you the value of rest and activity –
Balance between being and doing.

When you pause and go within, you have new eyes to see,
new ears to hear, new perception all around.
Give yourself this gift

Salal

gaultheria shallon

for realizing our power to forgive ourselves and others

Signature: Pink to white bell-shaped flowers with a narrow mouth bloom on one side of a long raceme. They resemble tiny Chinese lanterns, bearers of the light of forgiveness.

The purple berries are a food source for wildlife and were also eaten by many Indian people to provide vitamin C.

Forgiveness is another way of "letting go" and of not getting stuck in positions about our projections. It is rooted in non-judgment and a recognition that justice is not our job.

It is not the kind of forgiveness which judges the situation or person and then decides to be magnanimous and superior by forgiving. It is forgiveness which honours ourselves, others, and the flow of life.

Salal helps us to sort out and to assimilate life experience and frees us to view reality through the window of the Heart. It dissolves self-righteousness. When we are unforgiving, the energy in our Heart centre becomes blocked.

This is primarily an emotional and mental remedy. It clears stress at these levels and allows us the freedom and joy to experience the embodiment of Spirit, which manifests in mysterious ways.

The Salal Deva appeared during a journeying process. She was carrying a stem of the flowers which were all glowing brightly. The light of these tiny lanterns guided me through the tangled underbrush of the forest and led me to a waterfall. I noted that as long as I kept my attention on her light, my path was easy and sure. The minute I was distracted by some fear or judgment, the forest seemed hostile and unfriendly.

Chakra:	Heart
Meridians:	Heart, Small Intestine
Key Word:	Forgiveness
Challenges:	Grudges, Resentment
Affirmations:	I am forgiving.
	I forgive myself and release the past.

Salal – Forgiving

Forgiveness is for you and you alone.

My lantern-like bells will illuminate the darkest corners of
your heart and free you to love again.

Let go. Be free.

Salmonberry
rubus spectabilis

physical tonic; spinal alignment and structural balancing

Signature: *Bright pink flowers on 6 - 12 foot bushes with prickly canes.*

The name originated along the Columbia River where the natives ate the tender shoots with salmon roe. The berries are quite sweet and edible.

Another remedy of self-expression, Salmonberry works primarily on the physical body. At birth we take on a physical body, and through our life experiences and how we respond to them we create a map on which our energy blocks and holding patterns are discernible. Salmonberry works on bones and muscles and fascia and aligns the spine. It is an excellent remedy to use at the time of injury. Over the long term it can help with chronic misalignments of the physical structure if there are accompanying attitudinal shifts. Through the Bladder channel on the back we can access all the other organs through the back Shu points which run bilaterally on both sides of the thoracic and lumbar spine.

It is said that every thought we think and every feeling we feel are recorded in the physical. Although the results of this essence are reflected in the physical its effectiveness is due to its ability to erase the originating thought or feeling.

Chakra:	Third Eye
Meridian:	Bladder
Key Words:	Physical alignment, Physical expression
Challenges:	Physical, mental, emotional, and spiritual alignment
Affirmation:	I celebrate my physical embodiment.

Salmonberry – *Alignment*

Celebrate life. Embrace your physical form.

Experience your body as the temple for your Spirit.

Honour and care for it and it will reflect your inner Light.

Silver Birch
betula pendula

enhances ability to receive and to conceive; softens the need to control; dispels suffering and develops humility

Signature: *Birches are graceful light catchers who carry both male and female parts on different infloresecences on the same tree. The gentle catkins are preformed the season before and become tassel-like in the spring. The key feature of birch is its thin white paper bark, which has been used for paper and birch bark canoes by many cultures.*

Silver Birch is the catalyst for balanced female energy. It epitomizes "strength in yielding."

Physically this remedy will be used for healing the organs of reproduction. Emotionally and spiritually it will help with conception especially if there are mental or emotional blocks standing in the way. Metaphysically it will assist with the conception of new ideas, and bring them forth into manifestation.

Silver Birch can also be used to eliminate power struggles in relationship. When one person does not need to control the whole show it is easier to create agreement and harmony prevails.

Control is a very dominant feature in our North American society, especially for people who are trying to play many roles simultaneously. It is incredibly self-sabotaging behaviour. Trees would snap in half if they were as inflexible as some humans.

Chakra:	Heart
Meridian:	Spleen
Key Words:	Conception, Manifestation
Challenges:	Control
Affirmation:	I am flexible and strong. I am able to conceive.

Silver Birch – *Conception*

I am soft in my strength. I yield to the wind. I bend to the ice.

I move with the energy of "what is." I am the face of the feminine.

Let me show you how to be flexible in the face of challenges.

Let me show you how to dance the dance of life.

Let me impregnate you with the seed of possibility
in each new moment.

Let me show you how to tap into and fulfill the
blueprint of your life.

Snowberry
sympboricarpus albus

accepting life as it is, at the moment

Signature: Produces clusters of tiny pink flowers on bushes growing up to 5 feet tall. Its white berries stay on the shrub almost all winter. There is something about the enduring nature of this plant and its year-round visibility which is indicative of how its energy always embraces life as it is.

Snowberry dissolves resistance to "what is" and gently leads us to acceptance. Situations and experiences may not appear to "make sense." Nonetheless we can embrace them wholeheartedly.

Embracing "what is," even when it is painful, can lead to that exquisite experience of ecstasy. Snowberry guides us to this place of being fully alive in the moment.

The soul is a fragment of the Light. On its journey through life it encounters shadows and darkness even within itself. Only by acknowledging and embracing the dark can we move again into the Light. If we resist, the darkness intensifies.

In the symbology of the Tarot the correlation for this essence is the Devil. What could be a better symbol of darkness? But as James Wanless points out in the *Voyager Tarot,* devil spelled backwards is "lived" and marks the potential for full expression of life. He quotes Vivekananda, "See good and evil as the same; both are merely God's play." He also notes that the I Ching hexagram for the Devil is #16 – Enthusiasm. This word comes from the Greek "en theos," which literally means "in God."

Working through the Crown chakra we remember who we are and accept "what is" as a challenge. Snowberry fortifies the link between the Crown and Heart chakras and leads to vibrancy of the Heart.

Physically it is effective for chronic fatigue syndrome and seasonal affective disorders.

Chakras:	Crown, Heart
Meridians:	Kidney, Bladder
Key Words:	Acceptance, Enthusiasm
Challenge:	Resistance
Affirmation:	I embrace my life experience.

Snowberry – *Acceptance*

You humans often think that you are in charge –
that somehow you have failed if life isn't unfolding
exactly as you think it should.

Strive to work with the unfolding of events rather than
thinking that you know best.

There is wisdom in embracing.

Snowdrop
galanthus nivalis

for letting go, having fun, lightening up

Signature: Another very early spring flower it breaks through frozen soil to produce clumps of white bell-shaped flowers. Its ability to survive even the harshest winter conditions is symbolic of the Soul's ability to accept even the most difficult of challenges on the Earth plane.

Snowdrop combines enthusiasm, inspiration, and joyful exploration of life experiences. It embodies the qualities of personal power and leadership.

It dissolves energy blockages and personal holding patterns which prevent Qi energy from flowing freely.

Physically it impacts on disorders where freedom of physical expression is paralyzed or distorted in some manner – arthritis, multiple sclerosis, poliomyelitis, cerebral palsy.

It has a strong impact on the Kidney and Bladder channels and through these it strengthens the will and dissolves paralyzing fear. It helps us to get mobilized.

It links the Root chakra (survival), the Solar Plexus chakra (personal identity and emotions), and the Crown chakra (spirituality).

Even though it is poisonous it has been used in an herbal preparation, called nivalus, in eastern Europe in a wide range of conditions characterized by nervous tissue degeneration – eg. poliomyelitis.

It is extremely beneficial for severe Kidney Qi deficiency, especially when there are symptoms of cold as well.

Chakras:	Root, Solar Plexus, Crown
Meridians:	Kidney, Bladder
Key Words:	Hope, Delight, Release
Challenges:	Fear, Restriction
Affirmation:	I can let go and experience joy.

Snowdrop *– Hope / Delight / Release*

Imagine the vitality it takes to push through the frozen earth.
Imagine the delight I feel when I am above the earth and
bathing in the winter sun.

I offer you this same inner strength.
I will nourish your essence and warm your heart
so that you too can express your vitality.

Twin Flower
linnaea borealis

non-judgment

Signature: *A creeping ground cover plant with small shiny elliptic leaves and one stalk which produces two identical bell shaped pink flowers. The plant signature is the two identical flowers which shows up as the age-old symbol of the scales of justice. Its delicate pink colour symbolizes compassion from which no judgment can arise.*

Making judgments leads to rigidity and resistance. We can only release judgment when we are peaceful with ourselves, then we can greet every situation with a breath of release and with the deep knowing that what we put out we will get back. It is with this mental framework that we are able to be in the process of our lives without getting stuck on fixed positions.

Primarily a mental remedy it promotes an awareness that it is all much bigger than we are able to perceive and understand. Twin Flower fosters optimism and humility.

On another level it is for those who adopt a critical attitude towards everything and everyone, including themselves. Twin Flower gives us the gift of discernment and the ability to make choices which are in tune with our inner journey and without criticism of self or other.

Chakras:	Root, Heart
Meridians:	Liver, Gall Bladder
Key Words:	Peace of mind, Acceptance, Compassion
Challenges:	Judgment, Criticism
Affirmation:	I do not understand what anything is for, and so I accept what is without criticism.

Twin Flower – *Compassion*

Allow me to show you both sides of the coin.
Allow me to show you the paradox.
Allow me to show you the tension between yin and yang
that allows form to manifest.
Allow me to show you life in all its polarities.

And when you want to give up your judgment and your
belief in right and wrong, good and bad,
think of my pink bells and feel your heart.

Vanilla Leaf
achlys triphylla

affirmation and acceptance of one's self

Signature: *Growing in dark forests, it has two stalks, one which terminates in three large fan shaped leaves and the second which extends well above the leaves and produces a narrow spike of small white flowers. The flower is delicate, and at the same time upright and noticeable. It adopts a posture of self-esteem.*

Like the flower from which it is taken the Vanilla Leaf essence demonstrates both our groundedness and our desire to reach towards the fulfilment of our full potential. Associated with the Lung meridian in Chinese medicine it symbolizes the taking in of prana via the respiratory system and the conversion of prana to vital energy to sustain life. Vanilla Leaf reminds us to celebrate our uniqueness and the unique patterns we have chosen for our Earth plane experience.

This is a remedy of exuberance and joy and acceptance and primarily works via the emotional – how we feel about ourselves, to the mental – how we think about ourselves, and then to the physical. Physically it works on skin disorders and any physical problems which relate back to self-denigration and lack of self-love.

Chakras:	Third Eye, Crown
Meridians:	Lung, Large Intestine
Key Word:	Self-esteem
Challenge:	Self-loathing
Affirmations:	I love myself.
	I celebrate who I am.

Vanilla Leaf – *Self-esteem*

Do not feel small in relation to others. Make no comparisons.

Allow yourself to manifest your perfect infinite potential.

Express yourself. Show yourself.

Stand straight and tall in the spotlight of your Self.

Viburnum

viburnum carlesii

strengthens our connection with the subconscious and our psychic abilities

Signature: Viburnum blooms in clusters of pinkish-white flowers from which emanate an exquisite fragrance. The colour and fragrance are gentle inspiration for a relaxed, non-judgmental posture.

This remedy is an excellent aid to channelling, meditating, or centring. It helps us to really hear that "still, small voice within" and to be willing to trust it.

It accesses the "clear seeing" abilities of the sixth chakra and helps us to experience heightened awareness. Physically it affects the ears and the ability to listen. It also impacts on the brain and triggers the nervous system to relax through its resonance with the pituitary gland.

It relates to the Triple Warmer channel which is concerned with balance and harmony of the body, mind, and spirit. Also relating to the Spleen channel it helps us to experience our unity and oneness with all of life. It can be especially helpful in beginning dialogue with plant spirits and other devic life forms. Viburnum gives us the gift of accessing imagination and trusting our inner knowing.

Taken before going to sleep, it will assist in programming dreams to provide guidance for the problems of our daily lives.

Chakra: Third Eye

Meridians: Spleen, Triple Warmer

Key Words: Intuition, Channel, Relaxed, Insight

Challenges: Self-doubt, Insecurity

Affirmation: I am a channel for creative intelligence.

Viburnum *– Intuition*

You are blessed with an inner knowing.

Yes, there is a place in you which can be your comfort and your guidance. All you need do is stop and listen.

Let me take your attention from the cares of the world.

Let me introduce you to your inner guide.

Wallflower
cheiranthus

for hopelessness, endurance, preparedness; attuning to our own inner rhythms

Signature: *Fragrant yellow flowers which bloom prolifically on woody stalks.*

Wallflowers are very noticeable even if they are paralyzingly shy. This remedy will assist in communication about inner worlds. It helps cross the boundaries between seeing, feeling, and hearing type learners – "if you could see what I feel."

It dispels that sense of hopelessness which is often experienced when we feel misunderstood and like we can't find the right means to make ourselves understood.

"The world speaks to me in pictures, my soul answers in music," says Tagore. This is the gift of Wallflower. We can actually honour and even delight in the many manifestations of divinity in form. Wallflower is truly a medicine for saints and mystics – i.e. appreciation of the individual who can step to the beat of a different drummer.

Through its entry into the Solar Plexus chakra it cleanses the imprints of old emotional pain resulting from feeling like the "ugly duckling."

Chakra:	Solar Plexus
Meridian:	Stomach, Spleen
Key Words:	Expression, Sharing
Challenges:	Sensory deficits, Autism
Affirmation:	My senses are alive and I can share my perceptions with you.

Wallflower – *Communication*

In my world there is colour and music and fragrance.

In my world there is light and delight.

Go inside and see what you feel and feel
what you hear and hear what you see.
Awaken to the truth of your multi-dimensionality.

Weigela
weigela florida

helps to integrate experiences on the physical and emotional planes

Signature: *Cascades of pink bell shaped flowers grow on a bush 5 - 7 feet tall. The edges of the bells become 5 petals which look like an open jaw. The flowers are androgynous in appearance.*

When we trust that we are always in the right place at the right time our experiences eventually "make sense." Weigela helps us to realize what we are getting out of any given experience. We can then use this data for further growth by choosing to discard the pattern or alter it in some way. Weigela affects both physical and emotional patterns. For instance, we may hold a posture of being quite timid and shy, and as a result experience misunderstanding and isolation in social interaction. As we become willing to see ourselves as the source of our pain we can begin to alter the underlying patterns and thereby change the response of others to us. This is not a manipulative stance, but rather one of personal response-ability and empowerment.

It allows us to see others as our teachers and mirrors which reflect back to us our own negative, and positive, energy patterns.

The essence enters via the Throat and supports freedom of self-expression. It nourishes the Wood element and supports our ability to grow, even when conditions seem adverse.

This is a useful remedy to take at times of "accidents" and all seemingly unexpected physical and emotional traumas.

Chakra:	Throat, Third Eye
Meridian:	Liver, Gall Bladder
Key Words:	Integration, Alignment
Challenges:	Disassociation, Speechless
Affirmation:	I am an embodiment of wisdom.

Weigela – *Teaching*

There are no accidents. Everything that happens is part of
the infinite divine plan unfolding.

Your freedom lies in your ability to accept and to
respond to the situation as it is.

Windflower
anemone pulsatilla

spiritual tonic; provides grounding and inner security

Signature: There is a quality of timidity or shyness about this soft, furry, violet flower which appears on the prairies while the ice and snow are still on the ground. This signature resonates with the shyness that we sometimes feel about allowing our inner light to shine. It is said that it received its name because Windflower only opens when the wind is blowing.

Windflower is the essence which provides the security necessary to express our spiritual being. It allows the soul to dance, as the Windflower dances in the wind.

By allowing us to feel secure with our own originality, it balances our emotional responses. It encourages self-acceptance and self-expression and thereby allows for the unequivocal acceptance of others.

It is a remedy to work on the inner self, to connect with Be-ing.

Herbally it has been used as a sedative and analgesic. Homeopathically, one of its black letter symptoms is menstrual pain. As a flower essence it affects stomach disorders, both physical and emotional. In Chinese medicine the Stomach channel governs our ability to digest food and experience and to convert them into nourishment for the Body/Mind. We can feel grounded and secure only when we are nourished.

Chakras:	Throat, Heart
Meridian:	Stomach
Key Words:	Grounding, Spirit
Challenges:	Scattered, Spaced out
Affirmation:	I know who I am.

Windflower – *Spirit*

Soft and furry, delicate and mauve, I offer you the opportunity
to connect with the Light of your being – Spirit.
Feel my energy coursing through your body/mind.
Experience my softness, my rootedness, my ability to be in
touch with heaven while being deeply connected to the earth.

Yellow Pond-Lily
nuphar polysepalum

floating free of emotions and attachments; feeling strong and secure in my path; blesses relationships

Signature: Fragrant, yellow, waxy, cup-shaped flowers float on the surface of the water. Each is connected to its roots maybe five metres below in the water by a thick, fleshy stem. The centre of each flower is like a three dimensional mandala. Each flower is surrounded by heart-shaped leaves which also emerge from the rhizome on long stalks and float on the surface of the water.

This remedy helps us to work with the heart subtly. It allows us to float free of emotional attachments with grace and ease, while fostering a secure sense of self.

Yellow Pond-Lily reminds me of these lines from Tagore; *"The centre is still and silent in the heart of an eternal dance of circles."* The flower feels like a protective womb in which to make contact with the sacred self beyond the cacophony and pull of the emotional realm.

Through the Bladder channel we are granted the ability to see things anew and to release emotional patterns, so that we are able to move forward fearlessly and without being 'at the mercy' of our feelings.

Its connection with the Throat chakra allows us to express ourselves purely and without artifice.

Yellow Pond-Lily helps us to centre, to perceive differently and to act on our new information.

Chakra: Throat

Meridian: Bladder

Key Words: Strength, Security

Challenges: Attachment, Doubt

Affirmation: I am not my feelings.

Yellow Pond Lily – *Letting Go / Centering*

In the knowing of who I am, I float free.

In the knowledge of who you are, I let go.

No emotional baggage to weigh me down.

No emotional drama to consume my energy.

Flower & Sea Essence Kits

Anemone
anthopleura elegantissima

for acceptance of self and others by taking responsibility for one's own reality; allowing oneself to be organized by the universe

Signature: The colours are similar to those of watermelon tourmaline – a pink centre with green outside. These are both colours of the heart. When a sea anemone is approached, it curls in upon itself as an act of self-protection and loses its vulnerability and openness to life. Symbolically it looks like the eye. When our eyes are closed we cannot appreciate the wonder and oneness of life. Nor can we see our own part in creating our experiences and respond to life with an open heart. By the same token, it is also life supporting to choose to close one's eyes on occasion, and this is the wisdom of Anemone.

The remedy acts to open us to greater levels of awareness by aligning the mental body with our Higher Soul Purpose. Thus we realize that *I do create my own reality.* Every thought I think, every feeling I feel, affects the whole.

Anemone releases karmic stuckness in the Solar Plexus. The events and experiences of our lives always look different if we begin from the understanding that we have chosen them for our life script. Then free will of the highest order can be experienced – "How may I respond to this?" The alternative is resistance which always leaves us feeling tense, isolated, and alone.

Primarily a mental remedy, it is extremely useful in situations of physical pain. It allows us the freedom to move into the pain, instead of resisting it.

In Chinese medicine, the Liver channel governs the eyes. Anemone assists with physical eye problems as well as helping us to see ourselves, others, and the events of our lives from a perspective of personal responsibility.

The Liver energy is also the General in Chinese medicine. The General makes plans. Wise plans are made only when personal ego control is relinquished and we can see the big picture.

Anemone types are often over-controlling emotionally and mentally. The kinds of illnesses to which they are prone are tendon and muscle spasms and injuries. They are so busy controlling the intended outcome of their activity that they are unable to hear messages from the physical body about when it has had enough. Competitive athletes and super persons often manifest these traits.

Chakra:	Solar Plexus
Meridian:	Liver
Key Words:	Allowing, Empowerment
Challenges:	Victim, Powerlessness, Blame, Controlling
Affirmation:	I am able to respond with trust and openness.

Anemone *– Response - ability*

Only when you are able to respond from your higher Self
will your choices lead to inner peace. Only when you are
willing to accept that you have chosen this event as the
classroom for your learning will you be free.

Resistance to what is will lead to pain – at all levels.

Step back. Take another look. Take another breath.

And then choose your response.

Barnacle
balanus glandula

for attuning with the feminine aspect of the self; for developing radical trust

Signature: In form Barnacle appears very feminine. However it has an extremely hard structure and clings tenaciously to the rocks on which it lives. Its signature is symbolic of the strength available in our feminine nature.

When a woman goes into labour and gives birth it is an act of radical trust, of allowing the forces of Nature to flow through her and to guide her. In the same manner we can cultivate this radical trust in all aspects of our lives by embracing the feminine within.

Barnacle embodies wisdom, nurturing, fertility, and abundance. It is a useful essence for both men and women who may feel that they were abandoned by their female parent. It allows us to find the mother within.

It enables males to embrace their anima, or female soul qualities, and fosters deep respect and sensitivity towards the feminine.

Physically it impacts on the female reproductive system and is especially useful for releasing the energy patterns which create cysts and fibroids. It is also a powerful birthing remedy. It affects the pituitary gland and regulates its production and release of hormones. It also acts to harmonize the forebrain and the back brain which correspond respectively to our cultural development and our primitive patternings.

In Chinese medicine the Small Intestine channel is entrusted with the task of separating the pure from the impure. As children we trust the feminine to provide us with the nourishment necessary to grow and develop to independent adulthood.

Barnacle types may be obsessive about sorting things out. Their illness patterns can manifest as an inability to absorb nutrients and bowel dysfunction. Emotionally they will always appear to be seeking nurturing and nourishment from outside themselves.

Chakra:	Heart
Meridian:	Small Intestine
Key Words:	Intuitive, Yielding, Nurturing
Challenges:	Tough, Resistant, Stubborn
Affirmation:	I embrace the softness within.

Barnacle – *Yielding*

My external form is hard and jagged.
But within is a soft and yielding place.

And from here I emerge into the force of the ocean
to find my nourishment.

Let me show you how to connect with
your own inner softness.

Brown Kelp
nereocystis luetkeana

for shifts in perception leading to clarity

Signature: Brown Kelp looks like a tangled mass of long, rubbery strands with round bulbous floats. It reflects the immense mental confusion we will often tolerate before we are willing to take a leap of faith in order to see things differently. Fear often maintains the same fixed point of view even when experience shows us that it is not serving us. Even the slightest shift will bring a totally new understanding.

Brown Kelp helps us to take the leap of faith which can bring us back to our centre, the inner core of our being. It reminds us that "the knowledge which passeth understanding" is to be found within. It is very helpful for approaching new undertakings, especially those of a metaphysical nature, for it enhances the ability to go within and to feel comfortable there.

It balances the energy between the Root, or survival chakra, and the Crown chakra, our connection with the macrocosm. Often when we are fearful we go into old survival patterns instead of trusting the flow.

The Bladder channel is the controller of the storage of water and maintains adequate reservoirs of bodily fluids. Symbolically it controls what we are willing to bring to consciousness from the unconscious. If we are in fear or survival mode, we either block out information or, in the extreme, actually become disembodied for a while. This remedy helps us to feel safe while mapping unconscious territory.

Physically it dissolves back tension and affects bladder infections and ear problems, especially if the latter are caused by fluid imbalance in the middle or inner ear.

The Brown Kelp type tends to get in their own way through fear and confusion.

Chakras:	Root, Crown
Meridian:	Bladder
Key Words:	Clarity, Freedom
Challenges:	Confusion, Fixation
Affirmation:	I can let go of this position.

Brown Kelp – *Clarity*

When you learn to step back and "witness" your thoughts there will be no more confusion. Life will be easy and there will be more time and energy for fulfillment.

Chiton

mopalia muscosa

for gentleness which serves to break up and to dissolve blockages and tension

Signature: Ovoid shell with 8 hinged segments. When disturbed, it curls up to protect its soft interior. Most of the time it moves almost unnoticed, blending in with the landscape, along the rocks at the intertidal zone.

Primarily a physical remedy, Chiton helps us to live softly in our bodies. Instead of tightening up under stress, it assists us to stay soft. Its signature connects it especially with the cervical spine at the back of the neck and the thyroid cartilage at the front of the neck. It is a remedy of choice for whiplash or any other neck injury and also for conditions where dysfunction of the thyroid gland cause holding patterns in the body – eg. excess weight. It is a wonderful example of flexibility within structure and as an essence will help us to be more flexible within our own body/mind structure.

At an emotional level its oval shield-like form allows us a measure of protective energy from emotional trauma and pain. It would be a useful remedy to take before going into situations where the potential for emotional distress exists.

At a metaphysical level its 8 hinges represent abundance and prosperity at one level and when placed on its side the number 8 represents infinity. This remedy will assist us to move beyond the limitations of cultural conditioning and rigid beliefs and to encourage the full creative expression of the Liver channel. It allows us to receive some new information, perceive something in a new way, and have the ability to change course and act on this insight.

Chakra:	Throat
Meridian:	Liver
Key Words:	Flexibility, Gentleness
Challenges:	Rigidity
Affirmation:	I maintain flexibility within my physical structure.

Chiton – Gentleness

Live softly in your body. Indeed it is your temple –
the house of your soul.

Let it be a radiant reflection of who you really are.

Coral

pocillopora meandrina

for living in community; respect for self and others

Signature: *Tiny animals who come together to form colonies and create a shape that resembles a cauliflower head. They appear to be rock-like and inanimate and have a symbiotic relationship with tiny algal cells. Despite their calcified structure, they are alive and if walked on or broken off by humans, this live community is killed.*

Apart from its rich orange-red colour, a clump of Coral resembles the grey matter of the brain. The essence allows us to retrieve old, old memories and lost connections with the earth and how to be earthlings. It allows for self-expression (connection with the Throat chakra) in harmony with the divinity in our self and our fellow beings. It helps us to remember that we have no enemies, only fellow beings who have agreed to play roles in our script for our own learning and evolution. It cleanses old "stuff" held in the Solar Plexus chakra so that we are not held back by old emotion-charged memory patterns.

Both its signature and its connection to the kidney channel in Chinese medicine make it a very potent remedy for the brain and Central Nervous System. The Kidney is where our inherited Qi resides. It affects physical growth and mental potential. In this regard it would be a remedy of choice for any CNS dis-ease like post polio syndrome, Parkinson's, multiple sclerosis etc.

It would also be a remedy of choice for people who have lost part of their physical brain or been born without it, like hydrocephalic children who are already able to use one part of the brain to perform the function of a part of the brain that is affected by the disease. This remedy will encourage cell adaptability so that a viable cell will be able to take over the function of a missing cell.

Chakra:	Solar Plexus, Throat
Meridian:	Kidney
Key Words:	Harmony, Cooperation
Challenges:	Conflict, Fear
Affirmation:	I can live harmoniously in community. Only fear prevents me from living in paradise.

Coral – Harmony

Unity and diversity living together in harmony.

We are many and we are one.

Remember when you harm another,
you are harming yourself.

When you help another you are magnifying
your own inner beauty.

Diatoms
amphipleura pellucida

repatterning cellular memory; letting in the light

Signature: *Single-celled beings who look like light and are responsible for the shimmering phosphorescence in oceans worldwide. Observed under powerful microscopes diatoms resemble unique three-dimensional mandalas.*

Diatoms are immortal. Single-celled organisms do not die. They reproduce themselves as carbon copies of the first Diatom. In this way they manifest infinite potential through adaptability. They appear in many different shapes and sizes – spirals, triangles, circles with intricate patterns of which no two are the same. And they don't appear at all to the naked eye except as shimmering light.

Diatom essence can be used where the dharma or purpose of a cell has been forgotten as in cases of cancer and degenerative disease. Diatom will en-lighten the cell and assist with its return to normal if that is the soul's intent.

The phosphorescent shimmer in the Indian Ocean guided one of the space shuttles back to earth. As an essence Diatom has the potential to guide earthlings back to heaven and/or to bring heaven to earth.

Chakra:	Heart
Meridian:	Heart
Key Words:	Source, Love, Consciousness, Grace
Challenges:	Darkness, Stuckness
Affirmation:	Heart is my centre.

Diatoms – *Dharma / Purpose*

I am Light. I am formless and all forms.

My vibration will coax every cell in your body
to remember its divine plan.

Dolphin
stenella longirostris

appreciation for "all that is"; playful, lighthearted; interspecies communication

Signature: Spinner Dolphins are so named because of their natural ability to leap out of the water and spin on their longitudinal axis. These playful beings grow up to 2 meters in length and live in schools of twenty to forty but sometimes as many as several hundred. They have a long, narrow snout and a grey body with a light belly.

Dolphins are the Water creature manifestation of angels. They bring forth all the same energy for us – playfulness, lightheartedness, dancing, flying, fun energy. They are probably humans' first link with other dimensional consciousness from the animal kingdom. There are many amazing stories of dolphins rescuing stranded and exhausted swimmers and gently carrying them back to the safety of land. This remedy is a vital link for someone who feels profound alienation and loneliness and a sense of deep loss and abandonment living on the earth plane.

Dolphins have huge brains. Always people talk of their hearts in relation to dolphins and their recognition of their ability to be more than they are. This is a remedy of heart and mind expansion and transformation. Primarily connecting to the limbic system, the part of the brain where we experience a wide range of emotions from pleasure and sexual ecstasy to anger and fear, Dolphin is a remedy to transform linear mind into holistic feeling mind through the alchemy of connection with heart energy. Many people have seen this remedy lodging in the Heart centre, travelling up to the head and then spiralling out into other dimensions, indicating its power for expansion of consciousness.

Chakra:	Sacral, Solar Plexus, Heart, Throat, Third Eye, Crown
Meridian:	Spleen, Heart
Key Words:	Playful, Lighthearted, Higher communication
Challenges:	Seriousness, Melancholy
Affirmation:	I dance my life light heartedly.

***Dolphin** – Lightheartedness*

I am the angel of the sea. I spend my days in harmony.

Let me show you how to dispel your heaviness,
and dance like me.

There is nothing so serious or terrible that it can
snuff out the light of your soul.

When you are feeling heavy, call on me. I will lift your spirit and
nurture your soul. Why do you think that I leap out of the water?

– merely to express my delight in my ability to do so.

Hermit Crab
pagurus granosimanus

the ability to enjoy "alone-ness"; contentment & sensitivity

Signature: *As its name implies, the Hermit Crab lives quite a solitary life and moves from one vacated shell to another along the beach. It is a common sight to find its pincers and/or antennae emerging from an empty winkle or cockleshell. Its other noteworthy feature is that is scurries sideways, skirting danger and never meeting anything head on.*

Hermit Crab will help us through those dark nights of the soul when our alone-ness feels overwhelming. It will help us to reconnect with the soul whose journey is always alone, individual, and unique. With this understanding comes freedom. With this freedom and higher sense of self integrity comes the ability to be at ease in many different circumstances – physically, emotionally and mentally. In this regard it is a very useful remedy for travellers of inner space as well as outer space.

It diminishes fear.

In counterpoint to this ability to appreciate alone-ness it is also an effective energy pattern to introduce when someone is always avoiding – relationships, life, moving forward. It is for those who skirt the issues and who are so insecure that they are unable to enter and maintain authentic relationships.

Hermit Crab helps us to be comfortable with ourselves no matter where we are. It helps to quiet the mind and appreciate stillness.

Chakra:	Throat
Meridian:	Stomach
Key Words:	Contentment, Ease, Comfortable with self
Challenges:	Loneliness, Avoidance
Affirmation:	I am content and at peace with my solitude.

Hermit Crab *– Contentment*

Because I remember who I am
I can make my home anywhere.

Because I am satisfied with my own company
I am never alone.

My soul sings a hymn of praise to the divinity in all creation.

Jellyfish
aurelia aurita

for fluidity and letting go into the experience

Signature: *On the sand, where it is sometimes left when the tide goes out, Jellyfish looks like a clear insignificant gelatinous blob. When it is floating in water, it looks as graceful as an angel dancing. You can see its tiny fringe-like tentacles and four clearly defined chambers which look like the chambers of the heart, but are in fact its reproductive organs.*

Jellyfish is a birthing and re-birthing remedy.

Resistance creates pain. Holding on to anything, other than what "is" right now, creates blockage and stagnation.

Primarily a spiritual remedy, it connects us with the rhythms of our being and prevents rigid emotional and mental patterns from interfering with our experience of the NOW.

Jellyfish resonates with the fifth chakra, our centre for self-expression and communication.

In Chinese medicine, the Heart houses the Spirit. When the Heart is healthy the Spirit is calm and joyful and able to embrace life experience as it unfolds.

Physically Jellyfish dissolves the energy which creates arterial plaque and hardening. It also affects heart-related spirit disorders like depression.

As an emotional and mental remedy it dissolves bitterness and hardness in these bodies before the physical manifestations of dis-ease occur.

Chakra:	Throat
Meridians:	Heart, Heart Protector
Key Words:	Fluid, Flexible, Present
Challenges:	Stuck, Rigid
Affirmation:	Be Here Now.

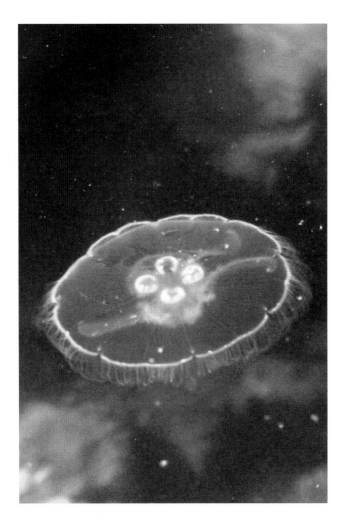

Jellyfish – *Embracing*

Through my transparency I am able to see
clearly through the window
of my heart.

Through my fluidity I am able to see
infinite possibility.

I offer you the gift of loving unconditionally.

Moon Snail
polinices lewisii

to cleanse the mind and let in light

Signature: *The signature of Moon Snail is the spiral pattern on its shell. Symbolically this can lead us deeper within or serve to guide us on meditative journeys to connect with universal Light.*

When the physical body is harmonized through the Triple Warmer channel, then the mind finds a comfortable dwelling place. In the ancient Chinese texts there was a picture of the human body with three fires in it. These fires were located in the lower abdomen, the solar plexus and the chest and represented the energy required to reproduce, to digest and assimilate nutrients, and to convert air or prana into oxygen for the cells. In Chinese medicine, the Triple Warmer channel is the ruler of balance and harmony as it provides communication for the whole physical network. When any part of the network is uneasy, the mind is also affected. So Moon Snail eliminates physical toxins which cloud the mind. Mentally, it is a tool for meditation and inner journeys. Another remedy for mapping unconscious territory, it harnesses the creativity of the Sacral chakra and helps us to explore any aspect of creative expression.

The challenge for Moon Snail types is to cultivate an attitude of innocent wonderment instead of becoming enmeshed in rigid thought structures.

Chakra: Sacral

Meridian: Triple Warmer

Key Words: Curiosity, Innocence

Challenges: Rigid Beliefs and Attitudes

Affirmations: I am free.
                   My mind is filled with Light.

Moon Snail – Illumination

Let me guide you in the spiral dance,

– the ever expanding circles of life unfolding.

Let me take you into Light so that you may appreciate the
wonder of Life itself.

Mussel

mytilus edulis

for releasing the burden of anger and to enable one to stand up straight

Signature: *Fan shaped shell with purple/black rough exterior. The shell lining is varying translucent shades of pink, blue, or violet.*

Anger suppressed is like the black outer surface of the mussel – dark, ominous, foreboding. Anger unleashed is equally black and threatening.

The energy of anger transformed allows the inner radiance of being to shine forth. It is like the inner surface of the Mussel shell – pink, blue, violet, soft, opalescent.

This is the remedy par excellence for victim consciousness which prevents us from being aligned with our inner power, strength and creativity. When anger is stored up, tension in the physical body results, especially in the neck and shoulders. Restriction in this area creates an energy blockage between heart and mind.

In Chinese medicine, Gall Bladder is responsible for making decisions and wise judgments. Unhealthy Gall Bladder energy is tight and controlling and never satisfied with the way things are – always judging, in a self-destructive way.

Mussel impacts on the second chakra, the centre of creativity and sexual expression. Anger often results when we are not expressing our creativity or when there is some experience of sexual frustration.

Physically it relaxes tense neck and shoulder muscles and affects headaches and dizziness resulting from this kind of tension. It is helpful for injuries like whiplash. It promotes the flow of bile and aids digestion.

Emotionally, Mussel resolves feelings of irritability, frustration and anger. This essence often comes up for someone who has been diagnosed as having a life threatening illness like AIDS, and where there is a feeling of frustration and hopelessness.

Chakra:	Sacral
Meridian:	Gall Bladder
Key Words:	Creativity
Challenges:	Irritability, Frustration
Affirmation:	I am creative and powerful.

Mussel – *Transformation*

Whoosh! An explosion and it's done.

The energy is moved, transformed,
released and it's over.

You are now free to move on to the next experience
without baggage.

Be grateful for this anger, this energy in motion.

Use it.

Pink Seaweed
corallina vancouveriensis

a grounding remedy; for patience before new beginnings; to harmonize thought before action

Signature: Although it is classified as a plant, Pink Seaweed is mainly composed of calcium. Even with this hard structure it maintains a posture of gracefulness. The vibrant pink of this tide-pool algae dances with the energy of change natural to its environment. The ocean fills the pool and then recedes in a diurnal cycle of ebb and flow. Pink Seaweed is both secure and flexible at the same time.

When we are secure in the power of our own being, we are like giant trees firmly rooted in the earth and able to adapt to changing conditions. With rootedness and flexibility we can accomplish whatever we set out to do. Pink Seaweed is the essence to use for new jobs, new schools, new relationships, new experiences. It helps us to move out of our "comfort zone" into the new and challenging. Change is a constant, a fact of life. We can either resist it or dance with it.

The meridian that is often affected when we are going through change is the Heart Protector which circulates the Heart essence to the other channels. If the Heart Protector becomes calcified and rigid, there is no joy or grace in our undertakings. Its secondary connection to the Large Intestine channel helps us to joyfully release the past, to make space for change to enter.

Physically, Pink Seaweed strengthens bones and teeth, in addition to being used for constipation. Emotionally, it softens the Heart Protector, and allows us to experience change with gracefulness and joy.

Chakras:	Sacral, Solar Plexus
Meridian:	Heart Protector
Key Words:	Grounded, Secure, Patient
Challenges:	Change, Inflexibility
Affirmations:	I am grounded and secure. I move in the flow of life.

Pink Seaweed *– Grounding*

Your heart is the ground of your being.

Let me enfold you in the warmth of my pink lace.

Accept yourself and give yourself time and space
to manifest your full potential.

Rainbow Kelp
iridaea cordata

alignment of front and back brain – i.e., reactivity and sensibility; alchemical transformation

Signature: *Living close to shore, this iridescent Kelp reflects as many colours as Fire Opals – from shimmering blues, greens, and purples, to fiery reds and oranges.*

This remedy helps us to attune to higher perception, the subtle energies which are the fabric of life. It increases sensitivity and balances the reactivity of the reptilian back brain with the sensitivity and potential of the front brain. Potentially a remedy for depression and inner states of darkness and mental confusion, Rainbow Kelp brings golden light particles into the darkness. It helps us to release, relax and connect to our light source again.

Rainbow Kelp connects with the Third Eye chakra – refined sensory perception and the Navel chakra – the adrenal glands and "the fight or flight response" and fear states.

Its affinity with the Triple Warmer channel helps to balance all the other energy channels in the Body/Mind, regulate body temperature, harmonize extrovert and introvert and thereby impact on social relationships.

Chakra:	Navel, Third Eye
Meridian:	Triple Burner
Key Words:	Alchemy, Potentiality
Challenges:	Reactivity
Affirmation:	I am able to respond with my full potential.

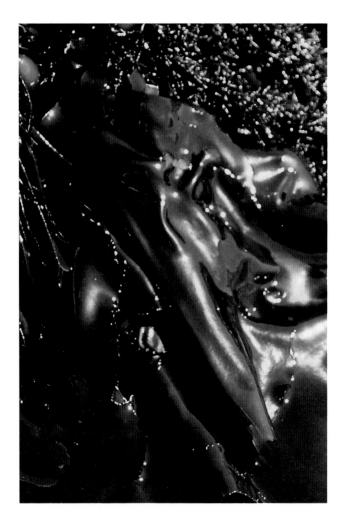

Rainbow Kelp *– Alchemy*

Your human body/mind is like a finely tuned instrument.

It can play the full gamut of human experience from
sensuality to divine bliss.

Give thanks for this miracle of who and what you are.

Sand Dollar
dendraster excentricus

to create a disruption of the mirage; coming to your senses

Signature: *The signature of Sand Dollar is the 5 beautiful petals on its surface. Beneath each petal is a small compartment containing a tiny white dove-shaped shell. Each little dove is a symbol of the liberation of consciousness that comes from listening to gentle messages from within.*

Sand Dollar helps us to become aware of the roots of our dis-ease.

This was the first sea essence. It came to us in response to a friend who was coping with an unusual cancer. With her it acted as the "great awakener" and she "woke up" to her participation in the creation of the dis-ease. She was then able to transform the energy and to redirect it into more productive channels for herself.

Primarily a mental remedy, it also impacts on the efficient, life-giving movement of Qi energy via the Metal element through the Lung channel. It assists with positive thinking which can only get effective results when underlying belief patterns and attitudes have been examined and released.

The physical body is the visible expression of underlying thoughts and feelings. Sand Dollar helps to uncover the underlying causes of dis-ease in the physical body. Because of its connection to both the Throat chakra and the Lung channel, it affects bronchitis, asthma, throat problems and self-expression.

Chakra:	Throat
Meridian:	Lung
Key Words:	Reality, Truth
Challenges:	Illusion, Limitation
Affirmation:	I am willing to expand my awareness.

Sand Dollar – *Truth*

This is your moment of liberation. A moment of true insight.

Embrace your inner knowing and be free.

Sea Horse
hippocampus

energizing the spine and central nervous system; accessing the 'wild one' within

Signature: With its horse-like head and long sinewy body, this little being gallops through the water. It is the only species where the male not only carries the eggs, but also gives birth to the offspring. For centuries it has been used herbally by the Chinese to tonify the kidneys and the lungs.

In Chinese medicine there is an image of the spirit of the Metal element of a fair young maiden wearing a white lace gown, with long flowing blonde hair, galloping on a powerful white horse. It is truly an image of the very Yin connecting to the most Yang. The Sea Horse embodies this very image, affecting the most refined aspect of human physiology - the nervous system and yet manifesting in the form of one of our strongest and yang animals. Sea Horse resolves and/or integrates the "paradox" of embodiment and allows each of us to express our own unique talents and abilities no matter which form we have chosen this time around. With this essence we can let go of our notions of how men and women "ought" to be.

At a physical level this essence may be used for any dis-ease and/or dys-function in the central nervous system - communication between the brain and either motor or sensory functions. It also benefits the lungs and assists them in taking in and utilizing more life force (prana, Qi) with each inhalation of breath. It is a remedy of choice for athletic training and physical endurance.

Its connection to the Governing vessel resolves stiffness of the spine and also allows the remedy to be dispersed to all the other meridians as needed through the connecting points on this channel.

Chakra:	Root, Sacral
Meridian:	Lung, Governing Vessel
Key Words:	Life Force, Expression
Challenges:	Paralysis, Lazy
Affirmation:	I feel the life force in my physical body. There is no loss of power in gentleness.

Sea Horse – *Life Force*

Jump on my back and gallop through the waves with me.

Express your vitality and divinity.

Sea Lettuce
ulva lactuca

embracing and healing the shadow; for dispersal and elimination of toxins

Signature: What appears to be a tuft of 4 - 6 bright green sheet-like leaves is actually one blade with ruffled edges and several splits. This leaf is transparent and slippery. It is anchored to rocks in the upper intertidal zone by a small discoid holdfast. Its chief feature is its transparent green-ness. It is eaten in many parts of the world as a condiment in soups and salads.

The gift of Sea Lettuce is its ability to recognize, to heal and to transform the dark side – the secret faults and hidden flaws of the ego personality which we prefer to keep hidden, even from ourselves. Perceived through the healing green transparency of Sea Lettuce, these blemishes are digested and absorbed and the real darkness is eliminated. The colour green brings oxygen and healing and is useful for decreasing heat. Sea Lettuce feels like a blanket which soothes and heals the lower abdomen. It can be used when healing is required for the reproductive organs or the bowels.

In the Indian tradition there is a wise one known as the "Eater of Filth." The task of this Elder was to listen with open, compassionate heart and non-opinionated mind to individuals acknowledging their worst sin, the evil in their hearts. His job was to digest their sinister thoughts and feelings and in so doing they were freed of their inner darkness. Sea Lettuce is a remedy of purification and release.

Chakra:	Solar Plexus
Meridian:	Small Intestine, Stomach
Key Words:	Purifying, Healing
Challenges:	Facing the dark side
Affirmation:	I shine the light of healing on my dark side. My dark side is dissolved in the green light of healing.

Sea Lettuce – Purification

Look at yourself through the window of my greenness and
see yourself clearly.

Let me help you to see yourself as healed and whole.

Do not leave any dark corner unlit.

There is nothing to hide.
Bathe yourself in the Light of Being.

Sea Palm
postelsia palmaeformis

meetings at the edge of breakthroughs in consciousness; balances "hurry for nothing" attitude

Signature: *Like gracefully swaying palm trees, Sea Palm gently responds to its environment. Even in the roughest waters, it maintains its grace and integrity.*

We can easily forget to be fully present when we get all revved up and think that we are "running the show." This remedy resonates for those who never take time to smell the flowers because they are so busy pushing the river.

Sea Palm is especially suitable for those who rush about doing, always doing. Their "busy-ness" is often a hindrance to success and to meaningful relationships. They can be paragons of efficiency, but at the expense of anything or anyone being meaningful or important to them.

They charge on, regardless of all opposition. Heavily caught up in a pattern of control and resistance, there is tension at the physical, mental, and emotional levels. This tension can usually be released only when some external crisis brings them to a sudden halt. They are the loud complainers when ill. These patterns are often related to self-worth issues and stem from feeling unloved and unwanted as a child.

The Sea Palm type craves nurturing and nourishment emotionally and physically, and will often suffer from digestive problems and eating disorders.

Chakra:	Heart
Meridian:	Stomach
Key Words:	Flowing, Allowing, Be-ing
Challenges:	Busy, Preoccupied, Controlling
Affirmation:	I am fully present.

Sea Palm – Be-ing

Thank you for my flexibility.

Thank you for my endurance.

Learn from me and bend with the
ebb and flow of life's tides.

Sea Turtle
chelonia mydas

for persistence, grace, commitment

Signature: *Weighing between 200 - 375 pounds at maturity, these amazing beings carry their homes on their backs. And while they may look clumsy and slow on land, in the water they are as graceful as a prima ballerina. Its shell has 13 clearly defined compartments - 13 being an esoteric symbol for transformation.*

Turtle energy figures prominently in the legends of many cultures. She is often described as carrying Mother Earth on her back. Her ability to survive in water or on land, as well as the fact that she carries her home with her wherever she goes, makes her very adaptable. Her shell is also like a shield which protects the heart and vital organs. The geometric design with the central compartments always numbering 13 is significant - 13 being the number of death and transformation. Personality-wise, Turtles can be slow and steady but if they are pushed they will either withdraw within their shells or snap fiercely at whoever is disturbing them.

As a remedy Turtle benefits the Spleen and assists it in its Earth functions of transformation and absorption of nutritive Qi. It helps those who tend to be "spaced out" and "ungrounded" to reconnect with solid earth energy - to get out of their heads and into being in their bodies and living on the earth.

At the level of Spirit, it helps us to find that 'spark of divinity' within - our soul and connection to the Source.

Chakra:	Heart
Meridian:	Spleen, Heart Protector
Key Words:	At home, Present, Available
Challenges:	Busy-ness, Awkwardness
Affirmation:	I "lumber" through my life with grace and charm.

Sea Turtle – *Grace*

Let me carry you my child.

Open your heart and follow me through the sea
and I will lead you to immortality.

Sponge
myxilla incrustans

everything is unfolding in perfection; nothing happens to me without my consent

Signature: *Soft and porous, sponges are the most primitive of the many-celled animals. They live in colonies and are capable of regeneration when part is broken off. They resemble the nephrons of the kidneys and feed by entrapping minute food particles floating through the water with their external "collar" cells. Many sponges emit a strong odour which makes them uninviting to predators.*

As the nephrons of the kidneys filter the impurities from blood so that it can be eliminated as urine, so the Sponge essence helps us to filter impurities from our minds and spirits so that we can be free. This measure of freedom allows us to embrace life fully and simultaneously "let go" with carefree abandon. Sponge helps us to relax into the perfect unfolding. It is about attachment and detachment and the ability to dance between these two polarities. It will be useful for those who tend to absorb energies from others and have no ability to transmute them.

Connected to the Stomach channel it assists with the digestion and absorption of emotions and ideas. Its connection with the Bladder channel helps us to maintain our own energy reserves and fluid balance by maintaining a posture of both active participation and passive observation.

The essence enters via the Crown chakra and fosters and supports union with the Divine.

Chakra:	Crown
Meridian:	Stomach, Bladder
Key Words:	Inner Peace, Wonder
Challenges:	Victim consciousness, Opinionated
Affirmation:	As I am able/willing to release judgment, hope and wonder blossom.

Sponge – *Wonder*

My gift to you is to walk the middle way,
to dance between polarities and to find your way home.

"Staghorn" Algae
lessoniopsis littoralis

holding ground (sense of self) amidst turbulence and confusion; accessing higher consciousness

Signature: Sturdy holdfasts which resemble the horns of a stag anchor this Kelp at the lowest tide zone where it is whipped about by the open surf of the Pacific Ocean. Stags have been the companions of royalty for centuries and in many cultures. They are mythically associated with gentleness and are said to carry the "spirit" of kings. It is an edible perennial plant and may have as many as 500 blades.

When we really feel lost and alone and disconnected from our own divinity, this essence will help to re-establish the connection. The antlers of the stag are symbols of antennae which can connect us to higher forms of attunement and perception. Staghorn essence is beneficial to the eyes both physically and metaphysically.

Staghorn essence reawakens spiritual clarity. It promotes the qualities of steadfastness and gentleness. If we become brittle and set in our ways, we snap and break. If we can hold fast and attune with higher consciousness amidst the crashing and thundering waves of the ocean, we will survive. Gentleness dissolves more barriers than force.

Staghorn essence works with the Gall Bladder channel – physically to relieve tight and painful shoulders, and to improve coordination; mentally to help with clear thinking and decision making especially with regard to making choices which are life supporting and beneficial to physical and emotional health.

Chakra:	Root
Meridian:	Gall Bladder
Key Words:	Steadiness, Inner Security
Challenges:	Self-knowledge
Affirmation:	I remember who I am in the midst of conflict and turmoil.

"Staghorn" Algae – *Inner Security*

While I stand rooted and firm I am mindful of
Spirit enlivening me.

Let me attune your Body/Mind to earth and to heaven.

Starfish
pisaster ochraceus

for willingly giving up the old and allowing the experience of being empty; a grief remedy

Signature: Large central disk with five tapered arms in colours of yellow, purple, red, orange and brown. Numerologically, five is the number for freedom and change. In the symbolism of the Tarot, five is the inner teacher – wisdom. So Starfish is about freedom rooted in inner wisdom.

Like the Starfish who clings to a rock when on land and moves in an exquisite dance when released to the ebb and flow of the ocean, we too can move through experience without clinging and paralyzing our inner resources. Often the death of a loved one provides us with this kind of opportunity to let go and to experience the wound of loss. Emptiness is prerequisite to fullness.

This essence helps us to appreciate the unique soul path of each individual and to remember that "to everything there is a season and a time for every purpose under heaven."

Primarily a spiritual remedy, it enters via the Crown chakra and allows us to experience a deep spiritual connection with those we love, even when they are no longer in physical form.

The Large Intestine channel is the great eliminator and carries away impurities from the body, mind, and spirit, leaving us pure and brilliant.

Grief is a great initiator, and when we can embrace it, all that is left for us to experience is love.

Chakra:	Crown
Meridian:	Large Intestine
Key Words:	Willingness, Releasing
Challenges:	Attachment, Clinging
Affirmation:	I accept the unfoldment of life.

Starfish – *Releasing*

Let my star bless you with the ability to let go.

Life is a dance, a journey, a symphony.

How can you experience it to the fullest if you are
clinging to any single moment?

Surfgrass
phyllospadix scouleri

for courage, strength, and power rooted in stability and flexibility

Signature: *The signature of Surfgrass is its intense emerald green colour which balances and harmonizes the Heart centre. It promotes fearlessness.*

Surfgrass encourages integration of opposites by embracing paradox. Then true courage can be achieved – the courage to be.

It is a remedy to achieve goals, not from ego desire, but from that place within ourselves which knows our life purpose. In this regard it is particularly useful for athletes who strive for excellence – to express their god self in their activity. Surfgrass strengthens the will and provides us with our second wind.

It benefits the Kidney and physically affects kidney dis-ease, infections, inflammations and calcifications. It balances the adrenal glands and allows us to use adrenaline in a life supporting manner – "stress without distress." Emotionally, Surfgrass alleviates fear and helps us to move into our seat of courage, the Heart chakra.

In Chinese Medicine Kidney stores the vital essence, or life force, and governs the energy reserves of the entire body. It plays a vital role in the maintenance of homeostasis in the physical. Surfgrass affects the larger definition of homeostasis – i.e., balance and harmony among body, mind, spirit and emotion.

Surfgrass types can be wishy-washy and undirected or willful and self-destructive. This essence helps to harmonize this polarity.

Chakra:	Heart
Meridian:	Kidney
Key Words:	Courage, Flexibility
Challenges:	Pride, Ego
Affirmation:	I am powerful and flexible.

Surfgrass – *Courage*

In my watery green grass you will find nourishment
for your own essence.

I bless you with courage and perseverance and the will
to pursue your perfect unfolding.

Urchin
strongylocentrotus purpuratus

for safety and psychic protection

Signature: Sharp purple quills are the signature of sea Urchin. Inside, the little sea creature is vulnerable and soft. We are protected when we stay in touch with universal light via the crown chakra.

A powerful remedy to use when charting unknown territory, like past life regressions or exploration of energy connections with people in this life.

Primarily a spiritual essence, it expands the mind to include access to stored memories from previous incarnations or early childhood.

People who were abused as children often take refuge in abusive behaviour patterns towards themselves – alcoholism, eating disorders and even suicidal tendencies. Urchin can provide the safety required to explore and to dispel the energy which created these patterns. At another level it can provide safety from any psychic assault on our Being.

Mentally it alleviates worry and obsessive thinking. Emotionally it affects compulsive behaviour and addictions.

Urchin also helps to dispel panic attacks and other respiratory problems which are common when we do not feel safe. This is probably due to the fact that in the creative cycle of the five elements of Chinese medicine, Earth/Spleen is the mother of Metal/Lungs. A severe imbalance in Spleen could easily manifest as Lung and respiratory symptoms.

Chakras:	Crown, Solar Plexus
Meridian:	Spleen
Key Words:	Exploration, Safety, Focus
Challenges:	Fear of the unknown
Affirmations:	It is safe to explore my hidden potential.
	I am protected when I bring more awareness to light.

Urchin *– Safety*

Come and rest within the softness of my shell.

In my three-dimensional mandala you are safe.

Let me surround you with my purple spines.

As I provide a safe haven for small sea creatures
I will provide a sanctuary for you.

Whale
globicephala macrocephalus

enhances ability to communicate through vibration and sound; expansion of human consciousness; ability to contact the record keepers

Signature: *Pilot Whales grow up to eighteen feet long and live in families of up to twenty members off the coast of Hawaii. They are black and have large round heads. These whales have teeth and primarily eat squid, fish and sometimes other marine mammals. They communicate with sound over distances of up to 2 miles.*

Whale essence is a remedy of choice for healers. It will enhance both auditory and kinaesthetic perception. If you want to expand your ability to sense energy and to transmit energy with your hands, Whale will assist with this desire. If you want to hear more subtle sounds even in the heart of a major city, use this essence either topically on your ears or take it orally.

Taking this essence will also enhance the ability to receive and to interpret impressions of a subtler nature – knowledge and information about where we came from, what our path is, and even future potential can be revealed when we are open to the possibility. Taking Whale essence and meditating with a record keeper quartz crystals will assist us in decoding the message contained in the crystal.

As a physical remedy it is a general tonic through its connection with Conception vessel which runs up the front midline of the body and Governing vessel which traverses the spinal cord. These two channels not only make up a primary circuit of Qi in the Body/Mind but can also directly influence all the other channels.

Chakra:	Third Eye, Crown
Meridian:	Conception Vessel, Governing Vessel
Key Words:	Telepathy, Clairsentience, Human Potential
Challenges:	Ethnocentricity, Arrogance
Affirmation:	I am able to access my full mental potential.

Whale *– Expansion*

I am the giant of the sea.

When you want to know what you're really capable of,
come to me.

Repertory of Key Issues and Flower and Sea Essence Correspondences

Mental, Emotional, and Spiritual Qualities

ABUNDANCE
- *Polyanthus, Barnacle, Fireweed*

ACCEPTANCE
- of self; able to access self-esteem – *Vanilla Leaf*
- of Self from a place of deep inner security – *Windflower*
- of others through seeing their point of view – *Harvest Lily*
- of situations by taking personal responsibility – *Anemone*
- of "what is" leading to non-judgment – *Twin Flower*
- of this moment - *Snowberry*

ADAPTABILITY
- *Douglas Aster, Coral, Diatom*

ALCHEMY
- *Rainbow Kelp*

ALIGNMENT
- *Weigela*

ALLOWING
- giving up control - *Anemone, Sea Palm*
- grief - *Starfish*
- channelling higher forces - *Barnacle*

APPRECIATION
- *Dolphin, Purple Magnolia, Wallflower*

AT HOME
- *Sea Turtle*
- in the body – *Purple Magnolia*
- in the world – *Arbutus*

ATTENTION
- *Blue Lupin*

ATTUNING
- with feminine aspect (anima) – *Barnacle*
- with masculine aspect (animus) – *Arbutus*

AVAILABLE
- *Chickweed, Sea Turtle*

AWARENESS
- attention – *Purple Magnolia*
- heightened/enhanced – *Anemone, Viburnum*
- expanded – *Sand Dollar*
- insight – *Chiton, Viburnum*
- perspective/perception – *Twin Flower*
- spiritual perception – *Death Camas*

BALANCE
- *Blue Camas, Fuchsia, Grape Hyacinth*
- after shock or trauma – *Grape Hyacinth*
- between intuitive and the rational – *Blue Camas*
- between front and back brain – *Rainbow Kelp*
- between action and passivity – *Sponge*
- emotional responses – *Windflower*
- in the midst of change – *Twin Flower*
- of energy – *Brown Kelp, Moon Snail*
- overall balancing – *Fuchsia*

BEAUTY
- *Alum Root, Harvest Lily, Indian Pipe*

BEGINNINGS
- *Death Camas*

BE-ING
- *Sea Palm*

BIRTH/RE-BIRTH
- *Candystick, Hooker's Onion, Jellyfish*

BONDING
- with mother – *Barnacle*
- with father – *Arbutus*

CENTRED
- *Periwinkle, Douglas Aster*

CENTRING
- through the ability to broaden perspective – *Ox-Eye Daisy*
- as part of meditation – *Goatsbeard*
- leading to channelling – *Viburnum*
- enhances ability to go within – *Brown Kelp*

CHANNEL
- *Viburnum*

CHOICE
- being able to make decisions – *Pipsissewa*
- being able to choose the simplest solution – *Lily of the Valley*
- in tune with our inner journey – *Twin Flower*
- ability to release limiting patterns – *Grass Widow*

CLAIRSENTIENCE
- *Whale*

CLARITY
- *Blue Lupin, Brown Kelp*
- of expression – *Lily of the Valley*
- of thought – *Blue Lupin*
- resolves mental confusion – *Brown Kelp*
- spiritual – *"Staghorn" Algae*

CLEANSING
- *Plantain*
- the mind – *Moon Snail*
- emotional – *Coral*

COMMITMENT
- *Pearly Everlasting, Sea Turtle*
- to a goal – *Forsythia*
- to right action for self – *Surfgrass*

COMMUNICATION
- *Bluebell, Wallflower*
- interspecies/higher – *Dolphin*
- understanding vibrational messages – *Whale*
- within the Body/Mind – *Moon Snail, Sea Horse*

COMMUNITY
- unifies group energy – *Harvest Lily*
- living in – *Coral*

COMPASSION
- for self through healing the inner child – *Fireweed*
- allows us to see through the window of the heart – *Salal*
- arising from non-judgment – *Twin Flower*
- for the dark side – *Sea Lettuce*

CONCEPTION
- *Silver Birch*

CONSCIOUS
- *Blue Camas*

CONSCIOUSNESS
- *Diatoms*
- abundance – *Polyanthus*
- breakthroughs in – *Sea Palm*
- expansion of – *Dolphin, Whale*
- higher – *"Staghorn" Algae*
- liberation of – *Brown Kelp, Sand Dollar*
- victim – *Mussel, Sponge*

CONTENTMENT
- *Hermit Crab*

COOPERATION
- *Coral, Harvest Lily*

COURAGE
- *Surfgrass, Douglas Aster*
- to experience change – *Death Camas*

CREATIVE EXPRESSION
- *Orange Honeysuckle, Chiton, Hooker's Onion, Moon Snail*

CREATIVITY
- supports creative expression – *Hooker's Onion*
- accesses creative potential of second chakra – *Orange Honeysuckle*
- exploration of creative expression – *Moon Snail*
- through transforming anger – *Mussel*

CURIOSITY
- *Moon Snail*
- joyful exploration of experience – *Snowdrop*

DECISIONS
- *Mussel, "Staghorn" Algae*

DECISIVENESS
- *Pipsissewa*

DELIGHT
- *Snowdrop*

DEVOTION
- *Pearly Everlasting*

DREAMS
- easily recalled – *Periwinkle*
- programming – *Viburnum*

EASE
- *Hermit Crab*

ECSTASY
- *Death Camas*
- embracing the moment – *Snowberry*

EMPOWERMENT
- *Anemone*

ENTHUSIASM
- through connecting with the Divine within – *Nootka Rose*
- through joyful exploration of experience – *Snowdrop*
- through acceptance of "what is" – *Snowberry*

EXPANSION
- *Douglas Aster, Whale*

EXPLORATION
- *Urchin, Snowdrop*

EXPRESSION
- *Sea Horse, Wallflower*
- communication – *Bluebell, Wallflower*
- creative – *Chiton, Moon Snail, Orange Honeysuckle*
- freedom of/to – *Candystick, Hooker's Onion, Weigela*
- physical – *Salmonberry, Snowdrop*
- self – *Easter Lily, Jellyfish, Sand Dollar, Coral*
- Self – *Camellia, Windflower, Sea Horse*
- sexual – *Mussel, Purple Magnolia*

FAITH
- *Brown Kelp, Poison Hemlock*

FANTASY
- *Goatsbeard*

FEELING
- *Purple Crocus*

FLEXIBILITY
- *Chiton, Jellyfish, Surfgrass, Pink Seaweed*
- due to an open heart – *Jellyfish*
- as a source of personal power – *Surfgrass*

FLOWING
- *Sea Palm*

FLUID
- *Jellyfish*

FOCUS
- *Blue Lupin, Urchin*

FORGIVENESS
- *Salal*

FREEDOM
- as a result of releasing limiting beliefs – *Grass Widow*
- through creative expression – *Hooker's Onion*
- through clear thinking – *Brown Kelp*
- to think differently – *Moon Snail*
- to fully experience feelings – *Starfish*
- personal – *Hermit Crab*
- of choice – *Lily of the Valley*

FREE WILL
- honouring the path of each soul – *Candystick*
- through "response-able" choice – *Anemone*

GENEROSITY
- *Douglas Aster*

GENTLENESS
- *Chiton, Lily of the Valley, Poplar, Sea Horse, "Staghorn" Algae*

GRACE
- *Alum Root, Diatoms, Sea Turtle, Camellia, Pink Seaweed, Sea Palm, Yellow Pond Lily*

GRATITUDE
- *Polyanthus*

GROUNDED
- *Pink Seaweed*

GROUNDING
- *Windflower, Narcissus, Vanilla Leaf*
- to harmonize thought before action – *Pink Seaweed*

HARMONY
- *Coral*
- in Body/Mind – *Moon Snail, Surfgrass, Viburnum*
- among energy centres/chakras – *Hooker's Onion*
- in relationships – *Coral, Pearly Everlasting, Silver Birch*

HEALING
- *Poplar, Sea Lettuce*

HONESTY
- *Easter Lily*

HOPE
- *Snowdrop, Sponge*

HUMILITY
- *Twin Flower*

HUMOUR
- *Hooker's Onion*

IMAGINATION
- ability to fantasize &/or visualize – *Goatsbeard*

INDIVIDUALITY
- *Windflower*

INNER DIRECTION
- *Orange Honeysuckle*

INNER KNOWING
- accessing inner knowing – *Blue Camas, Periwinkle*
- trusting inner voice – *Viburnum*

INNER PEACE
- *Sponge, Twin Flower*

INNER SECURITY
- "Staghorn" Algae
- feeling rooted and safe – *Pink Seaweed*
- allows the soul to dance – *Windflower*

INNOCENCE
- *Lily of the Valley, Moon Snail, Poplar*

INSIGHT
- *Viburnum*

INSPIRATION
- for creative endeavours – *Hooker's Onion*
- to move forward and express full potential – *Snowdrop*

INTEGRATION
- *Weigela*

INTEGRITY
- through connecting with Spirit within – *Arbutus*
- through integrating different aspects of self – *Easter Lily*
- maintained in the midst of turmoil and upheaval – *Sea Palm*

INTIMACY
- *Purple Magnolia*

INTROSPECTION
- *Red Huckleberry*

INTUITION
- *Viburnum, Barnacle, Blue Camas, Whale*

INTUITIVE
- *Barnacle*

JOY
- from feeling the connection with Spirit – *Nootka Rose*
- through celebrating our own uniqueness – *Vanilla Leaf*
- exploring life with joy and enthusiasm – *Snowdrop*
- through embracing life experience – *Jellyfish*
- expressing joy in activity – *Pink Seaweed*

LETTING GO
- *Poison Hemlock, Snowdrop*
- into experience – *Jellyfish*
- of dysfunctional behaviour patterns – *Fuchsia*
- of grievances – *Salal*
- of limiting beliefs and attitudes – *Grass Widow*

LIGHT
- *Hooker's Onion*

LIGHT-HEARTED
- *Alum Root, Dolphin, Hooker's Onion*

LIGHTNESS OF BEING
- *Fairy Bell*

LOVABLE
- *Fireweed*

LOVE
- *Diatoms, Fireweed*
- giving – *Douglas Aster*
- in relationship – *Pearly Everlasting*
- of life – *Nootka Rose*
- of self – *Vanilla Leaf*
- unconditional – *Lily of the Valley*

LOVING
- *Fireweed*

MANIFESTATION
- *Silver Birch*
- of our inner shaman – *Douglas Aster*
- of our divinity – *Alum Root, Wallflower*

MEDITATION
- as a tool in self-healing – *Goatsbeard*
- enhances ability to go within – *Viburnum*
- to access unconscious – *Moon Snail*

MEMORY
- *Periwinkle*

MOTIVATION
- *Forsythia*

NOURISHMENT/NURTURING
- *Barnacle, Narcissus, Red Huckleberry*
- craves nurturing – *Sea Palm*

OPENING
- *Purple Magnolia*
- to abundance – *Polyanthus*
- to the mystery of life – *Pearly Everlasting*

OPENNESS
- *Anemone, Bluebell, Camellia*

OPTIMISM
- *Twin Flower*

PASSION
- *Snowberry, Nootka Rose*

PATIENCE
- *Pink Seaweed*

PERSISTENCE
- see Willpower

PERSPECTIVE
- from the safety of the heart of life – *Ox-Eye Daisy*
- through accessing the whole brain – *Blue Camas*
- expansion of – *Anemone, Candystick, Pearly Everlasting*
- at times of trauma – *Grape Hyacinth*

PLAYFULNESS
- *Dolphin, Hooker's Onion*

POTENTIAL/POTENTIALITY
- *Rainbow Kelp, Whale*

POWER
- personal power to move forward in life – *Snowdrop*
- aligning with inner power – *Camellia*

PRESENT
- *Jellyfish, Sea Turtle, Chickweed, Sea Palm*

PRESENT MOMENT
- ability to exercise power of choice – *Pipsissewa*
- being fully present and able to respond – *Chickweed*
- embracing experience wholeheartedly – *Snowberry*
- letting go into the experience – *Jellyfish*
- embracing the experience of grief – *Purple Crocus*
- avoidance of – *Poison Hemlock, Sea Palm*

PSYCHIC DEVELOPMENT
- *Viburnum*

PURITY
- *Easter Lily*

PURPOSE
- alignment with Soul purpose – *Anemone*
- acceptance of life purpose of others – *Starfish*
- knowing our own life purpose from within – *Surfgrass*

RATIONAL/LOGICAL
- *Blue Camas*

REALITY
- *Sand Dollar*

REBIRTHING
- *Death Camas*

RECEPTIVITY
- accessing feminine/intuitive – *Barnacle*
- open to receiving abundance – *Polyanthus*

RECONCILIATION
- *Indian Pipe*

RELATIONSHIPS
- avoidance of – *Hermit Crab*
- commitment to – *Pearly Everlasting*
- group energy – *Harvest Lily*
- new – *Death Camas, Pink Seaweed*
- non-attachment to – *Yellow Pond Lily*
- transformation of – *Rainbow Kelp*

RELAXATION
- *Goatsbeard*

RELAXED
- *Viburnum*

RELEASE
- *Snowdrop*

RELEASING
- *Poison Hemlock*
- anger – *Mussel*
- the past – *Chickweed, Starfish*
- thoughts – *Fairy Bell*
- mental blocks – *Plantain*
- beliefs – *Grass Widow*
- emotions – *Yellow Pond Lily*

REMEMBERING
- *Periwinkle*
- who we are – *Blue Lupin*

RESPONSIBILITY
- present and available in this instant – *Chickweed*
- personal – *Anemone, Candystick, Pipsissewa, Weigela*

REVERENCE
- *Indian Pipe*

SAFETY
- *Narcissus, Urchin*
- while mapping the unconscious – *Brown Kelp*
- with intuitive knowledge – *Viburnum*

SECURE
- *Pink Seaweed*

SECURITY
- *"Staghorn" Algae, Yellow Pond Lily, Windflower*

SELF-ACTUALIZATION
- *Fuchsia*

SELF-ESTEEM
- *Vanilla Leaf*

SELF-EXPRESSION
- *Bluebell, Camellia, Coral, Sand Dollar, Weigela, Windflower*
- eliminating social masks – *Easter Lily*
- freedom to express self – *Weigela*
- free will – *Candystick*
- physical alignment – *Salmonberry*

SELF-REALIZATION
- *Camellia*

SELF-WORTH
- lack manifested as inability to receive – *Polyanthus*
- lack due to feeling unwanted as a child – *Sea Palm*
- nourished by – *Indian Pipe*

SERVICE
- *Pearly Everlasting*

SHARING
- *Wallflower*

SIMPLICITY
- *Lily of the Valley*

SOLITUDE
- *Hermit Crab*

SOURCE
- *Diatoms, Arbutus, Douglas Aster, Pearly Everlasting, Rainbow Kelp, Sea Turtle*

SPIRIT
- *Arbutus, Windflower*
- calling Spirit – *Indian Pipe*
- contacting Spirit – *Poplar*
- remedy for – *Hooker's Onion, Jellyfish, Starfish, Urchin*

SPIRITUAL CLARITY
- *"Staghorn"Algae*

SPIRITUAL TONIC
- *Windflower, Arbutus*

SPONTANEITY
- lightness and freedom of expression – *Hooker's Onion*
- enjoying physical experience – *Purple Magnolia*

STEADINESS
- *"Staghorn" Algae*

STRENGTH
- *Yellow Pond Lily, Barnacle, Mussel, Silver Birch, Surfgrass*

TELEPATHY
- *Whale*

TRANSFORMATION
- releasing habitual patterns – *Forsythia*
- of anger energy – *Mussel*
- of dis-ease energy – *Sand Dollar*
- spiritual rebirth – *Death Camas*
- alchemical – *Rainbow Kelp*
- through service – *Pearly Everlasting*
- of mind and heart – *Dolphin*

TRANSITIONS
- catalyst for change – *Forsythia*
- moving through change with ease – *Poison Hemlock*
- sudden and unexpected change – *Death Camas*

TRANSMUTATION
- of emotional toxins – *Blue Lupin*

TRUTH
- *Easter Lily, Sand Dollar*

TRUST
- *Alum Root, Lily of the Valley*
- of self – *Camellia, Pipsissewa*
- in the flow of life – *Anemone, Barnacle, Brown Kelp, Weigela*
- in our inner voice – *Viburnum*
- in our ability to make choices – *Pipsissewa*

UNCONSCIOUS
- *Brown Kelp, Moon Snail, Sand Dollar, Urchin*

UNDERSTANDING
- through shifts in perception – *Brown Kelp*
- from knowing we have chosen our script – *Anemone*

VISION/VISIONARY
- perspective – *Ox-Eye Daisy*
- seeing our own uniqueness – *Camellia*
- seeing through the eyes of a child – *Lily of the Valley*
- seeing others as mirrors of self – *Weigela*
- seeing the "big picture" – *Anemone*

VISION/VISUALIZATION
- *Goatsbeard*

WILLINGNESS
- *Starfish, Alum Root, Fairy Bell, Polyanthus*

WILLPOWER
- the will to change destructive behaviours – *Forsythia*
- strengthens the will – *Bluebell*
- to accomplish in activity – *Surfgrass*
- to let go of old beliefs – *Grass Widow*

WISDOM
- of the inner child – *Lily of the Valley*
- integration of inner knowing with outer experience – *Weigela*
- accessing inner wisdom – *Fairy Bell, Grass Widow, Periwinkle*
- of the feminine – *Barnacle*
- spiritual – *Arbutus, Red Huckleberry*
- of the body – *Orange Honeysuckle*

WONDER
- *Sponge*

YIELDING
- *Barnacle, Poplar, Silver Birch*

Mental, Emotional and Spiritual Challenges

ABANDONMENT
- *Arbutus, Nootka Rose, Barnacle, Dolphin*

ABUSE
- *Nootka Rose, Urchin*

AMBIGUITY
- *Fairy Bell*

ANGER
- *Blue Lupin, Candystick, Mussel, Orange Honeysuckle, Pearly Everlasting*

ANXIETY
- *Narcissus, Periwinkle*
- emotional – panic attacks affecting breathing – *Bluebell, Urchin*
- mental – overthinking, obsessive thinking, worry – *Urchin*
- spiritual – "angst" – *Arbutus*

APATHY
- *Periwinkle*

ARROGANCE
- *Whale*

ATTACHMENT
- *Douglas Aster, Starfish, Yellow Pond Lily, Hooker's Onion, Sponge*

AVOIDANCE
- *Hermit Crab*

AWKWARDNESS
- *Sea Turtle*

BITTERNESS
- *Chickweed, Jellyfish, Plantain*

BUSY/BUSY-NESS
- *Sea Palm, Sea Turtle, Fuchsia, Red Huckleberry*

CHANGE
- *Death Camas, Pink Seaweed, Forsythia, Fuchsia, Grass Widow, Orange Honeysuckle, Poison Hemlock*

CLINGING
- *Douglas Aster, Starfish*

CLOSED
- *Camellia*

COLDNESS
- *Fireweed, Purple Magnolia*

CONFLICT
- *Alum Root, Coral, Narcissus, "Staghorn" Algae*

CONFUSION
- *Blue Lupin, Brown Kelp, Periwinkle, Pipsissewa, Rainbow Kelp, "Staghorn" Algae*

CONTROL
- *Anemone, Lily of the Valley, Mussel, Silver Birch, Chickweed, Poison Hemlock*

CRITICAL/CRITICISM
- *Twin Flower, Plantain*

DARKNESS
- *Diatoms, Sea Lettuce, Easter Lily, Fairy Bell, Forsythia, Rainbow Kelp, Snowberry*

DENSE
- *Hooker's Onion*

DEPRESSION
- *Fairy Bell, Periwinkle, Blue Lupin, Grape Hyacinth, Jellyfish, Rainbow Kelp*
- post-partum depression – *Hooker's Onion*

DESPAIR
- *Blue Lupin, Grape Hyacinth, Periwinkle, Fairy Bell*

DISASSOCIATION
- *Weigela*

DISHONESTY
- *Easter Lily*

DOUBT
- *Yellow Pond Lily*
- self-doubt – *Viburnum*

DUPLICITY
- *Easter Lily*

EGO
- *Douglas Aster, Sea Lettuce, Surfgrass, Harvest Lily*

EMOTIONAL WOUNDS
- *Fireweed*

ETHNOCENTRICITY
- *Whale*

FATIGUE
- *Bluebell*

FEAR
- *Coral, Grass Widow, Snowdrop, Urchin, Blue Camas, Brown Kelp, Fireweed, Hermit Crab, Hooker's Onion, Jellyfish, Narcissus, Ox-Eye Daisy, Rainbow Kelp, Surfgrass*
- phobias – *Poison Hemlock*
- stimulating, i.e. becomes excitement – *Poison Hemlock*
- vague and non-specific – *Surfgrass*
- paralyzing – *Snowdrop*
- panic attacks – *Bluebell*

FEAR OF:
- abandonment – *Nootka Rose*
- death/life – *Snowdrop*
- scarcity – *Polyanthus*
- being judged – *Grass Widow, Bluebell*
- being separate from the group – *Grass Widow*

FRUSTRATION/FRUSTRATED
- *Blue Lupin, Mussel, Hooker's Onion*
- due to confusion about life purpose – *Candystick*
- due to blocked creativity – *Orange Honeysuckle,*
- in the face of the unexpected – *Pipsissewa*
- with our own negative behaviour – *Plantain*

GRIEF
- *Purple Crocus, Starfish*

GRUDGES
- *Salal*

GUILT
- *Camellia*

HATE
- *Vanilla Leaf, Forsythia*

HEAVY
- *Hooker's Onion*

HOLDING
- *Goatsbeard, Poison Hemlock, Chiton, Grape Hyacinth, Jellyfish, Salmonberry, Snowdrop*

HOMESICKNESS
- *Arbutus*

IDENTITY
- *Orange Honeysuckle*

ILLUSION
- *Easter Lily, Indian Pipe, Sand Dollar, Grass Widow*

INDECISIVENESS
- *Pipsissewa*

INFLEXIBILITY
- *Pink Seaweed, Silver Birch*

INSECURITY
- *Viburnum*

IRRITABILITY
- *Mussel*

JUDGMENT
- *Twin Flower, Mussel, Salal*
- fear of being judged – *Bluebell*
- judging others – *Plantain*

LAZINESS
- *Sea Horse*

LEARNING DISABILITIES
- *Blue Camas*

LIMITATION
- *Bluebell, Sand Dollar, Camellia, Chiton, Hooker's Onion, Grass Widow*

LONELINESS
- *Hermit Crab, Dolphin*

LONGING
- *Arbutus*

LOST
- *Orange Honeysuckle*

MASS CONSCIOUSNESS
- able to disengage from beliefs of others – *Grass Widow*
- able to "follow your bliss" – *Bluebell*
- examining individual beliefs – *Death Camas*

MELANCHOLY
- *Dolphin*

NEGATIVE THINKING
- *Plantain*

NEW BEGINNINGS
- *Death Camas, Pink Seaweed*

OBSESSIONS
- thinking – *Forsythia*
- with sorting things out – *Barnacle*
- thoughts like a "broken record" – *Pipsissewa*

OPINIONATED
- *Sponge*

OVERFOCUSED
- *Ox-Eye Daisy*

OVERWHELMED
- *Hooker's Onion*

PARALYSIS
- *Sea Horse*
- paralyzing fear – *Snowdrop*
- paralyzing shyness – *Wallflower*

POWER STRUGGLES
- *Alum Root*

PRIDE
- *Surfgrass*

PROCRASTINATION
- *Fuchsia*

PSYCHIC PROTECTION
- *Urchin*

PURIFICATION
- of the Mental body – *Plantain*
- change as a catalyst for – *Death Camas*
- releasing physical toxins – *Sea Lettuce*

REACTIVITY
- *Rainbow Kelp*

RESENTMENT
- *Chickweed, Plantain, Salal, Nootka Rose*

RESISTANCE
- *Fairy Bell, Snowberry, Anemone, Jellyfish, Purple Crocus, Sea Palm, Twin Flower*

RESISTANT
- *Barnacle*

RESTRICTION
- *Snowdrop*

RIGIDITY
- *Chiton, Lily of the Valley, Jellyfish, Moon Snail,*
- due to mental stuckness/bitterness – *Plantain*
- due to lack of integration within self – *Camellia*
- of the heart centre – *Jellyfish*
- from making judgments – *Twin Flower*

SADNESS
- due to loss of a loved one – *Purple Crocus*
- when we feel disconnected and homesick – *Arbutus*

SCATTERED
- *Windflower*

SELF-DESTRUCTION
- *Forsythia, Urchin*

SELF-DOUBT
- *Viburnum*

SELF-KNOWLEDGE
- *"Staghorn" Algae*

SELF-LOATHING
- *Vanilla Leaf, Forsythia*

SELF-RIGHTEOUSNESS
- *Salal*

SEPARATION
- *Indian Pipe, Poplar, Fireweed, Hooker's Onion*

SHAME
- *Camellia*

SHOCK
- *Grape Hyacinth, Fireweed*

SHYNESS
- *Bluebell, Windflower*

SLOTH
- *Fuchsia*

SOCIAL INTERACTION
- *Harvest Lily, Weigela*

SPACED OUT
- *Windflower, Sea Turtle*

SPEECHLESS
- *Weigela*

STRESS
- *Goatsbeard, Grape Hyacinth*

STUBBORNNESS
- *Barnacle, Camellia*

STUCK/STUCKNESS
- *Hooker's Onion, Diatoms, Jellyfish, Anemone, Chickweed, Plantain, Poison Hemlock, Salal*

SURVIVAL
- *Candystick*

TENSION
- *Goatsbeard, Brown Kelp, Candystick, Chiton, Harvest Lily, Mussel, Purple Crocus*

TIGHTNESS
- *Goatsbeard*

TONGUE-TIED
- *Bluebell*

TORPOR
- *Fuchsia*

TRAUMA
- *Grape Hyacinth, Candystick, Chiton, Hooker's Onion, Nootka Rose, Weigela*

UNCOMFORTABLE
- *Bluebell*

UNAVAILABLE
- *Chickweed*

UNGROUNDED
- *Windflower*

UNWORTHINESS
- *Polyanthus*

"VICTIM" CONSCIOUSNESS
- *Anemone, Sponge, Mussel, Pipsissewa*

WEARINESS
- *Nootka Rose*

WORRY
- *Narcissus, Death Camas, Pipsissewa, Urchin*

Physical Challenges based on the Energetics of Chinese Medicine

CARDIOVASCULAR SYSTEM:
- arterial plaque – *Jellyfish*
- body temperature – *Moon Snail, Rainbow Kelp*
- dizziness – *Mussel*
- hypertension (high blood pressure) – *Periwinkle, Surfgrass*
- oxygenation of blood – *Sea Lettuce*
- circulation – *Fireweed*
- tonic – *Lily of the Valley*

DIGESTIVE SYSTEM:
- improved flow of bile – *Mussel*
- stomach acid, belching – *Sea Palm*
- inability to absorb nutrients – *Barnacle*
- eating disorders (eating too much or too little) – *Urchin*
- weight problems (excess) – *Chickweed, Poison Hemlock*
- transformation & absorption of nutrients – *Sea Turtle*
- indigestion caused by emotional upsets – *Sponge*
- indigestion due to toxicity – *Blue Lupin, Plantain*
- blood & liver toxicity – *Plantain*
- headaches – *Blue Lupin, Plantain*
- fasting & cleansing – *Death Camas*
- food intolerances – *Grass Widow*
- nervous stomach – *Narcissus*
- improved digestion – *Windflower*
- general tonic – *Red Huckleberry*

ELIMINATION:
- general tonic for the colon – *Polyanthus, Starfish*
- bowel problems relating to stress & emotions – *Camellia, Starfish*
- inability to separate the pure from the impure – *Barnacle*
- heat & inflammation in the intestines (colitis, Crohn's disease) – *Sea Lettuce*
- constipation – *Pink Seaweed, Poison Hemlock*

ENDOCRINE SYSTEM:
- **Pituitary** – *Barnacle, Viburnum*
- **Pineal** – *Grape Hyacinth, Periwinkle, Whale*
- **Thyroid** – *Sand Dollar, Chiton*
- **Thymus** – *Jellyfish*
- **Adrenals** – *Surfgrass, Rainbow Kelp*

GENITO-URINARY SYSTEM:
- bladder problems – *Brown Kelp*
- kidney stones & inflammatory conditions – *Surfgrass*
- supports role of kidneys to cleanse blood & detoxify the system – *Coral*
- fluid balance & energy reserves – *Sponge*
- general kidney tonic – *Fuchsia, Snowdrop*

IMMUNE SYSTEM:
- lymphatic circulation & drainage – *Moon Snail*
- fortifying – *Goatsbeard*
- Chronic Fatigue Syndrome – *Snowberry*
- SAD (seasonal affective disorder) – *Red Huckleberry, Snowberry*

NERVOUS SYSTEM:
- C.N.S. (information between brain & spinal cord) – *Sea Horse*
- sensory & motor neurons – *Sea Horse*

- diseases (post polio syndrome, Parkinson's, multiple sclerosis) – *Coral*
- paralysis – *Poison Hemlock, Snowdrop*
- nervous disorders – *Periwinkle*
- nervous system degeneration – *Snowdrop*

Brain:
- front & back alignment – *Barnacle, Rainbow Kelp*
- right & left alignment – *Blue Camas*
- hydrocephalics & brain cell loss due to strokes – *Coral*
- limbic system – *Dolphin*
- clear thinking – *"Staghorn" Algae*
- expansion of brain potential – *Whale*
- choice making – *Pipsissewa*
- addictions – *Forsythia*
- depression – *Grape Hyacinth, Periwinkle*
- memory – *Periwinkle*
- autism – *Bluebell, Wallflower*

REPRODUCTIVE SYSTEM:
Female:
- cysts & fibroids – *Barnacle*
- inflammatory conditions – *Sea Lettuce*
- PMS premenstrual syndrome – *Easter Lily*
- menstrual cramps – *Sea Lettuce*
- surgery – *Sea Lettuce*
- birthing – *Barnacle, Jellyfish*
- birth traumas (for child or mother) – *Hooker's Onion, Urchin*
- menopause – *Orange Honeysuckle*
- surgery, miscarriage, abortion – *Candystick*
- stalled labour – *Poison Hemlock*
- general tonic – *Silver Birch*

Male:
- fertility – *Sea Horse*
- inflammatory conditions – *Sea Lettuce*
- surgery – *Candystick, Sea Lettuce*

RESPIRATORY:
- bronchitis, asthma, throat problems – *Polyanthus, Sand Dollar*
- general remedy for respiratory system – *Polyanthus, Sand Dollar*
- breathing (inspiration) – *Sea Horse*
- breathing easily – *Bluebell, Fairy Bell, Purple Crocus*
- general tonic for the lungs – *Arbutus*

SENSES: (SEEING, HEARING, FEELING, SMELLING, SPEAKING)
- refined sensory perception – *Douglas Aster, Purple Magnolia, Rainbow Kelp, Wallflower*
- eyes – *Anemone, Ox-Eye Daisy, Purple Magnolia, "Staghorn" Algae*
- ears – *Brown Kelp, Ox-Eye Daisy, Whale*
- feeling – *Purple Magnolia, Whale*
- smell – *Purple Magnolia*
- speaking – *Bluebell, Yellow Pond Lily*

STRUCTURAL: SKIN, BONES, AND MUSCLES
- muscle & tendon spasms – *Anemone*
- back tension – *Brown Kelp*
- bones & teeth – *Pink Seaweed*
- spinal alignment – *Salmonberry, Sea Horse*
- chest & upper back – *Fireweed, "Staghorn" Algae*
- neck & shoulder tension – *Mussel*
- cervical spine – *Chiton*
- physical tension related to grief – *Starfish*

- general body tension – *Chiton*
- improved coordination – *"Staghorn" Algae*
- sacrum & pelvic girdle – *Candystick*
- skin problems – *Vanilla Leaf*

Miscellaneous – Physical and Life Challenges

ABANDONMENT:
- feeling lost and homesick – *Arbutus, Dolphin*
- emotionally or physically abandoned – *Nootka Rose*
- feeling unloved and unwanted as a child – *Sea Palm*

ABORTION/MISCARRIAGE
- *Candystick, Sea Lettuce*

ABUSE:
- physical, sexual, emotional – *Nootka Rose, Sponge, Urchin*
- self-abuse – *Forsythia, Nootka Rose*

ADDICTIONS
- *Forsythia, Urchin*

ALCOHOLISM
- *Nootka Rose, Urchin*

ANXIETY
- *Narcissus, Periwinkle, Urchin*

AUTISM:
- *Bluebell, Wallflower*

BIRTH:
- *Barnacle, Candystick, Hooker's Onion, Jellyfish*
- stalled labour – *Poison Hemlock*

CELL MEMORY (LOSS OF ABILITY OF CELL TO DO ITS FUNCTION)
- *Diatoms*

CHRONIC FATIGUE SYNDROME
- *Diatoms, Dolphin, Snowberry*

DEATH OF A LOVED ONE: FEELING HEAVY HEARTED
- *Dolphin, Purple Crocus*
- allowing the experience of grief – *Starfish*

DEGENERATIVE DISEASES
- *Diatoms*

DEPRESSION:
- general – *Blue Lupin, Fairy Bell, Grape Hyacinth, Jellyfish, Periwinkle, Rainbow Kelp*
- feeling heavy hearted – *Dolphin*
- post partum – *Hooker's Onion*

DIVORCE:
- letting go – *Starfish*
- releasing bitterness & resentment – *Jellyfish*

DIZZINESS
- *Mussel*

EATING DISORDERS
- *Forsythia, Sea Palm, Urchin*

ENERGY/VITALITY:
- low energy – *Bluebell, Coral*
- rejuvenation – *Dolphin, Goatsbeard*
- physical endurance – *Sea Horse*

EXHAUSTION:
- fatigue – *Bluebell*
- general physical tonic – *Whale*

HEADACHES
- *Blue Lupin, Plantain, Mussel*

HOMEOSTASIS
- *Surfgrass*

HYPERTENSION
- *Periwinkle, Surfgrass*

MENOPAUSE
- *Orange Honeysuckle*

NEW BEGINNINGS
- *Death Camas, Pink Seaweed*

OBSESSIONS
- *Barnacle, Narcissus, Urchin*

PANIC ATTACKS
- *Bluebell, Urchin*

PHYSICAL PAIN
- *Anemone*

POST PARTUM DEPRESSION
- *Hooker's Onion*

PMS (PREMENSTRUAL SYNDROME)
- *Easter Lily*

SAD (SEASONAL AFFECTIVE DISORDER)
- *Diatoms, Grape Hyacinth, Periwinkle, Snowberry*

SEXUALITY/SENSUALITY
- enjoyment of the physical senses – *Dolphin, Purple Magnolia, Whale*
- sexual frustration – *Mussel*
- inability to express sexual energy – *Dolphin, Purple Magnolia*
- directing sexual energy into creative channels – *Orange Honeysuckle*

TRAUMA
- Suicidal – *Urchin*

WEIGHT REGULATION
- *Chickweed, Chiton, Poison Hemlock, Urchin*

WHIPLASH
- *Chiton, Mussel*

Appendix A

Gem and Crystal Essences

The gem and crystal remedies from Pacific Essences are lovingly prepared using the energy of both the Sun and the Moon in the Mother tincture. Gems and crystals resonate especially with the chakras and corresponding glands in the human body. Their ability to resonate with the human energy system is due to colour, chemistry, and crystalline structure. Through their crystalline structure gems are capable of emitting consistent, repetitive vibrations. The body in response will attune to these vibrations and come into equilibrium.

AMBER – illumination of mind and heart

AMETHYST – transformation of energy; protection

APOPHYLITE – cleanses resonances of "old stuff," physical or mental

AQUAMARINE – peaceful, calming and soothing; balances thymus

ARAGONITE – promotes self-reliance and inner security

AVENTURINE – aids with meditation and visualization

AZURITE – "gentling" of attitudes; awareness of perfect essence of all things

BLOODSTONE – alignment of energy centres

BLUE LACE AGATE – connects 6th and 7th chakras; inspiration and grace

CALCITE – decreases fear; increases dream memory

CARNELIAN – increases vitality; stimulates the liver to throw off impurities

CELESTITE – transports consciousness to celestial realms; enhances perception

CHRYSOCOLLA – harmony, balance, wholeness, integration; unifies 4th and 5th chakras

CITRINE – clearing of thought patterns to manifest what you want by attuning to creative light force

CORAL – connects us with our depths; symbolizes life force energy

CROCOITE – to let go of worry; to recognize thoughts before emotional reaction

EMERALD – enhances wisdom and projects love

FIRE AGATE – transformation towards harmony and love; heart tonic

FLUORITE – transformation and devotion; links matter with spirit via the Crown chakra

FUCHSITE – elevates emotions from unconscious to conscious and beyond to psychic and intuitive

GALENA – receptivity and microscopic intensity; helps to transmit thoughts

GREEN GARNET – purifies thoughts

GREEN TOURMALINE – eliminates mental and emotional toxins

HEMATITE – augments meridian flows

IOLITE – links up vision and communication

JADE – emotional grounding; healing deep emotional hurts

JASPER – physical tonic; balances body energies

KUNZITE – stabilizes pure love and joy in the heart

LAPIS LAZULI – transcendence of the ego; assists one to become a clear channel and to see others without judgment

LARIMAR – to become as a little child; delight and joy, wisdom and innocence

LEPIDOLITE – brain hemisphere integration; alleviates depression and allows for greater perspective

MALACHITE – reflects and mirrors that which is within

MOONSTONE – promotes vision and self-awareness

MUSCOVITE – aligns the endocrine system and chakras

OBSIDIAN – grounding and making manifest spiritual qualities

ONYX – absorption and transmutation of vibrations

OPAL – enhances feelings of "at-one-ment" between physical and spiritual; enhanced awareness

PEARL – absorbs and holds love energy; purity, beauty, compassion

PERIDOT – dissolves spiritual uncertainty

QUARTZ CRYSTAL – amplifies thoughts and feelings; acts on the thymus to balance the immune system; assists with the retention of information; decrystallizes congestion

RED GARNET – awakens great love and compassion

RHODOCHROSITE – connector of chakras via the solar plexus

RHODONITE – impacts breathing and speaking

ROSE QUARTZ – self-fulfilment and inner peace; teaches the power of forgiveness and repatterns the heart to love of self; dissolves burdens which suppress heart's ability to give and to receive

RUBELLITE – to express the exuberance and joy of love

RUBY – love and courage to express one's highest potential

RUTILE – to relieve fear and anxiety; balances disturbed energy patterns

SAPPHIRE – inspires faith and devotion; opens us to our spiritual nature

SELENITE – to focus one's own sense of inner truth; being in touch with thoughts at their source

SERPENTINE – stimulates psychic abilities and alleviates fear in relation to greater vision

SILICA – clears mental confusion

SMOKY QUARTZ – balances adrenal energy; purifies cloudy thought forms; uplifts level of consciousness

SUGELITE – attunes with mental body to see what's creating the physical problem; awakens innocence and wisdom

SULPHUR – softens rigidity and increases flexibility both physically and mentally

TIGER'S EYE – seeing and accepting diversity in oneness leading to right action

TOPAZ – light, joy, love; brings out Christ-like qualities

TOURMALINE – balances chakras and meridians

TURQUOISE – strength, balance, vitality

UNAKITE – right-mindedness leading to right action

WAVELLITE – being willing to give up resistance and to attune with the flow of life

Appendix B

The Goddess Remedies

The nine goddess remedies were made on New Year's Eve, December 31, 1990, with the energy of the Blue Moon. Each essence either encourages the qualities of the goddess archetype with which it is associated or assists in dealing with her challenges.

The essences are for both men and women. They will assist women to embrace the energies of the goddess as she manifests in different aspects of their lives. They will help men to recognize and to feel their own goddess energy within. The ultimate effect will be to enhance communication and understanding between the sexes so that we can move towards the consciousness of being humans together. They will help all who take them to acknowledge divinity within self and other.

The nine goddess remedies are:

Kali
- Hindu goddess of creation and destruction
- issues of power and destruction especially self-destruction
- expression of primordial energy; dancing the dance of life with passion and grace

Maya
- weaver of the web of illusion on the earth plane
- acceptance of self as an expression of divinity
- ability to contact the pure essence of being

Radha
- the female aspect of Krishna; together they represent the great love relationship
- devotion to self, other, and God/Goddess/All That Is

Shakti
- the coiled serpent at the base of the spine – kundalini
- powerful sexual energy of creation

Isis
- Egyptian goddess of fertility and the devoted lover/wife of Osiris
- can be used to attract a twin soul and also for self - transformation through grief over the loss of a soul partner

Sita
- Daughter of the Earth and friend of plants and animals
- to assist with communication with beings of the plant and animal kingdoms
- to cultivate gentleness

Demeter
- Greek goddess of agriculture and fertility
- issues of creativity, productivity, and fruitfulness
- to assist with the separation at childbirth, and the separations which occur throughout life between parents and children

Persephone
- Greek goddess of the Underworld
- helps to access wisdom and knowing in the unconscious
- assists with healing the inner child

Kuan Yin
- Chinese goddess of compassion and mercy
- to develop these qualities and to provide us with nurturance when our load is too heavy

Appendix C

Abundance

The Abundance essence is a combination of plants and minerals in a base of 60% pure spring water and 40% brandy which acts as a preservative. It aligns Body, Mind, Emotions, and Spirit to act in a unified manner to achieve individual goals while forging a connection with the larger flow of all of life. It promotes "abundance consciousness."

Taken orally, the Abundance essence alleviates self-doubt, encourages self-worth, and promotes willingness to receive and participate in the flow. It is an essence of transformation of consciousness.

The Abundance Oil is a pure aromatherapy oil which can be used for massage, bath therapy, or in an aromatic diffuser. It is a combination of the Abundance essence and the essential oil of Tangerine which carries the orange healing ray of creativity and productivity. The pleasing fragrance of Tangerine brings to mind the joy and wonder of Christmas – the feast of love, joy and abundance. It is both warming and soothing to the Body/Mind and helps to maintain the fine line of balance between the excitement and fear of new ventures. It frees us to participate fully in the adventure of life by gently releasing limiting attitudes.

The Abundance Program is a 22 day commitment to yourself. It is designed to be used while taking the Abundance essence orally and using the Abundance Oil on a daily basis.

The purpose of the 22 Day Program is to create a new framework for manifesting Abundance at any and all levels of your life. You may choose your focus to be money, relationships, work, family, or any area where you are experiencing lack or scarcity.

Each exercise is designed to release stuff which no longer serves you, or to assist you in creating a particular experience of Abundance in your life. Essentially the programme, along with the use of the Abundance Essence and Oil, will repattern cellular memory so that you can experience your own inner power to manifest exactly what you want.

The 22 Day Abundance Program has been translated into Spanish, Portuguese, French, German, and Japanese. We have also developed an Abundance Facilitator training programme and have certified our first facilitators in Argentina in 1997.

Bibliography

Bach, Richard. *Illusions*.
    Delacorte Press: 1977

Clark, Lewis. *Wild Flowers of the Pacific Northwest*. Sidney, B.C. Canada:
    Gray's Publishing Limited, 1976.

Choa Kok Sui. *Pranic Healing*
    Samuel Weiser, Inc. York Beach, Maine 1990

_____ *Advanced Pranic Healing*
    Institute of Inner Studies, Inc. Manila, Philippines 1992

Chopra, Deepak. *Unconditional Life*
    Bantam Books, New York 1991

_____ *Ageless Body, Timeless Mind*
    Harmony Books / New York 1993

_____ *The Seven Spiritual Laws Of Success*
    Amber-Allen Publishing, San Rafael, California 1994

Connelly, Dianne. *Traditional Acupuncture*: The Law of the Five Elements.
    Columbia, Maryland: Centre for Traditional Acupuncture, 1975.

Gerber, Richard, M.D. *Vibrational Medicine*. Santa Fe, New Mexico: Bear &
    Company, 1988.

Harbo, Rick. *Tidepool & Reef*. Surrey, B.C. Canada: Hancock House, 1980.

Judith, Anodea. *Wheels of Life*. St. Paul, Minnesota: Llewellyn Publications, 1987.

Lao Tsu. *Tao Te Ching*. New York: Random House, 1972.

McConnaughey, Bayard & Evelyn. *Pacific Coast*. New York: Alfred A. Knopf, 1985.

Raheem, Aminah, Ph.D. *Soul Return*. Boulder Creek, California: Aslan Publishing,
    1991.

Siegel, Bernie, M.D. *Love, Medicine & Miracles*. New York: Harper & Row, 1986.

Stark, Raymond. *Guide to Indian Herbs*. Surrey, B.C. Canada: Hancock House, 1981.

Stuart, Malcolm, editor. *The Encyclopedia of Herbs and Herbalism*. London: Orbis
    Publishing Limited, 1979.

Teeguarden, Iona. *The Joy of Feeling*. Tokyo: Japan Publications, 1986.

Thie, John, D.C. *Touch for Health*. Marina del Rey, California: DeVorss &
    Company, 1973.

Underhill, J.E. *Roadside Wildflowers of the Northwest*. Surrey, B.C. Canada:
    Hancock House, 1981.

_____ *Northwest Wild Berries*. Surrey, B.C. Canada: Hancock House, 1981.

Wanless, James. *Voyager Tarot*. Carmel, California: Merrill-West Publishing, 1989.

Westlake, Aubrey. *The Pattern of Health*. Berkeley & London: Shambhala, 1973.

Wood, Matthew. *SEVEN HERBS Plants As Teachers*. Berkeley, California: North
    Atlantic Books, 1986.

About the Author

Sabina Pettitt is a lover of life, people and Nature. She brings this passion to all aspects of her healing work – as an Acupuncturist, a Counsellor, a Flower Essence Practitioner and Developer.

Sabina is dedicated to wholeness and self-actualization both for herself and for her clients. She sees life, people and plants as energy unfolding – the Mystery. Perhaps this accounts for her attraction to, and involvement with, Vibrational Medicine.

In 1983, Sabina co-founded Pacific Essences, a company dedicated to exploring the therapeutic value of plants of the Pacific Northwest.

In 1985 she was guided to make remedies from plants and sea creatures from the Pacific Ocean. A first in the vibrational pharmacopoeia, the Sea Essences have proven to be a valuable new frequency in the repertory of vibrational medicine, and now include such amazing energies as Pilot Whales, Sea Horses, Spinner Dolphins and Green Sea Turtles.

In 1991, Sabina organized and hosted the second international flower essence conference with 35 speakers and over 200 delegates from around the world.

In 1992 she developed the Abundance Program, a combination of essences, aromatherapy, and processes to empower people to live the lives they choose and to feel deeply connected to the flow of life. The program has now been translated into Portuguese, Spanish, German, French, and Japanese.

Since 1993 she has travelled around the world teaching about the healing connection between the Nature kingdoms and human beings. Through Pacific Essences she offers an annual certification training on Energy Medicine™ in Victoria.

In 1997 she was the keynote speaker at a Natural Therapies conference in Buenos Aires and addressed 1200 participants. In the same year she was also a main speaker at the Findhorn Conference on Nature Healing Humanity which attracted 300 delegates from around the world.

She has studied Ayurveda with Dr. Deepak Chopra, as well as being certified as a Primordial Sound Meditation teacher by him.

Her spiritual training with Master Choa Kok Sui in Arhatic Yoga and Pranic Healing is an ongoing commitment to healing herself and the planet.

Sabina lives in Victoria, B.C., with her husband Michael, and practises Acupuncture and Counselling out of Pacific Acupuncture and Holistic Health Clinic. She also travels worldwide and teaches about Energy Medicine™.